THE CHRISTIAN PAGAN

THE CHRISTIAN PAGAN

A Naturalistic Survey
of Christian History

By
John H. Burgess

Mimir Publishers Inc.
Madison, Wisconsin

First edition

Know the Past, the Present, and the Future

Printed in the U.S.A.
by
Worzalla Publishing Co.
Stevens Point, Wisconsin

Transposition

. . . God created earth and brought in light. He made sky in the middle of water, and gathered it into one place to let dry land appear. This He called "Earth." Therefrom He let grass, herb, tree and fruit grow. Then He made beasts and cattle. He spoke: "Let us make man in our image to have dominance over fish and fowl and cattle."

Man was made.

God planted a garden in the East, and there man lived amongst rivers and trees and food aplenty. There was a Tree of Life, and a Tree of Knowledge. The garden was free to man, save that he was not to eat from these Trees.

God saw that man was alone and needed someone, so when man slept God took from him a rib. From this He made a woman.

A snake from the garden came to man's woman and taunted her — she was not free. She could not eat from fruit of the Tree of Knowledge. The woman replied that surely she would die if she ate of this fruit. The snake said, "No!" God knew if she ate off the Tree of Knowledge she would become wise and know right from wrong.

. . . The woman tried the fruit; she enticed her husband to have some. Then they became wise and knew right from wrong. They were naked and covered themselves.

When God found that they had covered themselves, He knew they had done what He had forbidden. The man said his wife had tempted him to eat of the fruit. God turned to the woman and asked how she had come to do what He had forbidden. She told of the snake that had induced her to do it.

God found the snake and cursed him to crawl through the dust on his belly all the days of his life, and He produced enmity between the snake and the woman, and their progeny. God condemned the woman to sorrow and bear children in grief; thereafter she would be bowed and dutiful to her husband. The man, He said, must work and sweat, and, now that he was wise, must suffer anguish and seek knowledge throughout all his life.

God said that man had become as one of the Gods. He now knew right from wrong. Fearful that he would eat from the Tree of Life, and live forever, as the Gods, God cast man *from the garden, and forbade his return. From there man moved into fields, where he toiled and sweated, and worked the substance of the Earth from which he had been made. . .*

—Creation according to ancient Hebrew, as given in the Pentateuch, with authorship ascribed to Moses (14th to 15th century, B.C.)—Now thought to have been written by later Hebrew scribes and based on older Babylonian mythology.

. . . Zeus (Jupiter) conceived of animals and entrusted their keeping to Epimetheus who provided a place beneath the heavens for all. Epimetheus gave his animal charges such things as strength, size, speed and cunning. To each he gave a special excellence to enjoy while they inhabited the earth. But when all was done he had been so generous with the others that he had missed one. He was perplexed, and sought council with his brother, Prometheus. He told Prometheus of the one animal for whom he had nothing left to give.

Prometheus pondered his brother's plight; then he gave to this remaining animal the greatest gift of all—the shape of the gods, and the ability to walk upright, and to rule over all the other earthly things. He gave this animal, whom he called "man," a spark from heaven to light his mind. He also gave him the divine gift of fire.

Zeus was furious. Prometheus had acted without the consent of Him, who was the supreme god, and had given to this animal things that were not his to give. Zeus chained Prometheus to a rock, and made him suffer long in punishment for this unpardonable transgression.

Then Zeus met with other of the gods to take vengeance also upon man, with whom Prometheus had been so generous above all the other animals. They contrived a woman to wrack vengeance upon man. She was called "Pandora" for she too was gifted as no other mortal, with beauty and wit, cunning, deceit, and curiosity; and they gave her one final gift—a box, which she was never to open.

She went as wife to live on earth with Epimetheus who suspected not the treachery of such a gift of beauty as Pandora who came from the gods.

Pandora lived happily with Epimetheus, until she one day looked into the box given her by the gods, for they had also given her curiosity, while admonishing her never to open the box. It was thus that all the evils of man began, for when the box was opened, out escaped greed, avarice, and malice, pain and hunger, and all the horror the gods had put there. When she finally struggled to force the box closed, only hope had not escaped, and remained for the salvation of mankind. . . .

. . . Creation according to Greek mythology.

TABLE OF CONTENTS

LIST OF FIGURES

LIST OF CHARTS

LIST OF TABLES

FOREWORD

I was first struck by the marked dearth of factual data on Christianity some ten years ago when called upon to teach Christian history. In seeking extra-Biblical sources for instruction, I became frustrated and confounded, particularly after examining the prolific works of Christian proponents for other than a monolithic historic structure. An objective survey indeed seemed impossible; but yet I became increasingly obsessed with the need for an unbiased clarification of Christian origins. This first meant almost categorical rejection of the inexhaustive but stereotyped popular versions covering the life and passion of Jesus, then turning instead to modern factual material on the cultural acculturation, assimilation and diffusion processes, together with the realization that the early pagan cults were indeed the fertile ground into which the seeds of primitive Christianity had been sown.

Historical treatises are perhaps disconcertingly vague in any context, even those with benefit of the most disciplined scholarship. Hindsight is always obscured by blind spots, confounded with the filtering and distorting of the intervening past and colored by the exigencies of the present. The history of Christianity is this, but, more, it is, indeed, a kind of hoax, cluttered and rigidified in the ossified character of theological partisanship that yields neither to fact nor uncertainty. Of the hundreds and thousands of such pseudo historical treatises on the life of Christ, only fear and reverence have supported the theses, or, worse, a kind of conditioned predisposition of credulity that perpetuates delusion upon delusion, and reinforces the vagary of imputed revelation. Needless to say, scholarly works are available to inspire healthy skepticism and respectful research. Sanday, Larson, Clemen and Davies, to name a few, are writers bearing respect for available, or unavailable, historical data on Christianity. Leastwise they recognize conjecture and speculation, and hesitate to formulate a historical sequence, or do so only with misgiving.

How Christianity came about, indeed, may be a moot question, for it further goes without saying that even the best sources are speculative. The Bible, containing the Pentateuch and other Hebrew books, the Synoptics and the Book of John in the New

Testament, in all honesty, just as the Apocrypha, must be considered spurious in a literal non-cryptic sense. Paul was a believer, and an arbiter among the Gentiles. Contemporaries of the period, such as Josephus, Philo, Pliny and others, were selective in their narrations, and either did not or could not observe in identity the founder of Christianity.

The birth of Christianity can only be vaguely discerned, albeit respectfully researched, but the modern perspective in Christianity may perhaps bear more scrutiny. The events of Christian growth, i.e., of the institution, have marked the centuries. These may be sampled and studied, and delivered to the scholar or lay thinker in the light of a modern understanding of cultural anthropology, social psychology and the acculturation processes. Then might he see Christianity in clear vision, in the perspective of his times and problems, that he might better choose his own way.

Charles Pearce, early 20th-century American philosopher, described "faith" as "thought coming to rest." Surely in these times of anxiety and potential universal annihilation, a man can be neither privileged nor permitted to relax his thinking.

The preponderance of Roman Catholics in the Western New York area, in which I resided for many years, provided an extreme but typical milieu for observation of the modern American religious complex. I am grateful to my many Protestant as well as Catholic friends and associates who have helped me with interpretations of the dogma; though now in the perspective of a religionist this discourse may seem merely to be the rantings of an infidel. I have seen the way in which lives are directly influenced or lived through imposed interpretations of dogma, in blind authoritarianism built into their orientation since childhood. This has fascinated, perplexed and alarmed me; for, while I feel a deep affection for many who are Christian, I cannot share their tacit acceptance in an age that demands even a ruthless assessment of our institutions and beliefs.

The primary perspective of this present survey is historical, i.e., non-partisan, since without this there is a complete lack of basis for Christianity. The Christian scene is viewed with sharp criticism, for without this there is no hope for Christianity.

Throughout all interpretations, a social-psychological bias has predominated due to my personal academic background and discipline.

As a further contribution to the study of Christian origins, doctrines and practices, this work may be of value in pointing up the likely developmental processes with a not heretofore-developed candid emphasis on essential pagan foundations, (i.e., in the polytheistic sense) as well as in presenting a synthesis of a historical and an openly critical point of view. However, in the main, it is hoped that in the spirit of this writing further reshaping of emphasis might be encouraged. By increasing the depth and breath of the fund of knowledge with which we regard our religious heritage, as we mature in our history as a Christian nation we might become more critical of fundamentals, important not only to the development of our people and institutions as a progressive society, but to the intellectual evolution of individuals as human beings, who are neither bees, nor ants, nor praying mantises.

J. H. Burgess
1968

THE CHRISTIAN
PAGAN

A Critical Survey of Christian
History

by

John H. Burgess

I

The Search For Meaning

Apathy about the foundations of the Christian faith is perhaps the strangest of all enigmas in our technological society. Here an attempt is made to confront this perplexing situation.

Chapter 1

The Birth and Life of Christianity

Christianity, perhaps as any institution, might be likened to an organism. Yet the literary license and liberty taken in using such an analogy for Christianity may be highly objectionable. It is a sacred institution, not amenable to such analysis, claim its proponents.

In the perspective of this writing, however, Christianity is taken to be a kind of macrocosm, a now gigantic organic being that developed prenatally in an Oriental-Israeli-Eurasion-Greco-Roman uterus, and has matured in a predominantly West European culture. Today the anatomy and physiology of this supra-organism is made up of many functioning organs, tissues and cells. Some of these die, others grow and spread. We may ask if the organism is healthy and wholesome, or morbid and cancerous. Does it live a life that will sustain itself and society, and, in its mature wisdom, promote the human society that gave it life, or has it become senile?

Perhaps this analogy, however, is only superficially objective. Perhaps it really cannot touch us personally, nor relate to the deeply personal meaning of Christianity. Yet some such device, that may help us to regard our faith more objectively, is imperative if an understanding of modern religion is to be achieved; or we will remain hopelessly lost in the "faith of our fathers." Truly the nature of Christianity, as an institution in and through which we operate, will never be realized if we do not first step back and examine it. For to describe a hole, we must be out of it as well as in it.

There are of course among us Presbyterians, Baptists, Methodists, etc., of Protestantism, and those within the hard core of Roman Catholicism and its fringe area of the Orthodox and the Episcopalian beliefs. In the United States there are over 200 such Christian sects, each numbering at least 100,000 constituents.

Thus in all probability we have been reared Christian, with little or no provocation to question the faith. But, we might ask, why were we not indoctrinated as Hindu, or Moslem, or Taoist, or Buddhist, or Confucianist? Why are we not Jewish? If Christian, why are we Protestant or Orthodox or Roman Catholic? If we are one thing and not another, how do we contrast, in what ways are our beliefs different? Why do we believe as we do? In this train of questioning we must, in all conscientious circumspection, probe these beliefs, and lay bare the fundamentals about our own faith. On the other hand, we might silently resolve to suppress such questions in some vague apprehension or malaise lest it be heresy, things about which one should not ask, for they are for priests and only men of God to know.

Christianity is based on faith. It is the pure beauty, strength, serenity, and security of unquestioning implicit faith. Christians tell us ". . . it is only as little children . . " that we come to know. If this be so, then, truly, God help us! Certainly, we live in times of ever-increasing complexity. Modern society has advanced in virtually all areas of endeavor. Transportation and communication technology, war making capability, medicine and physics, indeed, all branches of science are developing a modern world of limitless perspective. We are now on the threshold of radically new vistas in space; a radically different outlook on the nature of the universe is now in the offing. We may talk from our living room in Canton, Ohio, or Sunnyvale, California to a home in Schwaz, Austria, or Brest, Russia, within a few minutes for relay plugging to be completed. We can fly from New York to Paris in less than six hours. We can span oceans and continents to strike a city with millions in population, and extinguish its vitals and life in less than a half an hour by Intercontinental Ballistic Missile. We keep man living for years longer each succeeding decade and improve his chances of being born alive, and surviving childhood.

Have we prepared man, are we preparing our children, for life among what may well be monsters of progress? In order to regiment him more precisely, we have made him less a man and more an automaton, the virtually hapless victim of our mass propaganda media. Man is being transcended today by the fantastically impersonal machinery of technology through the unprecedented control of communication media by massive institutions and their propaganda.

Certainly it can be only in self-conscious introspection as well as extraspection, that the remarkable species of man might survive. He will otherwise fast lose himself and his individuality because he dare not question. We can ill afford such national schizophrenia. Consider, for example, the land of the Hindus and Jainists where animals are so sacred that man must perish and the lesser species survive. In such a way does man live in blindness, oblivious to his far-reaching capabilities. It might well be disastrous for our own nation to live with such blind perspective. Only through examining ourselves and the institutions of our time can we achieve the necessary insights to meet exigencies of the technological changes confronting us.

We are said to be a Christian nation, a nation of God; but more importantly we might consider the effectiveness with which we are meeting our challenges. These are not questions about whether or not God is with us, nor we with Him, but that if what we are doing will bring men happiness and peace, and hasten world union, and bring about realization in the intelligent control of individual men. Are we, for example, preparing our children, who will truly (not the meek) inherit the earth? Are we showing them the ways of progress, and teaching them tolerance and forbearance in the tedium of a useful productive life? Or are our teachings and institutions binding them with irrelevancies? Must they continue to live with the equivalent of the white elephants and sacred cows that run rampant among the superstitious and deprived? Must they inherit the kind of emotional hogwash yet harassing our generation, cluttering issues and still restricting future generations in the direct confrontation of increasingly worrisome problems arising from technological change? Indeed, critical circumspection seems essential. We must examine ourselves, our faith, our institutions, critically, if we are to survive as individuals and grow, if we are truly to promote "domestic tranquility", support our nation in just causes and, let us hope, the community of nations, to check vicious monolithic systems in our time such as Communism or Fascism, and perhaps the most alarming trend within our own culture of unscrupulous commercialism.

If it is heresy to look at one's beliefs, and ask where they lead, then let us be heretic! If we must rip the fibre of our beliefs to work out the solution to even a single central issue, this we must do; for a better future life will not come from superstition and magic, nor simply in the name of Jesus, nor Allah, nor the disturbed viscera or "gut feelings" that generate theistic philosophies.

If we ask that when we die, do our egos not survive, and will we not ascend to greater heights and joy and peace—and find the answer is "no", then still we must go on. When we ask, does not a master plan exist? Is there not purpose and meaning in the universe? Cannot any man see the golden thread? And again we find the answer is "no", we must go on. For this is a cataclysmic age; the time is right, not for revolution, but for realization, a time to see, to think and ponder the problems of our time unfettered.

This appeal is for us to look deeply into what, as Christians, we believe. We must, each of us, in a most conscientiously intellectual effort, consider these religious questions with an open mind, and to discuss even our most sacred beliefs without fear of losing what we may actually never have had.

If a reader turns from this book with deeper convictions, more firmly entrenched precepts, binding and blinding, and further obscuring the issues and problems, this writing will have been in vain. On the other hand, if he begins to consider his position in the Christian religious world in light of his evolved biological and social being, if he becomes able to trace the ramifying lines in his Christian heritage to their primitive origins, then a realization will have been accomplished; and the life of Christianity will continue to become a self-conscious one, without bigotry, and with new hope, not in the "Second Coming," but for enlightenment in our time.

Chapter 2

The Belief in Natural Man

It is the persuasion of the naturalist to be concerned with investigation, observation and theoretical formulations based on measuring, observing, collecting and compiling of concrete evidence. It was just so in Newton's work that brought about the internal combusion machine and rocketry, in Einstein's formulations that led to the development of nuclear weapons, and in Ohm's work that is the precedent to the multiple electronic gadgetry we find all about us. This persuasion is also cogent in the naturalist's approach to the study of man, for only as man learns profoundly of what his nature consists, can he learn of what he is capable of becoming. He must study how natural conditions have developed without human control before he might otherwise become endowed with the wisdom necessary to mold the processes, to bring them under his human direction.

The evidence is now overwhelming that man developed during a two-thousand million year period, evolving from ancient ancestral stock. During the last half-million year span, multiple races evolved under myriad environmental conditions and naturalistic circumstances. No evidence nor criteria are indicated that Yahweh favored one or the other of either races or individuals, nor that divergence from a common stock was the case in the creation of man. Rather, the development of each human race seems to have occurred independently according to naturalistic principles of adaptation and extinction in different geographic localities and climates. He first appeared as a pre-human ape, perhaps in a random, yet adaptive, evolutionary fashion, like the Australopithecene, the Java man, the Pekin Man, and the Pithecanthropus Erectus. Then came others, like Neanderthal Man and Cro Magnon Man, assuming a more human-like shape, and dropping down from the trees to become varieties of man as we know him—with his vestigial tail, and the salinity of body fluids from ancient sea waters. He is now born only with rudimentary reaction patterns, the remnant reflexes of a brachiating episode—the palmer grasping reflex to hold himself to a branch, or the sucking reflex to ingest nourishment when he can do nothing else.

The Haeckel theory holds that individual development tends to parallel that of the species as it changed over eons of time, viz., "ontogeny recapitulates phylogeny." The cell division from conception tends to portray the history of man's entire evolutionary development. (This, of course, holds for any species.) In the case of the human embryo-fetal development may be observed the fluid unicellular origin of the fertilized ovum, gill clefts of his marine ancestry, the appendages of a quadruped, a prehensile tail, a monocular, then binocular visual structure, the opposing thumb and great forebrain. Perhaps many such features have developed randomly, without even so-called "selective evolution" operating, let alone a "divine plan." Perhaps many were merely random mutations in the solar-earth gravitational environment, which, however, we may proudly attribute to an act of God in His zealous whimsey. Indeed, there are few thoughtful and observing men who deny the facts of evolution. Man has a primordial nature. His body functions he shares with the lowliest amoeba—to take nutrient and reproduce.

But the human organism has a unique intracellular integrity, and the organism resides in a complex community of ideas, and functions in a network of communication that does, in a sense, not begin in time. His artifacts and social devices have been transmitted for generations even throughout the entire life of his species. His organism operates in a community of ideas, but his bodily functions continue as an undeniable product of his biological evolution.

The biology of the human organism is, in a manner of speaking, in conflict and competition with that of all other organisms. It generates in the womb. There it may not be in conflict, except as the mother's body cells are depleted and compete for nourishment. Nor does the human organism gain its life often at the expense of others in a litter characteristic of many other animal forms. But when the human infant emerges into the sun, it must meet its competition. It clings to survive, later to forage and hunt, and seek its own, and then to receive or transmit its germ cells to repeat its life cycle—he in tumescence, penetration, ejaculating the flagellating germ cells, she in raised pelvis to receive the spermatazoa in enveloping, ensnaring and encysting egg cells.

Perhaps it cannot be completely accepted by Christians that man's inherent nature, rather than being "evil", is biological. In this view, the individual's needs are often in conflict with those of the community. In times of scarcity, when the earth was scorched and game could not be found, and berries were dry, and the tribe could not support new individuals, his needs and those of the tribe were in conflict. Nomads were driven away. Reproduction was checked—the individual could not discharge his semen, nor she receive it as natural biological functions. Thus did taboos and tribal laws originate. Such fundamental tribal objections are with us today in forms no different from those of cave dwellers. Some observers, for example (cf., C. Jung), interpret the massive organization of the modern Church to be simply holier-than-thou archetypes, born of instinctual tribal patterns, but that the rigidity and massiveness of the complex theological structure completely obscures the basic origin.

The unique assets, yet, perhaps paradoxically, liabilities of the human organism, are its sensing and perceptive capabilities. Some of these it shares with other animals or are even inferior to theirs; but what man sees, touches and feels, smells, or hears is tied in with the massive complexity of his forebrain. He retains, abstracts, and verbalizes. He becomes apprehensive, and his entire primitive physiology responds and reverberates when pained or conditioned. Man remembers. He is burned or pricked, or bloodlet, and he feels pain. Strange intense noises frighten him, for they harken danger; odors and tastes bring back whole experiences. He remembers the wind blowing in his face, when he was wet or dry, when his tissues cried to be fed and grow, when his bladder was full, then empty, and his colon was gorged with feces, and excreted and smelled, and his stomach swished until it was full. He remembers from whence he came, that a member of his loins erects and enters into a union with the female carcass. And throughout his life he has been awed and entranced by the wiles of nature—a leaf that moves and spins in the wind, clapping thunder and bolting electrical charges of lightning, the cold pallor of a bare-faced disc that shines in moon glow. From his memory of such things in the reacting body of man, comes his ideas—the idea, for example, of elongated forms, the shape of his reproductive organ. Out of such a context, in his higher mental processes, he abstracts such ideas as birth without the process of union and cell division. In abstracting about crop cycles, man made first-fruit offerings to the gods that they might increase the yield. Such offerings became actual human sacrifices, and, later, systematized symbolism, as in the sacrificial death of Jesus.

Man is seen to conceive in reason and fear, and he perceives that the cause of happenings must occur as he devises them. The wind blows as he might blow with mouth and lungs; so he conceives of gods in his own image. Man becomes angry, hates, and loves; so do the gods, whom he fashions as controllers of the forces of nature. As he is dutiful to, and reveres his mother, so does he also worship one who is pure and abstract—the Virgin Mary; or he may hate and denounce one like his father, whom he reveres as a dark figure of authority; or he may hate and rebel. The things that appear good and evil, he conceives to be composed of spirits, the substance of which, he fails to realize, comes from his own life and acts; and from the distress and relief he has known in his extreme animal propensities for anxiety and guilt, he formulates the principle of "original sin." As his family group is ruled by a central mother or father figure, or the tribe by a chief, a king or premier, so a higher authority must govern the world and the universe, one who is good and protects, as well as one who is evil and punishes.

The tragedy of such a contemporary outlook is simply that men still do not understand the origin of their distress and biological natures. Rather, they think in absolutes, which crystallize and sustain the ancient beliefs. In early Rome, the world was believed to be governed by forces manifested in nature by the cycle of day and night, the seasons and weather, the growth and decay of living things, and such events in human life as puberty, marriage and birth. These were conceived as spirits of action called "numina." Many were deeply personal, such as those that controlled crops and herds, and fecundity. These were petitioned.

Rituals were established to bring favor from the commonly recognized spirits. The relationship was thought of almost as a kind of relationship between men who might bestow and receive favors in mutual benefit. Gods and goddesses, such as Flora, the flowering goddess of corn, were coded and popularized. The gods, too, were rewarded with honey and milk and cheese, in amount equal to favors requested. Later state gods became universally accepted in the great city state of Rome. Splendid temples were erected to Apollo, Jupiter and Juno. The gods grew and flourished as Rome grew.

Such a multiplication of gods becomes the rule among believing men. Monotheism has perhaps evolved potentially as the greatest peace maker, but the individual gods and the sons of gods, such as Jesus, Mohammed, and Buddha, are different. The one God is yet a different God for each creed, as is the potential for conflict.

In a sense, the true salvation of man does not lie in a faith in God, nor in any of His sons, but solely in man's penetration of his own nature, a depth of understanding that cannot come from belief alone and codified institutional dogma. As an animal, man avoids pain and seeks solace for his discomfort. It is confusing and painful to question ancient authoritarian postulates, to undertake an on-going open-minded search for facts in control—but society, if it is to progress and grow, must raise such questions.

Let the theologian, may we submit, in our time relax his bigotry. Let him attempt to fathom the mystery that becloaks the thinking of such large masses of men. Let his scholarly study be one of authenticating the natural man in a formal, systematic, non-supernaturalistic inquiry into why men have come to believe as they do, and to lay bare the dangerous pretenses in our modern age. Let him bring to light whatever can be ascertained in a naturalistic context about the dominating power of Christianity where it beclouds issues, and blocks inquiry. In such efforts, the theologian may turn from the easy life of dogma, and, if still devoted to an ideal, may undertake the tedious task of sound social integration, resolving the tormenting cultural conflicts born of technological change.

Chapter 3

In the Beginning

Christian reverence and ritual is built into the tradition and heritage of the Occident. The practices are complex and the beliefs are, for one not indoctrinated, strange and perplexing. There is the eucharist of bread and wine given by the priest to an initiate in mass; the body and blood of the god-man is thereby transubstantiated. The communicants are then fused with Him to enter into His Kingdom. There is the belief in the Immaculate Conception, of the Mother Goddess, Mary, of a miraculous sin-free birth, she who bore Jesus. There are beliefs in eschatology, the ending of all things in Heaven and Hell, Purgatory or Limbo. Those in a state of grace are believed to join the Heavenly Father in celestial realms. In a Parousia, He shall come again to establish His Earthly Kingdom. These are but a few of the doctrines to which an individual is subject in catechism and Christian practices.

The Man Jesus, about whom the doctrine revolves, is the second person of the Trinity. It is about Him, and His Mother, Mary, that the Christian Calendar is structured with such feast days as the Annunciation (March 25th), Christmas (December 25th) and its preparation in Advent, the Circumcision (January 1st), the Epiphany (January 6th), Candlemas (February 2nd), the Transfiguration (August 6th), and the Easter cycle of moveable feasts and fasts which begin at Lent going into the Holy Week of Easter and the Ascension. Sunday is the Christian weekly memorial of the Resurrection, and Friday commemorates the Crucifixion. These are modern man's beliefs. The associated punishments and rewards dominate his life to a very considerable extent.

[13]

THE CHRISTIAN PAGAN

a. Reasons for Religion.

Semantically, the word "religion" is often bandied about in a confused manner to include any pensive act or humanlike disposition. Russell sees any religion as having three aspects evidenced to a greater or lesser degree in a given culture: (1) the church, (2) the creed, and (3) the code of morality.

The word "religion" comes from "relegere," or "religens," meaning to revere the gods; or from "religare" meaning to bind men together. According to Tolstoy, religion is the link between man and God. It becomes a peculiar means by which man may realize his relation to the super-human or supernatural mysterious forces on which he finds himself dependent. Other definitions coming from medieval and mystical thought have it as a connection between the human soul and a mysterious spirit dominating the world with which man might feel himself to be united. Tolstoy saw a plurality of religions as necessary for the expression of man's relation to the Infinite or God. These differ at different periods, but they have always been the chief motive in human society. Since man first became rational, according to Tolstoy, he neither has nor could live without religion.

Tolstoy has perhaps been somewhat presumptuous in the latter generalization to see all societies, primitive or otherwise, as practicing some form of religion. We might cite many segments of modern society, as well as the so-called "Golden-Age" of Greece. In many cases when religion is practiced at all, it is used for purposes of exploitation, and otherwise is held in contempt by a sophisticated intelligensia.

In Russell's analysis he finds that everywhere primitive religion was tribal rather than personal. It related the needs of the tribe to the gods with magical incantations for their appeasement. Cultural anthropologists also find a distinction between magic and religion. Magic presupposes powers to be inherent in the magician or some object, e.g., stones, the elixir of life, monkey paws, or rabbit's feet. Religion is an appeal to a presumed higher power for intervention. In medieval Christianity, magic and religion were intermixed. Satan, as well as the Deity, could work miracles, but Satan worked them for evil men.

Garstin postulates that magic and religion thrive best in ignorance where control over the physical environment is limited. A society possessing no apparatuses nor methods for the investigation of the nature of things, nor system of logic and experimentation for objective control, is more likely to accept a religious system than a secular one. When a society is seen to lack investigative methods, animism, magic, and taboos are supported on the emotional grounds of fear, and on the faith that custom and habit dictate. Their sole means of understanding the universe is by postulating spirits. Whenever elements of chance and accident operate, hope and fear have a wide play, and a spiritual entity is interjected. (cf., "Act of God" clauses in the insurance policies of modern society). Monotheism explains physical and social events in terms of a single spiritual being. When the nature of physical and social events become understood, with actual controllability demonstrated, effective religious dominance wanes.

b. Dynamics of Religion

A search for fundamentals from among the proponents of Christianity may yield only circular reasoning. We must, therefore, look outside the system. Such views as those of religious scholars, anthropologists and psychiatrists have offered fundamental insight frequently not found among Christians.

1). *Religious Scholars:* Religious scholars observe that those objects and natural phenomena assuming importance to a hunter, nomadic and pastoral peoples, agrarian, urban or military societies, have been venerated throughout the ages. Heavenly bodies, the sun, moon, and stars, served a primary function for nomads. These gave them a frequently life-saving directional orientation. The rain and sun, of fundamental importance to growth and the fruit of harvest, are worshipped when agricultural conditions provoke anguish and apprehension. Agrarian societies have frequently demonstrated to the gods, in open fields, how to reproduce. They have offered first fruits and animal sacrifices to petition. Today we have in our own society the saying of grace in thanksgiving as a minimum tribute. For today there is in this less apprehension about a full table as a result of modern methods of irrigation and natural controls over agriculture.

[15]

Von Ogden Vogt cites as the most effective practice of success-ful rulers to be in adopting of the prevailing religions or ideologies to enhance their authority. By this means voluntary participation by subjects is achieved. Through the ruler's identification with popular ideologies and ceremonies, social solidarity and stability are promoted. Early fertility rites promoted security among the people. Sacrifices ameliorated guilt and anxiety, and celebrations provided a sense of exhilaration and fulfillment. Kings and chiefs instrumenting these practices have either been priests themselves, or the priests and medicine men have been at their sides thoroughly identified with their office. Augustus Caesar, at the turn of the Christian era, recognized the need for identification with a deity. This astute emperor enhanced his political strength by restoring scores of Roman Temples and attempting to revivify waning Roman beliefs. Elizabeth I issued the Act of Uniformity in England to enforce common worship, which gave the British subjects an intense cult unifying and stabilizing the nation to this very day. Evangelist Billy Graham, a man close to God Himself, once considered running for the office of the Presidency of the United States. Modern U. S. politicians since Kennedy now find it necessary to have political cohorts among those of Roman Catholic faith to obtain support from this faction. Benedictions by priest and ministers are made before the government bodies enter into congressional sessions, or before a new president is sworn into office. The inaugural addresses of every U. S. president in history carry copious references to God. It is indeed necessary that an individual running for any political office apologize for lack of religious affiliation and to state publicly his faith in God.

2). *Anthropologists:* We also turn to anthropologists for explanation on the dynamics of religion. Bidney cites the anthropological theory of animism as a central dynamic of religion. This holds that the contrast between the living individual and his corpse is the primitive perception through which religion operates. The spirit flies in sleep. In dreams, it leaves the body to return in waking. The dead move no more. They were warm, real and intimately close to us. Then they became still. The vital quality has gone. The phantom of the self has left the body. It is then still. Yet, the soul, the memory of those dear, will live with us forever. Pluralistic animism, the view that the spirit flies from man in death, is seen as a phase in the evolution of culture. This pluralistic spiritism then evolves in the culture to become a collective singular spirit, the one spirit of man, God, who is beneficent and protective if we heed His wishes.

3). *Psychiatrists:* Psychiatric orientation today may also lend some insight into the nature of man's religious bent. Psychiatrist Fromm-Reichmann views the tensions induced in man, or his anxieties, as traceable to his inherent infantile dependency. Born completely dependent, save for a few reflexes, nourishment must be literally poured into him. The infant's every need must be met through the solicitude of others and in his being in the good grace of his parents. "Separation" fear develops lest he be parted from those who meet his very survival needs. Such "separation anxiety" prevails in his psychology even unto death. The death situation itself is extremely anxiety provoking, since it involves this separation. The theological hereafter (Heaven) becomes something of an antidote to separation fears in a promise of being sustained in a togetherness after death.

Throughout life, individuals tend to react to the images instilled in the early interpersonal patterns when they were first dependent. These early images, cast in the dependent period of life, distort later images of those they meet as adults. The persistence of these early expectancies frequently results in disillusionment and erroneous evaluation of peers, accompanied by feelings of isolation and insecurity. This compulsive adhering to early patterns of evaluation interferes markedly with personal growth in developing realistic values. The individual thus clings to infantile interpersonal patterns, unable to grow emotionally nor to modify his thinking. The treatment of such disturbances in an adult consists of developing insight on the origin of the tensions, and learning to live with the recurring anxiety-provoking conditions of infantile dependency.

Realities in man's appraisal of his culture are essential to his control of anxiety. He seeks to sustain his religion which is made up largely of his infantile images. It is about these infantile anxieties that myths and even modern theology have devel-

[17]

oped. These latter are not only transmitted, but sustained by infantile anxieties that prevail and disturb the modern adult. Anxiety is aroused and evidenced in any attitude of self doubt, verbal or nonverbal, or in general doubt about the belief system in which an individual has oriented himself. To disbelieve is to lose control of one's ideomotor tendencies in the posture of belief, and to distrust any devices of reason.

Modern psychiatric goals are to develop "self realization," and "self actualization" in the individual, that he might be delivered from any feelings of stagnation, sterility or "psychological death," that he might have the freedom for the development of his talents, skills and perceptive power within a realistic value system. The religious mind, as seen by a psychiatrist, may be bound together by infantile "separation anxiety," but ultimate growth of the individual lies in his understanding and developing realistic mature adult values.

c. The Christian Origins

Etiologies of religion may be speculative, but of one thing we are certain: that we are not Hindu, Moslem, Buddhist, Shintoist, Jew, nor Christian simply through some divine scheme. We have been trained and disciplined in every facet. The process is one of acculturation, cross-cultural transition from a primitive individual outlook to the elaborate faith and ritual of organized religion, which then becomes a wholly personal thing when assimilated that makes us veritably a part of the religious tradition. In like manner must the whole of Christianity have been born. It grew as its evangelists moved among those trained and disciplined in similar religions. Christianity was, we might say, assimilated in, or adapted to the older religions.

Beliefs were many at that point in history when the Christian cause was being espoused. Judaism itself, in the centuries preceding and following the turn of the Christian era, had undergone many transformations from Persian, Oriental and Hellenistic influences, since its earlier Babylonian origin. Egyptian elements were grafted onto the primitive theology in the Mosiac period centuries before the world of the Mediterranean was to come under the yoke of Rome. Polytheism characterized the early period. In the redacted Book of Genisis, of Babylonian origin, for example, is found such polytheistic reference, viz., ". . . for they were cast from the garden, lest they eat fruit of the Tree of Life and live forever as the gods . . . "

A later trend toward monotheism was evident in the Egyptian Aton, the Persian Mithras, and the Hebrew Yahweh who later became the Christian God, Jehovah.

Hebrew culture merged throughout history, as even today, with that of the empires to which the Hebrews became subject, and the lands to which the people migrated. Babylon prevailed until late in the 6th century, B.C. After the Babylonians, the Persians reigned supreme until the Alexandrian period in the 4th century B.C. Greek influence dominated the Mediterranean and civilized world, reshaping Hebrew thought and religion even after the conquest of the Romans. At Alexander's death, his generals assumed rule. Syria fell to the Seleucidae and Egypt to the Ptolemies. Judea lay between and went first to the Ptolemies, then to Syria. The Maccabean revolt against Syria made Judea a partially independent state under the Asmonean priestly line, until the Roman conquest in 63 B.C.*

This socio-political world at the time of Christ, its tradition, characters, and mythological-theological doctrines, was precisely the soil in which Christianity was to grow. The ancient myths, as related by Frazer and others, are primitive and inconsistent, and reveal essentially undisciplined thinking. Nonetheless, it was out of these that Christianity evolved, as it merged with these ancient cults, finally to crystallize into the tradition we know today. When Paul of Tarsus in Cilicia wound the mainspring of the Christian movement, in his work among the Gentiles about the Mediteranean world of the first century, prototypes of primitive man's religion abounded. Man's wonderment about the ruler of nature, his anxieties about survival, the growth of crops and care of cattle, his early cannibalism, sexual license and taboos, and his continuing search for a better existence, are seen to have operated in the pagan rites of Osiris,

---

* A word about historicity: Accuracy in reporting, even in an age of scientific discipline, can be seen to suffer at the hands of each reporter. Frederick Bartlett's work in serial learning several years ago clearly demonstrated the way in which new doctrines are conventionalized according to tradition. Many devout Christians, for example, may read "Fetters in Christendom" as "Fathers in Christendom."

Aphrodite, Adonis, Ishtar, Dionysus and Attis. It was from among the constituents of these religions in Damascus, Asia Minor, Achaia, and Rome, that such men as Paul and Peter preached the doctrine of Christianity; and from these territories grew the Christian Church we know today.

Suggested Further Reading

1. Bartlett, F. *Remembering* Macmillan Co., N.Y.
2. Bidney, D. "The Concept of Value in Modern Anthropology." in *Anthropology Today* University of Chicago Press 1953
3. Coon, C. S. *The Origin of Races* 1962
4. Ferm, V. (Ed.) *Ancient Religions* 1950
5. Fromm-Reichman, F. "Psychiatric Aspects of Anxiety." in *Identity and Anxiety* The Free Press of Glencoe, Illinois 1960
6. Garstin, L. H. *Each Age is a Dream* Bouregy and Curl, Inc., N.Y. 1954
7. Henderson, J., et al. *Patterns of Myths* 1963
8. Murdock, G. "The Common Denominator of Cultures." in *The Science of Man in the World Crisis* (Linton, R. (ed.)) 1945
9. Pelikan, J. *The Riddle of Roman Catholicism.*
10. Russell, B. *A History of Western Philosophy.* 1960
11. Russell, B. *Religion and Science.* 1961
12. Scott, J. "The Analysis of Social Organization in Animals." *Ecology* V. 27. p. 213-221.
13. Sierksma, F. *The Gods as We Shape Them.*
14. Tolstoy, L. *What is Religion?*
15. Vogt, Von Ogden "Emotional Stability and Government." *The Humanist* V. 23, Jan. 1963 P. 16f

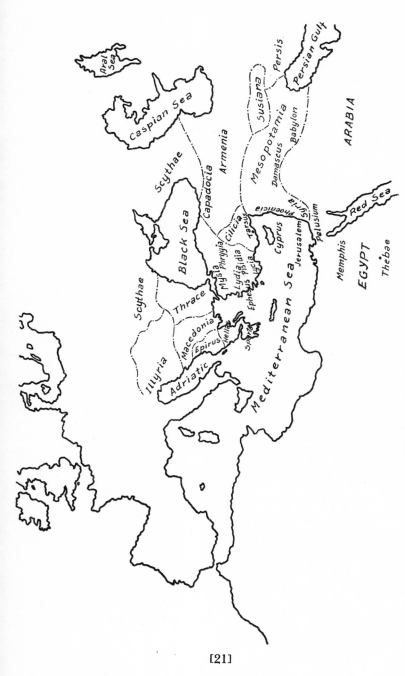

Fig. 1. Ancient Territories of the Mediterranean

[21]

II

Hebrew Background

of

The Judeo-Christian Tradition

Both Islam in the East and Christianity in the West are given precedence by Judaistic tradition. Religious scholarship must assume a fundamental comprehension of this tradition, particularly when considering the origin of contemporary Jewish-Christian antagonism.

Several extensive historical treatises are available to the reader, but a brief outline is presented here in order to provide the necessary background material for understanding the Christian complex we know today. Only as we learn profoundly of what the Jewish heritage consists, will we come to appreciate that the true nature of Christianity is not rooted in Judaism, even though traditional deicidal blame is placed on the Jews.

Chapter 4

Hebrew Antecedents

Some 20,000 years ago an ice cap covered the Northern hemisphere smothering the land masses of Northern Europe as far south as Italy. With the ice came extinction of animal life. Modern civilization began in the Middle East in the womb of Iranian-Sumerian culture some 8,000 years ago. (See Figure 1). It was carried thence to Egypt even while the northern regions were not yet fully recovered from the ravages of the glacier. In the north, the scattered people were still savages and cannibals. Out of the Iranian--Sumerian cultural complex the Hebrews emerged. The word, "Hebrew" (Ibhri) means "crossing over." Thus it was that northern tribes of Semitic people crossed over the Euphrates River in migration westward. The legendary Abraham, Isaac, Jacob (Israel) and his twelve sons, were perhaps men of these tribes. They were then not likely followers of Yahweh which was written into scriptures by Hebrew scribes of a much later period. These later scribes also wrote up the traditions of creation and the great flood in Genesis as it had been handed down from Babylonian mythology.

Much of the old Testament material (cf., Ex. xxi) was derived from the writings of King Hammurabi of Babylonia, and early Sumerians. Hebrew script was developed from Canaanitish, Phoenician, and Egyptian, as was Aramaic (Syrian), the language of Jesus, in which later Hebrew documents were written, including Jewish Christian books. Authorship of the Bible, the chief source of history for theologians, is spurious. Traditionally, the Pentateuch is claimed to be the writing of Moses. It is now evident, however, that scribes returning from the Persian exile wrote these books several centuries after the traditional Mosaic flight from Egypt. The Hebrew story of creation evidences Babylonian influence of the 6th or 7th century, B. C. In Babylonian tradition, the god Ea established his dwelling place over the water (Refer to Frazer). The city of Babylon, the central fane of Ea, was created on the nether waters. Compare this with the God of Genesis who built the sky in the midst of the water. "Eden," the paradise of the Hebrew Adam, is a word that meant "plain" in Babylonia. Reaction to sexual rites of the Babylonian fertility goddess, Ishtar (cf., also Aphrodite and Astarte) is also evident in the Eden story in repressed or symbolic form. It was Eve who was responsible for the fall of man. Ishtar called for sexual tribute in the Babylonian matriachal society (i.e., sacred prostitution, sexual orgies and castration rites, etc.). The severely patriarchal Hebrews evidenced extreme resentment of Ishtar in the condemnation of Eve for being both tempted and temptress through the phallic symbol—the snake. Many Christian theologians interpret the serpent in Genesis as Satan disguised. This blocks historical perspective and fails to take into account the Hebrew pre-cultures and the context in which Judaism developed.

Early Hebrew tribes were found throughout Palestine, east of the Jordan, north to Dan, and south to Beersheba in Northeastern Egypt. In Egypt, the tribes were Babylonians, Hittites, and Assyrians. These early nomads were all polytheistic. It was from this early conglomerate cultural background that the group identity of the Jews later emerged.

Chapter 5

Tribal Identities

The Jews have been a thoroughly devout and segregated religious people thoughout their history, beginning approximately eight centuries before Christ; in scriptures their God Yahweh, during the centuries preceeding Christ, was extensively defined in doctrine and placated in ritual. Their theocratic culture and nationalism, minority status, and ostensible disdain for Gentiles has frequently led to extreme antagonism and inhuman persecution of their members. (Strangely, such persecution tends to intensify, perpetuate, and reinforce group identities, cf., also, fourth century Christians). In a 3,000-year period, vicious Jewish annihilation was attempted by the Assyrians under Sennacherib, the Babylonians under Ahasuerus, Antiochus Epiphanes, Titus of the Caesar family, Hadrian, and by various factions during the Inquistition, and by the Germans under Hitler.

The Lord, in scriptures, admonished His people that they should heed His wishes and commandments; if they did as they were told they would be given the leadership of the world. It has been a real and personal expectancy for the Jews throughout their history—just as the Passover has reminded them yearly for 3,000 years that Yahweh will smite their enemies and spare their own. They were the chosen people, a people who to this day survive unassimilated throughout nations of the world. Elijah, to precede the Messiah, is still awaited at the Passover meal in many Jewish homes.

It is written that the Lord is all powerful and watches over His people. They need not gird themselves for He is there to do for them, as He held the sun still for Joshua and parted the Red Sea for Moses in the exodus from Egypt. When they neglected His praise and commands, then came the chastisement, humiliation in captivity, slavery, poverty, and persecution, while persecutors merely became the instruments of Him, Yahweh, who would bring His people back in their worship.

In historical perspective, Yahweh may have been an adaptation of an earlier Egyptian monotheism. The Egyptian god Aton emerged under the Pharoahs Amenhotep III and IV in the 14th century, B.C. During a period of a developed, prosperous culture in the rich fertile land of the Nile valley, Amenhotep III (Ikhnaton) first espoused the universality of Aton, a one-god creator and protector of all mankind. Ikhnaton decreed the abolition of Osirian-Amen worship, its temples and priesthood; for a brief period an extensive brotherhood-of-man emphasis was given in the worship of this unitary God. It was short-lived, however, for Osirian worshippers again assumed control, and condemned Aton as a false god.

Historically, the Israelites were in Egypt during this period as migratory shepherds. They may well have benefited from the liberal brotherhood and sanction to all men proffered by Ikhnaton's Aton. Moses, though considered mythical by many scholars, may have been a royal Egyptian in the 13th century, B.C., who was still a protagonist of Aton and was duly ostracized by the Osirian priesthood. Then, as an outcast for his heresy, he may have turned to the foreign nomads, the Israelites. He would offer them his god, the father of all men; the Israelites, who once enjoyed freedom and equality under Ikhnaton's "one God," were now enslaved under the hostile Osirian priesthood and Pharoah Rameses II. Late in the 13th century, B.C., the Egyptians were at war with Libia. This interval may have been when the Israelites fled from Egypt. Judeo-Christian folklore portrays the Israelites, under the leadership of Moses, fleeing from the tyranny of Merneptah, son of Rameses II, crossing a lake of reeds at the Gulf of Suez, while a windstorm shallowed the water with pursuing charioteers becoming mired in the mud. This narration became the high point in Hebrew exodus tradition, in later folklore attributed to Yahweh's intervention in the parting of the Red Sea.

The exodus tradition was written at least four centuries after Moses. The Book of Exodus describes the Mosaic covenant at Mount Sinai (an area within the Sinai peninsula in Egypt). The Decalogue or "Commandments" were formulated, in tradition, to bring together other Semitic Tribes from the desert and steppes of Arabia, by giving them the supernatural sanction, of a jealous and warlike "Lord of Hosts" who dwelt at Mount Sinai. The brother of Moses, Aaron, became the high priest of the covenanted tribes—the sons of Jacob who were called Israelites.

After the death of Moses the Israelites moved toward Canaan (Phoenicia). Then, under a sheikh named Joshua, they joined other Semites east of the Jordan, skirmishing for landed areas when their intrusion was resented. Likewise, they infiltrated Phoenicia among the Canaanites, attacking weakly fortified cities, but settling largely in the hills. They were gradually assimilated by the Canaanites, but retained strong Israelic identity. Later scribes colorfully attributed the Israeli movement into Palestine to Yahweh's intervention in giving His people the "Promised Land."

Yahweh was the Lord of Hosts (God of War). Other gods, within this same period, however, were also habitually worshipped, such as Ashtoreth in fertility rites, and Baal in agriculture. The god Aton, once universal in intention, had perhaps become a provincial god for the Israelites, a war god, the select god, "Yahweh." As God of the Israelites they sought his favor, and He theirs. Yahweh sanctioned usurping and exploitation among extra tribal peoples; but unto each other they must be true and love their neighbors as themselves. They thought of themselves as the first born, only begotten, chosen and beloved people of Yahweh.

The preachment of Osiris bore kinship to the later Judaistic formulations. Compare, for example, the following from the Osirian "Repudiation of Sin."

". . . Hail to thee Great God of Truth and Justice. I have not committed inequity against men. I have not oppressed the poor. I have not caused the slave to be ill-treated of his master. I have given bread to the hungry and drink to him that was athirst, and have clothed the naked with garments. I have not blasphemed. I have not stolen. I have not made false accusations. I have not slain any man treacherously . . . "

Compare also the Pharaoh Amenhotep IV's, later called "Ikhnaton," (meaning "profitable to Aton"), hymn to Aton (meaning "sun" or "light"):

". . . Manifold are thy works, one and only God whose power none other possesseth; the whole earth hast Thou created according to Thine own understanding. When Thou was alone didst Thou create man and beast both large and small, all that go upon their feet, all that fly upon wings; yea, all the foreign lands . . . Thou settest all in their place and providest all with their needs . . . Thou art the life of life; through Thee men see . . ."

Early Judaism, as other Semitic religions of the Assyrians and Babylonians, was solely concerned with banding the people together in this life. It held no interest in a hereafter. Moses was their first great traditional leader. To him later scribes attributed the commandments and insistent worship of Yahweh. In the 12th century, B.C., the Israelites are portrayed as thrusting into Palestine, and under the sanction of Yahweh, thieving, plundering, killing, and driving out the inhabitants. These, the Philistines, Canaanites, Ammonites, Moabites, Amalekites, Jebusites, and Edomites grew in hatred against the Israelites, and the Israelites lived perpetually in conflict or on the brink of war.

Chapter 6

The Rise and Fall of the
Hebrew Empire

In the year circa 1025 B.C., the scattered loosely-organized Israelites under separate sheikhs or judges, united under a single ruler for more effective defense. A king was chosen, Saul, and ritualistically acclaimed "Yahweh's Anointed."

Then David, late in the 11th century, B.C., came to power in Israel having ruled over the tribe of Judah. On the death of Ishbosheth, son of King Saul, David was popularly chosen king. He conquered, and ruled over the independent city of Jerusalem to make it the religious and political center of Israel. There he built a palace on Mount Zion ("the city of David") and a brief period of peace, national unity and prestige was enjoyed under a people's government. After conquering Jerusalem, David extended the empire into Syria to the north and east across the Jordan. The empire flourished in independence under David. He became traditionally the Lord's Anointed beyond all others, psalmist, poet, and romantic hero.

Solomon, the second son of David and Bathsheba, assumed rule of Israel at the turn of the 10th century, B.C. Under his rule the kingdom attained its widest extent. Solomon avoided war by adding to his harem the daughters of potential enemies. A royal chapel was built during his reign, —a temple to Yahweh, excelled only by the luxury of his own palace. Yahweh worship then became increasingly centralized in Jerusalem. The God of Sinai became supreme. Royal splendor assumed magnificent proportions with the grandiose temple and royal palaces; but the taxation imposed on the people to attain this courtly luxury brought discontent. Solomon's alliance with heathen courts and his alien wives and concubines also provoked discontent of the prophetic party.

It was King Solomon who was accredited, though now historically questionable, with the writing of Proverbs, Ecclesiastics, the Song of Solomon, the Apocrypha, and the Wisdom of Solomon.

When Solomon died, Rehoboam, his heir, was petitioned by a people's representative of ten tribes, to reduce taxes. Rehoboam refused and promised only greater burdens. Upon such provocation the ten tribes of the North seceded. The North became Israel, with capital at Samaria. The southern kingdom was comprised of only Judah and Benjamin, with capital at Jerusalem.

Civil war between these two states raged intermittently until Samaria of Israel was finally destroyed by Assyria in 721 B.C. The weakened nation, never again to achieve greatness, was made prey by neighboring powers with the people humbled and their property plundered. The divided kingdom of Judah in the South and Israel in the North, was increasingly used as a pawn for intrigue by the great powers of Egypt, Assyria, Babylon, and Persia. Under constant threat of war, many Israeli refugees, as well as those of the South, fled to Media and Mesopotamia.

Great numbers of prophets arose in the vicissitudes of Israel and Judah under the constant menace of the great mideastern powers of that era. They spoke in the name of Yahweh who proclaimed Himself God of the chosen people of Israel (and Judah). The prophets admonished the people that Yahweh must be worshipped exclusively. As ethical monotheism advanced, Yahweh's ethical commandments, requiring justice, mercy, benevolence and righteousness, were to be obeyed. Disobedience incurred the wrath of Yahweh and His retribution. The prophets, however, found logical necessity in reconciling the constant peril and plight of the chosen people when favored by such a powerful God as Yahweh. So it was that the role of the chosen people was explained to those outsiders who, too, were righteous but not among the chosen. It was said that the chosen were made to suffer because of sinning. In apocalyptic revelation as related by the prophet Amos it was prophesied that the chosen people would be carried off in captivity beyond Damascus (a prophecy that was first historical fact.) Yahweh was concerned with others than the Jews, but the chosen people were His messengers and divine servants who would carry His Word beyond their land.

After Samaria had fallen to the Assyrians the northern people were assimilated in intermarriage and lost tribal identity. Judah, alone, remained intact, as a pitiful remnant of the once-great Hebrew Empire.

Chapter 7

The Eternal Messianic Hope

The Hebrew nation came into being under Saul, it achieved greatness under David, and wallowed in courtly luxury under Solomon. This persists as the tribal memory of the Jews to this day.

At the turn of the 6th century, B.C., the sole remaining organized remnant of Hebrews was then in Judah of the South, where the people were in abject submission to Assyria. It was only through cunning, intrigue, and selective patronage of military powers that the nucleus of the Jews was then sustained. A priestly hierarchy developed, together with the highly codified Kosher system and theocracy that characterizes orthodox Jewry. This was built about the tradition of Zadok, a high priest of David and Solomon, and of the priest brother of Moses, Aaron, and the traditional assistant priests, the Levites.

Covenants with Yahweh, His commandments, the priestly mandates, strict laws, and admonitions bound the people together—this too was reinforced by the unceasing hope for the resurgence of the Hebrew nation. The scribes and prophets took up the cry and promised high expectancy for the triumph of the chosen people. A great leader, just as King David had been, would come again, and under the holy sanction of Yahweh, in fact an anointed one, a Messiah, (cf., "Christos," Gr.) would lead the Jews to world conquest. More, the Lord God Himself, when His people had consumed themselves in devotion and obedience, would strike the foreign nations of the world, and make all men dead or Hebrew. This was the national paranoia, that may account for the strength of the Jewish fraternity.

In the year 587 B.C., Egypt invaded Judah. King Josiah of Judah was killed in battle and Pharaoh Necho installed his son,

Jehoiakim, to reign over Judah. One year later Jerusalem fell to Babylonia, just as the Prophet Jeremiah had warned the people it would. They had not, in the seesaw struggle for power raging about them, paid tribute to the nation in ascendancy, Babylon, and the new conqueror exiled them; into Babylon the exiled Jews carried with them their laws, tradition and their God, Yahweh.

Under Nebuchadnezzar of Babylon, Jerusalem had been again plundered and the people of Judah remained in submission. Three years later, the Jews remaining in Jerusalem rebelled, and regained the city, but the city was recaptured, and, this time, thousands of Jews enslaved. The Babylonian-appointed King Zedekiah of Jerusalem, twelve years later, revolted in league with the Jews, but this, too, was short-lived, for the Babylonians again took the city laying it in almost complete ruins. All but a few Jews were exiled to Babylonia. The land of Palestine was then virtually depleted of Jews.

In succeeding generations Babylon was overthrown by Persia in the greatest extent of the Persian empire (See Figure 2). The Persian imperial policy permitted a measure of Jewish functional autonomy. Descendants of the exiled Jewish expatriates, who had nurtured their idea of Yahweh throughout the years of their captivity, returned to the promised land. The Jewish religious community had intermingled with the religions of the Persians and the Babylonians. Yet the exclusiveness in their relationship with Yahweh prevailed.

The Temple in Jerusalem was rebuilt and, in the tradition of David and Solomon, advances in Judaism were achieved. The country continued to be the battle ground for Egypt and Persia. Many harassed Jews left as refugees to settle in Egypt—in southern Egypt a Temple to Yahweh was built during this period.

In their many migrations, the "Jews" as the Persians had come to call the people of Judah, assumed many variations in their religious outlook. Zoroastrian influences, in such precepts as an after life, became evident. The idea of sacred water, as the Hindus regarded the Ganges, became common among prophets and soothsayers in the Yahweh context. Then came the Greeks late in the 4th century, B.C., who were eventually to provide the

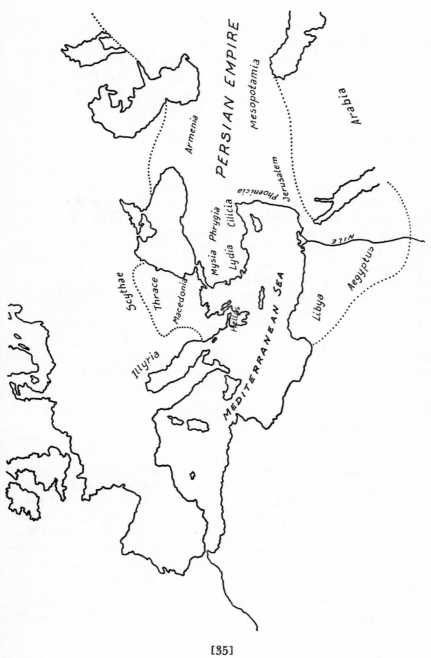

Fig. 2. The Great Persian Empire (500-300 B.C.)

groundwork immersed in the Yahweh cult for the extensive Christian dogma inherent in modern culture.

Macedonians defeated the Persians. In 333 B.C., Alexander the Great entered Jerusalem. He granted, as the Persians had done, functional autonomy to the Jews, and established a Jewish colony in Egypt called Alexandria. When Alexander died in 323 B.C., his generals, Ptolemy and Seleuces Nicator, vied for control. Ptolemy assumed control in Egypt and Nicator in Syria. Ptolemy captured Palestine in 302, B.C.; then Antiochus III of Seleucid assumed control. The latter became a self-proclaimed Epiphanes, meaning "appearance of God." He attempted to abolish the Jewish religion, desecrating the Temple and ordering the massacre of thousands of devout Jews. The Temple became used for Zeus worship, in the offering of swine's flesh to the god Zeus. The practice of Sabbath observances and other Jewish rites was punishable by death. Seleucus Nicator had established the Seleucidae dynasty (312-64 B.C.) at Antioch to rule over Bactria, Persia, Babylonia, Syria and part of Asia Minor. Jewish culture and religion was thus extensively modified under the Hellenistic influence of Seleucidae, and the Ptolemies who were the Greco-Egyptian rulers during this period. Greek culture during the post-Alexandrian period had spread throughout the Mediterranean. The Jews were no less influenced than were other cultures.

When Antiochus IV Epiphanes became king of Seleucidae in the second century, B.C., the religion of Jerusalem was again subject to forceful suppression. The Temple was desecrated, and the Dionysiac-Eleusinian sacrifice was instituted. Jews, who refused to accept the cult, were persecuted by these Greeks; yet the apostates, the Jewish infidels, were regarded among Jews with greater venom than were the Greeks themselves. A Jewish family, Hasmonaeans (Maccabees, meaning "hammer") who were zealous religious patriots, headed a revolt against Antiochus, inciting battles which were to last several decades. Mattathias (circa 180 B.C.), a priest of Judaism, founded the Maccabee dynasty. He was the first to take a stand against the persecutions.

Mattathias and a small group acted in protest against the heathen Hellenistic practices and fled to the wilderness of Judah.

They were soon joined by devout Jews, and eventually moved into the villages and cities where they renewed the worship of Yahweh. When Mattathias died, a son, Juhadah or Judas Maccabaeus, assumed command of the patriots. Under his leadership they reconquered Jerusalem. It was then that the Temple was purified and holy service to Yahweh resumed. Thus, today is celebrated this renewed dedication (Hanukkah) to Yahweh.

Judas fell in battle after completing an alliance with Rome. Judah became again an independent nation under his brother Simon. Simon was later to be treacherously murdered by his son-in-law, Ptolemy. Simon ruled in Jerusalem until 106 B.C., followed by his son, John Hyrcanus. The successor of Hyrcanus, Janneus, in political intrigue had crucified 800 Pharisees to ascend to a throne of Judea. His sons, Aristobulus II and Hyrcanus, vied for the throne which was no longer that of a king but of a High Priest. Then came Rome, when Pompey entered Jerusalem in 63 B.C.

During the Maccabean period, the Essenic movement had begun as a protest against the debasement of Judaism, and the failure to follow the mandates of the prophetic Yahweh, who would not save his people while they transgressed. Essenic creed became one of zealous devotion to the Torah for righteousness. For Essenes the belief was real and personal, and the only salvation was a supernatural intervention by an Anointed One of Yahweh. In the Essenic scriptoriums the writings of the prophets, such as those ascribed to Isaiah, were copied. There also were written the discipline and rules of their unique creed. Later rulers of the Maccabee family (Asmoneans) had leaned less toward religious piety, which characterized the Pharisees, and more toward the platform of political material progress of the Sadducee Party. This was to what the Essenes were reacting.

When Rome assumed power in 63 B.C., the Jews were once again subject to a foreign nation. Their very survival as a people was threatened, for their Yahweh cult was discouraged and regarded contemptuously. Through Roman citizenship and intermarriage they could easily have become assimilated. Instead, Messianic hopes arose anew. Their tradition was in search of a leader, such as Abraham who fathered their tribe, or Moses who had led them from Egypt, or David who had brought them greatness, peace and prosperity, or the early Maccabees who had renewed their aspirations of triumph. It was promised in the scriptures: ". . . may the Merciful One permit us to live on to the days of the Messiah!" The hope for such a Messiah was centuries old. It was a compounded one—of a divine miracle maker, of a strong leader who would reunite the Jewish nation, and deliver the people from the tyranny of conquering despots.

Messianic definitions differed among the secular Sadducees, the pious Pharisees, and devout Essenes; but, the rumble of age-old Messianic prophecies, the hope born of a degraded nationalism and the thunder of the then contemporary prophets instilled optimism in the breast of every Jew, a fever of expectancy in many, and in some a paranoid self-aggrandizement who considered themselves the Messiah.

When Herod died in 4 B.C., open sedition broke out. Any strong personality was accepted as king among the bands of Jews who would win their rights. Publius Varus, Roman governor of Syria, crucified two thousand Jews during these revolts. The rebellious Jews were forever giving trouble:

Judas the Gaulonite (Zealot) in 7 A.D., led a major insurrection that was crushed and continued underground.

Theudas (44 A.D.) led thousands into the wilderness. In divine inspiration, they were to march straight through the Jordan dryshod as Joshua. These uprisings, however, were also quelled.

Sicarri, a secret society of assassins, vowed to the cause of nationalized Jewry, operated surreptitiously, typically moving in crowds on holy days and knifing Romans and others of their enemies.

Provocation to rebellion was perhaps justified. Roman procurators commissioned bandits to steal, murder, and pillage on a percentage-take basis. Such corruption and lawlessness developed, as was inevitable, into open war against Rome in 66 A.D. The Romans viewed all this as outlandish and intolerable, that of all their empire, Judea alone should rebel.

From within came the incessant cry of Messiah, and pretenders to messiahship—John of Gischala, Eleazor the Zealot, and Simon of Gioras. Such men as these aroused the impoverished and resentful against their own—the wealthy. "Kill the oppressors," came the cry. Priests and men of wealth were murdered, records were burned so that debts would be cleared away. The poor thus joined into the insurrection, as well as those with the fervor of expectancy in the apocalyptic messianic creed.

Titus of Rome made concessions, but the Jews would have none. Meanwhile, the internal strife reduced many to the eating of dung, and even cannibalism. The armies of Titus lay siege to Jerusalem for eight months. Almost complete devastation followed. Nearly one and one-half million Jews were killed, or starved or sold into slavery.

Less than a century later, Bar Cochba began the final Jewish revolt. Jerusalem was again razed and all Jews exiled, and this time forbidden to return. Late in the first century A.D., the Jews were thus removed from their homeland; not until midway into the 20th century, A.D., were they in any measure to resettle.

The national history of Jewry had been one of turmoil and conflict. In a thousand years there were only brief respites in strife from within and without. Enmity was all about, first from those into whose lands the Hebrews had intruded when infiltrating Palestine. Internal conflict split them into Judah and Israel. They were subsequently wracked upon by the invading Assyrians, Babylonians, Persians, Greeks, and finally the Romans. Through it all a prototype monotheism, such as that of the Egyptian god Aton, had developed in the war god Yahweh. The cult of Yahweh was not unmaleable. Other Semitic cults and religions, such as Ishtarism and Zoroastrianism, served to mold its later theology. Buddhism moved in from the East with the swelling Persian Empire of the 5th and 6th centuries B.C. Hellenistic enlightenment, during the Alexandrian period, briefly damped the cult and brought Orphean-Dionysian, Pythagorian, and Platonic influences. From Rome came the influence of Mithra. As the prophets decried the contamination of Yahweh by these foreign cults, so were they influenced. Jewish sects came eventually to parrot and believe, as did others about the Mediterranean, that a god man would rise from the dead and redeem His people. And so began the story of Jesus.

Suggested Further Reading

1. Albright, W. *The Archaeology of Palestine and the Bible* Fleming H. Revell Co., N. Y. 1932
2. Albright, W. *From Stone Age to Christianity* John Hopkins Press, Md. 1946
3. Anati, E. *Palestine before the Hebrews* 1963
4. Arnold, M. *Isaiah of Jerusalem*
5. Bokser, B. Z. *Wisdom of the Talmud* The Citadel Press N. Y., 1962
6. Charles, R. H. *The Apocrypha and Pseudepigrapha of the Old Testament in English Supra* The Clarendon Press, Oxford 1913
7. Charles, R. H. *Religious Development Between Old and New Testaments.* Henry Holt, 1913
8. Frazer, J. G. *Folklore in the Old Testament* The MacMillan Co., London, 1919
9. Frazer, J. G. *The New Golden Bough* Doubleday & Co., Inc., N. Y., 1961
10. Gray, G. B. *A Critical Introduction to the Old Testament* Charles Scribner's Sons, N. Y., 1913
11. Gordon, C. H. *Before the Bible: The Common Background of Greek and Hebrew Civilizations* Harper & Row, N. Y., 1963
12. Hamilton, H. F. *The People of God*
13. Howlett, D. "Faith and History" in *The Atlantic Monthly* April, 1956
14. Kenyon, F. *The Bible and Archaeology* Harper & Brothers, 1940
15. Kramer, S. *The Sumerians: Their History, Culture and Character* 1963
16. Leslie, E. *Old Testament Religion* The Abingdom Press, N. Y., 1936
17. Marti, K. *The Religion of the Old Testament* Putnam's Sons, N. Y., 1907
18. McCabe, J. *The Forgery of the Old Testament*
19. Milley, C. R. *The Prophets of Israel* Philosophical Library, Inc., N. Y., 1959

20. Oesterly, W., and Robinson, T. *Hebrew Religion* The Mac-Millan Co., N. Y., 1930
21. Peake, A. S. *Problem of Suffering in the Old Testament* Alec Allenson, 1947
22. Pfeiffer, R. H. *"Introduction to the Old Testament"* Harper and Brothers, N. Y., 1941
23. Robinson, T. H. *Prophecy and Prophets* Charles Scribners, Sons, N. Y., 1923
24. Robinson, T. H. *A History of Israel* Clarendon Press, Oxford, 1932
25. Skinner, J. *Prophecy and Religion* University Press, Cambridge, 1922
26. Streane, A. W. *The Age of the Maccabees* Eyre & Spottiswood, London, 1898
27. *Westminster Historical Atlas to the Bible* Westminster Press, 1945
28. Wollman, T. P. *The Graphic History of the Jewish Heritage* Shergold Publishers, Inc., N. Y. 1963

III

Gospel and Non-Gospel
Narrations of Jesus

Jesus is the exemplary model of being we are exhorted to follow. He is God's Anointed, the Christ, ordained to lead the Jews and all men in the ways of righteousness and salvation. In recent decades we have learned that Jesus, as Paul of Tarsus, was all things to all men. He was, above all else, a "Salvation-of-God" creation, whether in fact created by man or God. If we are to establish the reality of Jesus, apart from theology, historical, psychological, sociological, archaeological—every source of evidence available—must be employed. In this quest we might ask, was He the Son of God, the Son of Man, or the Son of Mythology?

Chapter **8**

Jesus — If He Were Man

Before assuming an analytical posture in examining the Gospel Jesus, or Jesus the man, we must again study the human individual in the perspective of modern psychology. William James, an early American psychologist, once contrasted culture-borne, complex man with simple animal forms. Imagine yourself as your dog, he proposed. There is nought in you then of fancy and creativity. Sunsets that inspire a human poet would for you, as a dog, mean only a time for the food plate. You never wonder about existence. The universe is, because you are in it. You can think of nothing apart from it. You have no literary facility nor imagination. You never ponder philosophically about from whence you came nor are to go. The world is never abstract in fancy, but concrete and physical. But when you are man, you live in a culture abounding with artifacts that provoke and symbols that stimulate.

A society of men, confronted with myriad such problems as those of disease, unemployment, or threats of war, is provoked to think and to discuss cures, economics or theories of state. Such problems are often of no interest to any great numbers of citizens, but now, when they become involved, are baffled, thwarted, puzzled and frustrated. Each is driven to model, project, ponder and reflect, and to think out solutions. Symbolic representative images are substituted for action to avert the final and possibly disastrous results of overt action. Each man's thinking necessarily occurs in his external environment, a cultural matrix that initiates and supports his thinking and acting. It does not, as is sometimes implied, occur in a biological or social vacuum. A man's thinking cannot consist of disembodied ideas immaculately conceived in an isolated consciousness. Thinking, above all else, bears the imprint of a social matrix. Even the mere presence of others, in overt, subtle communication, will alter the course of a man's thinking. His thinking is stimulated by theirs, but it flattens out and becomes "conventionalized." Frederick Bartlett, several decades ago, demonstrated the stabilizing effects of social conventions upon the individual's thinking. As a man communicates, the subjects that dominate the interest of those whom he addresses are commonly familiar ones. The cultural background establishes the way a group sees an event, and stabilizes an individual's thinking within the social framework. The implied differences are resisted. Thus, the "Portrait D'Homme" abstract figure presented to subjects by Bartlett for successive serial reproductions, became the face and image of man. A peculiar Egyptian hieroglyphic-like figure became the common cat as it was successively transformed by subjects in an Anglicized culture. It was by such a process that the Egyptian goddess Isis became the goddess Persephone in the Hellenistic culture. The culture of a society, its traditions, dominant images and symbols, in such a manner, regulates and controls individuals' thinking. No matter how radical in perspective differences may be, the cultural norm must dominate. Language itself is like a museum collection of ancient tools, passed down through the ages. In a sense, the language uses the individual, though he would deny that words are anything but his tools. Yet, the words of a love song command his sentiment, or a hymn eulogizing the Savior evokes his reverence, or the proposition of angels dancing on a pin head emerges for his analysis.

A cultural framework bore Jesus of Galilee. When the theological shell of modern Christianity has been split open, we must realize that Jesus was a cultural man. His membership in a socio-economic class instilled a perspective or a point of view. As a result of immediate cultural influences, he acquired a trend in his thinking. This he verbalized fluently and understood only within the framework of his culture. His outlook emerged in a demoralizing society and he reflected on the Messianic solutions as conventionalized in the Hebrew culture.

To account for the creativity of Jesus as given in the Gospel is presumptuous. A well-established, critical historical perspective is necessary, really, to understand Jesus as a teacher. Detailed information is essential, covering His interpersonal relations, schools and teachers under whom He studied, audiences whom he addressed, the Zeitgeist—the philosophical and cultural climate of his times, the social political trends of which He was an exponent, as well as the idiomatic forms and critical standards of those under whose influence his apprenticeship was served. (See Figure 3). It would be necessary that these pressures and influences be explicitly determined. Then would the Gospel of Jesus become intelligible. Then would the man Jesus be seen as but a half-way house, wherein evolved the shadowy substance from which the Christian Church was formed.

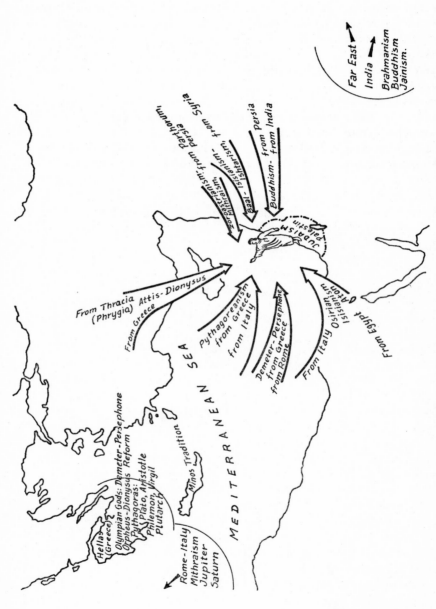

Fig. 3. Religions and Ideologies Influencing the Gospel Jesus

Chapter **9**

The Gospel Narrative Bases of Christ

Christianity is founded theologically almost exclusively upon the books selected and redacted by early and later Church fathers.

Bible interpretations are the cardinal points of difference among Christian sects, particularly between the Protestant and Roman Catholic. Individual interpretation is permitted among Protestants, while the Roman Catholic Church assumes sole authority in interpretation (cf., notes in Roman Catholic bibles directing interpretation).

Extant manuscripts include the 4th century Greek Codex Vaticanus, and Codex Sinaiticus, 5th century Codex Alexandrinus, and 6th century Codex Bezae. Most ancient fragments of the old testament are the 2nd century, B.C. Papyrus of Nash, and the recently found Dead Sea Scrolls.

The original Roman Catholic Latin translation was the Vulgate of St. Jerome. English versions were the Douay or Rheims-Douay published by Roman Catholic scholars at Rheims in 1882 and in Douai, France, extensively revised by Archbishop Challoner. New Roman Catholic translations were undertaken in the Westminister version in England, and in a Revised Rheims-Douay edition.

Protestant bibles were first developed by John Wycliffe in translating the Latin into English, and the later Lollard revisions of the 15th century. William Tyndale's translation from Hebrew and Greek was the first published Protestant bible in 1525-26, which was later reworked as the Bishop's Bible in 1568. Versions contemporary with the original Tyndale Bible were those of Miles Coverdale and Thomas Matthew. Coverdale's was the first version adopted by the British Crown in 1539.

The Geneva Bible was also developed during this period by Protestant Calvinists. The authorized version of the King

James Bible of 1611 was composed by a committee of churchmen headed by Lancelot Andrewes (a literary work ranked with
those of Shakespeare). Revised versions have been recently completed, including the Revised Standard versions of American
scholars published in 1952, and the New English Bible.

Biblical content coming from such continous redactions, of
course, may be highly suspect. The original biblical content itself is also of dubious origin. Common literary practice of Hebrew scribes, as well as that of later writers of the New Testament, was apocalyptical revelation in ascribing prophecy and
authorship to a hero of the past. This would be analogous to a
20th-century writer completing an article on the plight and in-
spirations of America, historically documented, yet ascribing authorship and prophecy to Abraham Lincoln. In such a manner
as this, many of the books were written as ascribed to authorship
of Moses, Solomon, Isaiah, Daniel, and the Twelve Patriarchs;
this is also evidenced in the books of the New Testament. Scribes
tended to develop the text and narration according to their own
partisanship and interest. Take, for example, the Book of Daniel. Here the author's intention is quite clear. He wished to
convince Jews that Yahweh would protect any Jew who refused
to obey a sacrilegious ruler (e.g., during the periods of Antiochus
Epiphanes of the second century). The author's narrations
were frequently unfactual, while the strength of his persuasion
was quite obviously fanatical. Recently discovered tablets of
baked clay prepared under King Cyrus, ruler of Persia near the
turn of the 5th century, B.C., have refuted the historical validity of the Book of Daniel. The alleged Babylonian king, Bel-
shazzar in Daniel was fictious. Babylon was not taken in war,
but was peacefully surrendered to Cyrus, and not Darius. The
practice of apocalyptical revelation is also evident, since no writer
could have described the Chaldeans as they are in Daniel until
after the period of Alexander. The author of Daniel must have
lived several centuries after Babylon's fall. His facts were inaccurate; his motives obviously Judaian.

The earliest Christian manuscripts now extant are those from
the fourth century. Original New Testament fragments were in
Greek, none of which are now available. Church fathers up until the fourth century had had abundant opportunity to edit and

make redactions necessary to resolve theological controversies in gaining proponents. French, German, and Anglicized old and new versions of the bible have also been obviously subjected to unique cultural perspective and expediency. The King James version, for example, gave literary flare in the then embellishing Anglicized rhetorical convention.

The first New Testament documents were written in a kind of mixed Greek, called Judaeo-Greek (Hellenistic). The Septuagint (Greek version of the old testament) as used in Egypt, Asia Minor and Palestine, was in this language. The spoken language and idioms of this period are obscure, but they seem largely to have developed as a hybrid language adapted to commercial transactions between Greek and Jew. Of the Synoptics, Mathew, Mark and Luke, Mark was written the earliest at about 60 to 70 A.D. (This may be so, since Mark was with Peter in Rome during this period.) Mark is generally considered to be the most authenic of the three gospels presenting a more common narrative basis, i.e., Mathew and Luke appear to be expanded versions of Mark. Mathew and Luke were likely written early in the second century, with expansions and redactions occurring late in the same century (cf., the Virgin Birth). The Book of John is obviously a theological fabrication, with all traces of any historical accuracy lost. It was written with the obvious intention of compromising existing pagan doctrines around the 2nd century, of, by, and for Gentiles. The Grecian Logos doctrine is also apparent, when Christ has become the Word (absolute and unchangeable) made flesh. Jesus was here considered to be a human being, into whom at Baptism the word of God entered as imminent power. His kingdom, in John, is not of this world, which repudiates the central orientation of the Judaistically-oriented Synoptics heralding an earthly kingdom of Christ. In the Book of John all that is required to be a Christian is to love one another; this disregards the celibate communistic precepts prevalent in the Synoptics. Other differences of candidly Grecian terms in the Book of John include:

1) Jesus has good relations with His family.
2) He openly proclaims Himself to be Christ.
3) He no longer rejects His family, nor do they seek to carry Him home because He is beside Himself.

4) He makes no unproven prophecies.
5) He no longer casts out devils (Zoroastrian influence on Judaism) .
6) He no longer condemns the rich.
7) He assumes the role of Dionysus and makes and gives wine at the Cana wedding.
8) It is the populace who proclaim Him entering Jerusalem —not merely the disciples.

The reasons apparent for such sharp departures from the Synoptics were fundamentally to make Jesus Christ acceptable in Grecian cultural terms, and to support the Greek practice of monogamy and property rights. The growing clergy could not survive such communistic elements as espoused in the Synoptics Gospel Jesus; rather, they sought monetary and political support of the Greeks by formulating creeds and dogmas that would be acceptable to them. The Book of John made possible an implicit faith in the pre-existing Christ, and this became the practical basis for the Gentile universal Church. The Grecian emphasis purveyed for communicants mansions in the celestial realm. It thus relegated to a vague status the chief emphasis of the Synoptics, the Parousia, viz., an earthly kingdom where Christ would reign.

The Books of Mathew, Mark and Luke, due to emphasis on geneology and the triumph of the Jewish people, seem by contrast to the Book of John to have been largely of Jewish origin. Mathew was likely a severe Hellenic redaction of an earlier Aramaic version strongly espousing the Jewish Christian sect. In the more thoroughly Greek version in the Book of John, Jesus became more like a Greek mystery soter. He became God. The Greek stoic Logos Doctrine inherent in the Book of John was later to develop into the Trinitarian dogma.

The earlier strongly Judaistic Christian gospels, as that according to the Hebrews, were later apparently destroyed by Gentile Christians.

The Apocrypha (meaning "kept hidden"), consisted of sixteen books including the Gospel According to Peter, Gospel Fragments of Fayum, Oxyrhyncus, Pseudipigrapha, Book of Jubilees, Testament of the Twelve Patriarchs, the Protevangelium of James, Gospel of Thomas and Acts of John. Several traces of these apocryphal works have been studied by both scholars and theologians alike. (cf., the scholarly work of the late Reverend James Donehoo.) The accepted gospels contained in both Protestant and Catholic bibles need not be considered to be historically more valid nor authentic than were those of the Apocrypha. Rather, they have achieved their status solely through the judgment of early Church fathers who considered them to be more edifying of the dogma.

We have seen that the first four books of the New Testament were writen one or two centuries after the period covered in the life of Jesus, in fact, after the Epistles of Paul were written. The books themselves were not written by the nominal authors presumed to be apostles. Luke (1:1-4) is admittedly a documentation of traditional beliefs, and disclaims first-hand knowledge. Mathew, on the other hand, may have been developed from the apocryphal work credited to him, the "Gospel According to the Hebrews." All may have drawn from a document of likewise unknown authorship available at the time, the "Sayings of Jesus." The geneological portions were Judaic, while virgin-birth references were Greek pagan redactions. The Book of John confounds the chronology given in the other gospels as well as confuses the local geographic travels of Jesus. Complete agreement among the gospels obtains only in the arrest, trial and crucifixion of Jesus. The Gospel of Peter later even elaborated on this basic drama, embellishing it with supernaturalistic voices at the crucifixion. The crucifixion drama was also readily adaptable to pagan conventional drama and pageantry (cf., the Osirian and Eleusinian mysteries).

Early Christian growth was often promoted by deception and Church forgeries. Passages in the writing of Josephus mentioning Jesus as Christ have since been disproven as fraudulent. Independant testimony is also lacking in the 1st century writing of Justus of Tiberius, a native of Galilee and historian whose works, *The Wars of the Jews,* and *Chronicle of the Jewish Kings from Moses to Agrippa,* were available until around the 9th century, A.D. The educated Roman, Tacitus, describing the superstitious Christian cult in Rome in the 2nd century, merely refers to the tradition of Christ, who allegedly suffered death at the hands of a Roman procurator, Pontius Pilate. There have thus been no extra-gospel sources supporting the historicity of Jesus.

That the historical Jesus lived is, however, more than a matter of loose conjecture or faith in the holy books. The evidence is found in the extensive Christian movement 60 years after His demise, the interpersonal interaction that had apparently occurred between Him and Mathew, and Peter who was later known in Rome. It is also given credence by the credibility of such men, apart from superimposed mythology, as Zoroaster, Guatama, Mahavira, John the Baptist, and Julius Caesar. When we accept these as historical figures, we must, by analogy, accept the historicity of Jesus. Historians, however, frequently have misgiving about the gospel sources, which disagree, and are often raked with inconsistencies. Several such inconsistencies include:

1) John the Baptist both did and did not recognize Jesus as the Messiah (cf., John 1, 29, 34, and Matt. xi, 2,3)

2) John the Baptist was, and was not Elias, the harbinger of the Messiah (cf., John, 1,21 and Mat. xi, 14)

3) The father of Joseph (Mary's husband) was Jacob—no, he was Heli (cf., Mathew 1, 16 and Luke iii, 23)

4) Mary and Joseph fled into Egypt with the infant Jesus—no, they did not flee, but returned to Nazareth (cf., Matt. 11, 14, 15, 19, 23 and Luke ii, 22, 39)

5) Jesus went into the wilderness after his baptism—no, He went to the Cana wedding (cf., Mark i, 12, 13 and John ii, 12)

6) Jesus preached his first sermon on the Mount—no, it was on a plain (cf., Matt. v, 1, 2 and Luke vi, 17, 20)

7) John was in prison when Jesus went preaching into Galilee—no, he was not in prison (cf., Mark i, 14, and John i, iii, 22, 24)

8) Jesus told the disciples to go forth with neither staff nor sandals—no, they should take staff and sandals (cf., Mark vi, 8,9 and Matt. x, 9,10)

9) Two blind men cried for His mercy—no, only one (cf., Matt. xx, 30 and Luke xvii, 35, 38)

10) Two men came possessed from a tomb—no, only one (cf., Matt. viii, 28 and Mark v, 2)

11) A centurion sought Jesus to heal his servant—no, it was the messenger of the centurion (cf., Matt. viii, 5, 6 and Luke vii, 3, 4)

12) Jesus was crucified at the third hour—no, it was the sixth (cf., Mark xv, 24, and John xix, 14, 15)

13) Judas conspired with the chief priests before the Last Passover Supper—no, it was after (cf., Luke xxii, 3, 4, 7 and John xiii, 27)

14) Both thieves reviled Jesus in execution—no, only one, the other rebuking the first (cf., Matt. xxvii, 44 and Luke xxiii, 39, 40)

15) Vinegar mingled with gall was offered to Jesus on the cross—no, it was wine with myrrh. (cf., Matt. xxvii, 34 and Mark xvi, 23)

16) Three women came to the sepulcher—no, it was two—no, it was only one (cf., Mark xvi, Matt. xxviii, 1 and John xx, 1)

17) Jesus arose on the third day—no, it was the second (cf., Matt. xii, 40, and Mark xv, 25, 42, 44, 45, 46, xvi, 9)
The women told the disciples of the resurrection—no, they did not tell anyone (cf., Luke xxiv, 9 and Mark xvi, 8)

18) Jesus ascended from Bethany—no, (cf., Luke xxiv, 50, 51 and Mark xvi, 14, 19; also Acts 1, 9, 12)

19) Christ is equal with God—no, He is not equal (cf., John x, 30 and Matt. xxiv, 36)

20) Christ judges men—no, He does not judge (cf., John v, 22, 30 and John xii, 47)

21) Christ was all powerful—no (cf., Matt. xxvii and Mark vi, 5)

22) The Law was changed by Christ—no, it was not (cf., Luke xvi, 16 and Matt. v, 17, 18, 19)

23) Christ came to bring peace—no, He came to make war (cf., Luke i, 76, 79, ii, 13, 19, and Matt. x, 34)

Such inconsistencies as these can be explained only in a realization that different points of view and partisanships were involved. The cause was not one of fidelity in describing, in the discipline of an historian, an historical figure. Rather, such zealous partisanship resulted in distortion and cluttering of tradition, at the center of which was a conglomerate, martyred hero. The facts employed were devices selected to give credence to gospel narrations. For example, the Persian Magi made pilgrimages in the Fravashi tradition; some, at this period, journeyed through Palestine proclaiming Emperor Nero to be the God Mithras. In the gospels, they came to hail the birth of Jesus. The Annunciations of the Sheperds may have been liturgical compositions adopted in Luke and coming from the Mithraic pagan doctrine. The slaughter of infants ordered by Herod, of which there is no other historical evidence, may have been fabricated to fulfill the prophecy of Rachel (cf., also the flight of Mary and Joseph to Egypt). The preachments of Jesus could also have come from documented Essenic formulations which bear many similarities to principles espoused in the gospels. Also, the narrations want much for consistency (cf., Mathew's Sermon on the Mount and the scattered utterances in Luke). The home of Jesus, Nazareth, is also historically dubious in this period. Josephus made no mention of this town during his extensive recruitment for the war against the Romans in the middle of the first century, nor is it given reference elsewhere.

Gospel sources are highly suspect as invalid and unreliable documents about the life of Jesus. They rather appear to be conventional or traditional superstructures, perverting history according to the time and culture in which they originated. From these, there is but little basis to address the subject of an historical Jesus.

Chapter 10

Contextual Non-Gospel Sources

The historicity of Jesus is commonly accepted among scholars, though they remain perplexed by the inconsistencies in the gospels, the spurious authorship, and the lack of historical verification. For this reason, many have become intensely interested in leather scrolls recently found about the Dead Sea. The scrolls have been positively dated at around the first century B.C. or A.D. In dating and translation, a veritable wealth of data has been compiled on a peculiar Jewish sect that existed around the time of Jesus called the Essenes. Scholars have long been familiar with this sect historically as described in the writings of the Jewish historians, Josephus and Philo. They were a minority group in Palestine who were extremely devout, and often subjected to severe harassment at the hands of orthodox Pharisees and the irreligious-politico Sadducees. Little had been known of the Essenes, who were, to all intents and purposes, highly secretive in their codes and rituals out of fear of being persecuted. Members of most Essenic sects were celibate, highly disciplined, and sworn to guard the precepts and sanctity of the group. The workings of the sect have been revealed over the centuries as their hidden documents have been found and translated. These included:

1) The Book of Enoch, found in Abyssinia in the 18th century, was composed around 180 B.C. with portions dating to 70 B.C. Pythagorean elements, somewhat paralleling the content of the Book of Daniel, are evident.

2) The Damascus Document was found in Cairo, Egypt, at the turn of the present century. Content revealed an early phase of the Essenic holy movement when Judaism predominated.

3) Testament of the Twelve Patriarchs, or the Didache, was composed around 120 B.C. In it, each of the twelve sons of Ja-

cob deliver an ethical monologue essentially that of the Sermon on the Mount.

More recent findings include:

4) St. Mark's Isaiah Scroll (Kept at St. Mark Monastery). This contains the complete book of Isaiah.

5) Hebrew University Isaiah Scroll, contains the Book of Isaiah, Chapters 36 to 66 and parts of earlier chapters.

6) Midrash on the Book of Habakkuk (commentary on sacred text) bears reference to a "Teacher of Righteousness."

7) The Manual of Discipline, or the Order of the Community, describes a covenant of steadfast love in which members are united with God. The spirits of light and truth and darkness and error, the rule of order, entrance requirements, and penalties for infringement are described, together with a thanksgiving prayer.

8) The War of the Sons of Light with the Sons of Darkness— describes a conflict between the righteous and the wicked.

9) The Thanksgiving Psalms are twenty Psalms similar to those of the Old Testament.

10) *Lamech*, written in Aramaic rather than Hebrew, as are the others, contains expanded chapters from the Book of Genesis.

As an historical observer, Philo Judaeus of Alexandria, in his *Quod Omnis Probus Liber*, written about 20 A.D., described the members of the sect as indifferent to money, worldly possessions, and pleasure, and being kindly, equitable and amiable. They lived in colonies and admitted any traveling member of their sect to share in their belongings, having a common fund for food and clothing. Pliny, in his *Historica Naturalis*, about 70 A.D., wrote of Essenes as living on the west side of the Dead Sea, without women, among palm trees, growing in number by the joining of new members. Josephus, in his *Wars of the Jews*, described the three Jewish sects, the Pharisees, the Sadducees, and the Essenes, the latter of whom pretended of severe discipline. The Essenes were themselves chaste, but sought out the children of others while they were yet docile and pliable for learning, and formed in them the beliefs and manners of the sect. They decried the lascivious behavior of women, and condemned their universal infidelity. Essenic groups lived in many cities and went freely among their sects. Their piety was extreme. In a work day they praised their God before departing for work in their trade. Each day at noon they returned and bathed their bodies, dressing in white garments. They ate in the presence of a priest who offered grace before and after the meal. They returned then to work, and came back to supper in the same manner. The Sabbath was devoted to rest, worship of God, and the study of Mosaic Laws. They were permitted their own accord to offer succour to such as deserved it, and who stood in need. They dispersed only righteous anger and restrained passion. Theirs was fidelity and honesty without swearing to God, and they took pains in studying the ancients and chose what was most advantageous for their souls and bodies. Their vows were in piety to God and justice to men, to hate the wicked and assist the righteous, to love truth and reprove lie tellers, and keep secret the doctrines of the society. They were organized into four classes, and, indeed, of such rigidity that if the lower of these should so much as touch the higher, the higher was required to cleanse himself.

In the war with the Romans late in the first century, members of the sect were tortured, their flesh stretched and distorted, burned, torn to pieces in an effort to induce them to blaspheme their legislator or eat what was forbidden, and tell what they were pledged to keep in trust; yet, they tormented their tormentors with smiles in their pain as they died expecting to live again. For they believed that bodies were transient, but souls, from the subtile air, were only temporarily joined with bodies to be released from the bondage through death to rejoice in a heaven. This was a place beyond the ocean (as the Greeks believed) which was oppressed by neither storm, rain, snow nor sleet, but caressed by gentle breezes. The damned, they believed, went to dark and tempestuous dens of unending torment. Thus the vehement inclination of bad men to vice was restrained by fear and expectation that they would suffer eternal punishment after death. Among the Essenes were also those who undertook the telling of things to come through reading of the holy books, and using several purifications, thus being conversant with the discoveries of the prophets. There were those, too, who lived as Essenes but believed in the succession of their kind through the bearing of children, yet without regard for body pleasure.

In the *Antiquities of the Jews*, Josephus delineates the "Party line" of Sadducees, Pharisees and the Essenes. The Sadducees denied fate and claimed that we ourselves are the cause of good. They held that we receive evil only from our own folly. Sadducees developed as a party during the Maccabean period, called the Zadokites in the name of Zadok, a high priest of King David. In the pre-Christian era they were the educated and wealthy class of political nationalists. The Zadokites subsequently split into Sadducees, (who became economic conservatives, increasingly less religious), and Chasids. The Book of Daniel was written by a Chasid. Chasids further diverged into the Pharisees and Essenes. The Essenes (originating circa 145-100 B.C.) became religious extremists, considering that fate governed all things, and that nothing befell man that was not according to its determination. Pharisees fell midway between the extremes of the Sadducees and the Essenes. The Essenic doctrine held that all things could be ascribed to God. The goal of all men was to achieve righteousness. Essenes offered no sacrifices in the Temple, but applied their own pure lustrations while completely addicted to virtue. The Pharisees developed temple worship and such externalized formal discipline as in rules concerning the Sabbath and dietary practices.

The Essenes were yet Jews devoted to Mosaic tradition, but examination of their doctrine indicates they had been profoundly influenced by Persian Zoroastrian and Grecian Pythagorian precepts. They considered the ephemeral existence inconsequential, thus giving formal allegiance to whatever civil power ruled. Their leader, or hero image, was a claimant to prophetship, called the "Teacher of Righteousness." The "Teacher" had traveled and studied extensively among the Persians, the Indians, the Greeks and the Asians. In their tradition, the "Teacher of Righteousness" suffered persecution at the hands of the Maccabees. During a Passover celebration he was condemned to be exiled for Essenic heresy; but he taunted and tormented those who condemned him, insisting that their calendar was fallacious, as were their holy days. His sentence was changed to death. He was executed during the Passover Festival, establishing (or perpetuating) a tradition, which Jesus later was to assume. This "Teacher of Righteousness" personified for the Essenes the essential sacrificial God-Man, for whom the sacred meal was celebrated, viz., the body and blood of their savior god (cf., also the Jewish legend of Yeshu adopted in the persecution and virgin-birth stories).

The esoteric religious documents of the Essenes were kept secret, since they contained heresy that could subject the group to further persecution as revolutionaries, violating the Law as enforced by the Pharisees. The Essenes refused to take oaths, nor did they celebrate the commonly accepted holy days. They ignored temple worship, and rejected marriage and private property. Their "Teacher of Righteousness" had become a kind of martyr during the Maccabean period. He was believed by the sect to be the Messiah, to have arisen from the dead, ascending into heaven to return as the Son of Man, and fulfilling the Danielic prophecy. Such rebels as John the Baptist may also have been Essenes. He held in common with the Essenes a hatred of Pharisees and Sadducees and may have been an erstwhile Essenic prophet who heralded the coming of a new Messiah, to fulfill the prophecy of Isaiah.

Organization of the Essenes was rigid. There were Priests, their assistants, the Levites, the lay members, and novitiates. Membership rites and requirements included:

1) The first year an initiate underwent an inner transformation in acceptance of the Essenic practices. He was subjected to preliminary examination by a board, to be probationary for one year while submitting initially to the discipline.

2) He was again given examination by the board to determine if he had indeed adopted Essenic ways; he was then admitted to the novitiate.

3) A second year of probationary status was required, followed again by examinations; if passed the second time, the novitiate was admitted to the sacred meal and his belongings accepted into the community.

4) A third year of trial was required before being given the most demanding examination; if passed, he became a brother, to be admitted to the sacrament of the eucharistic wine, and to full council in the assembly.

Punishments of the sect exacted for infringement of the society's rules varied:

An offender was excluded from the sacred rites and one-quarter of his rations was withheld. Offenses included withholding wealth or calling a brother a fool (three months), interrupting a neighbor (10 days), gossiping (one year). Murmuring against the community was punished by temporary expulsion, and betraying the order, permanent expulsion.

The monastic scheme was after Isaiah; a group of members, chosen for their exemplary conduct, went to the Qumran Monastery to establish a place of God in the Wilderness (Isaiah 40). Most continued to live in a thiasoi (small community) while working in a normally employed capacity. The chosen were supported in their work and study by the common fund. So it was that on the shores of Lake Asphaltitis (now the Black Sea), that the sect established the Qumran Monastery for this was truly a place in the wilderness with barren shores, ridges and crevasses, where earthquakes rocked the land, and malodorous sulphur emanated from the water. Here was the place, as in Isaiah, where, when the "Anointed One" should come, the crooked would be made straight, and rough places plain, where on the barren shores would grow trees for food, whose leaves would never fade nor fruit be diminished, because the waters would come from the place of the everlasting sanctuary. The Essenes became extinct in their original form after the annihilation and banishment of Jews from Israel by the Romans in 70 A.D. The new Jewish sect of the Christians, paralleling and succeeding that of the Essenes, was marked by such events as follows:

1) *37 B.C.*: Antigonus, the last of the Maccabean line, was succeeded by Herod the Great in Judea.

2) *37 B.C. - 4 B.C.*: Herod the Great completed splendid buildings at the seaport of Caesarea, and restored the Temple in Jerusalem.

3) *4 B.C. - 34 A.D.*: Herod Antipas ruled in Galilee. He married his brother's wife, and was rebuked by John the Baptist. Antipas was defeated in battle by Aretas, the father of his first wife. Herod Archelaus reigned in Judea until 6 A.D., when removed by Rome. After Archelaus, administration of Judea was assigned to a Roman Procurator, who reported to the Governor of Syria. Pontius Pilatus held this office from 26 A.D. to 36 A.D.

4) *34 A.D. - 44 A.D.*: Agrippa ruled as the last Jewish king in Galilee; then Rome assumed full authority.

At the beginnings of Roman secular decadence, in its vast impersonal administration, beleaguered by political corruption, the Jewish sect of the Christians emerged. Under Roman Procurator Pilatus, tensions between Jews and Romans increased. Jews were inordinate religio-nationalistic fanatics who considered the Romans sacrilegious. After 44 A.D., Palestinean Governor Antonius Felix ruled with an iron hand and crucified Jews en masse for minor infractions. The Sicarii became organized in retaliation as a militant Jewish group who harassed the Romans and made their life in Palestine indeed hazardous. Romans were knifed or otherwise assassinated as they walked on the streets. During this time the Jewish Christian movement began, similar in both doctrine and practice to that of Essenes and the convenanters at Qumran. Christians became known as the Sect of the Nazarenes, possibly from the word "netzer," meaning scion or offspring in the Messiahship of David who was the offshoot or son of Jessie. "Nazarene" and "Christians" thus may have meant, "Believers in the Messiah," with nationalistic as well as religious overtones.

In 64 A.D., the Roman Gessius Florus ruled in Judea. His administration was fraught with licentiousness and corruption. Dissenters were massacred in vast numbers while social injustices and brigandage were rife. Local rebellions finally resulted in overthrow of the Roman garrison, and eventually war was declared on Rome under Pharisaic leadership. Christians and Essenes alike fled across the Jordan, refusing to fight in the rebellion. Josephus, later to gain renown as an historian, was placed in charge of an emergency government, mobilizing and recruiting citizens throughout Palestine for the defense of Galilee. The external strife, the conflicting factions of Sadducees and Pharisees, the impassive Essenes and Christians, and the misdirected, fanatically nationalistic Zealots, split the Jews internally with ineffectual mobilization against the Romans. Killing of Jews among Jews aided the Roman onslaught. Late in the summer of 70 A.D., the outer court of the Temple was set afire. Fighting went on, even as burnt offerings were made to summon the help of Yahweh within the Temple. Then came its final destruction.

The Qumran monastics might have seen in the Roman Wars the time of Yahweh, when He would turn his hand against the Kittim (invading Romans). This was then, perhaps, the period when the Essenes secreted their documents in caves, intending to return, which they were nevermore to do, after Yahweh had fulfilled His promises. The Essenes thus became extinct through their own closed system of delusions, while the Christians were reaching out to the Gentiles to expand and multiply.

Chapter II

Politico-Religious Climate
at the Time of Jesus

Prophets abounded in Palestine at the turn of the Christian era. These were, for the most part, a fanatical group, whether Zealot, Pharisee, Essene or of Far Eastern origin, who went barefoot, and clothed in castoffs. They identified with, and espoused, as the Buddha, the impoverished, and the oppressed. They detested the rich. Thus their following grew among the poor and the pariahs, who were like the outcasts of India, having neither property, position, nor status. Yahweh prophets furiously decried heresy, and, because of large following, had always carried extensive influence (cf., John the Baptist). It was the prophets who earlier had followed David, and promoted him to become king. Their creed, in all its intensity, prospered most in periods of oppression and depression. It was then that their following increased, and fulminations against the wicked and rich were perpetrated with much success. All misfortunes were attributed by the prophets to transgressions against Yahweh and His commandments. After Soloman, many had turned from Yahweh and worshipped the agricultural god Baal, and the fertility goddess, Astoreth. For more than two centuries, Yahweh declined in power. Elijah alone, in the Northern kingdom, espoused the "cause of the Lord," even while Queen Jezebel, wife of King Ahab, entertained the prophets of Baal and Astarte in her very court. In Judah, altars of Baal and Astarte were widespread, but in the northern kingdom of Israel, Yahweh had even been denied. It was for this reason, according to apocalyptic revelation, that the Ten Tribes of the north were destroyed.

At the destruction of Israel to the north in 704 B.C., King Hezekiah of Judah practiced the utmost servility in diplomacy that

Judah, (Greco-Roman name, Judaea or Judea, is used interchangeably) might survive before the onslaught of Sennacherib's Assyrian armies. Very severe requirements were imposed in Judah's capitulation. It was then that Hezekiah turned again, with religious fervor, to the Lord God of Israel. Pagan temples were destroyed, with shrines, and sacred prostitution abolished. Again were heard the protestations of prophets against blood sacrifices to Yahweh—in the slaying of rams, lambs, he-goats, and bullocks, to lay before the altar of Yahweh. This was a practice, they decried, that had come up from the heathen.

At the turn of the 6th century, B.C., the Temple came finally under control of Yahweh priests. They consolidated their position by putting into script their history and ceremonials. The sacerdotal law (i.e., that of the divinely inspired priesthood) of the Hilkiah was condemned by Jeremiah as a distortion of Mosaic law. Yet, thenceforward, the Mosaic Law, as written, governed the Jews and reinforced their identity by forbidding marriage with heathens.

Ezra returned from exile in Babylon to rule Jerusalem midway in the fifth century B.C. It is now evident that he was the most instrumental of priests in systematically compiling and editing the documents that were to make Judah as much a theocratic priest state as it was a nation. The new priesthood moved quickly with their expanding political power and authority. They forbade prophecy, especially any that conflicted with the written word. Their rule was established as a covenant with Yahweh, in the same way that the original commandments were flashed by Yahweh to Moses. These scribes employed the method of apocalyptical revelation, i.e., a traditional figure in Hebrew legend such as Moses, Enoch, Abraham, or Elijah, was purported to have pronounced prophecy, and/or divine revelation down to the moment of writing. Then the historical facts which supported the alleged prophecy to date lent credence to that which was prophecied to come after. This was a device often used to establish credulity and control.

The code of the early scribes was straightforward and law oriented. They treated not of eternal rewards or punishment. According to the Book of Psalms, Ecclesiastes, and even as late as that of Job, we are only of dust and to dust shall we return. During the Seleucidian period, (2nd to 3rd century, B.C.), the Zoroastrian-Pythagorean-Osirian beliefs in immortality, resurrection, supernatural judgement, hell, heaven, eternal reward and punishment, began to make their appearance. In the Book of Isaiah, for example, are found such passages as: " . . . dead men shall live again . . . " In Daniel: " . . . the dead shall live, some to everlasting life, some to everlasting contempt. . . . "

The Sadducees resisted such doctrines, while the Pharisees, according to the first century Pythagorean writer Josephus, increasingly adopted such precepts, and considered all souls immortal subject to everlasting reward and punishments. Later rabbis, the orthodox priests of whom Pharisees were the prototypes, eliminated these doctrines, perhaps as a reaction to their centrality in Christian dogma. The Messianic hope of the ancient Hebrews, however, has prevailed. Rabbi Moses ben Maimon, (11th century, A.D.) whose works *"Mishne Torah"* (Second Law) and *"Guide for the Perplexed and Others,"* have extremely influenced modern Jewish thought, considered it mandatory for Jews to expect a Messiah. Messianic descriptions have changed with the years. Several of these Messiah precepts follow:

8th Century B.C. - a great human leader, descending from King David with divine approval and intervention, would gather the 12 tribes of Israel into Judea as a unified kingdom to which all Gentiles would pay allegiance, and whose religion the entire world would embrace. (Found in Isaiah)

2nd Century, B.C. - an all-powerful superhuman being, the "Son of Man" surrounded by myriad ministers, destroying enemies of Israel, calling the dead from their graves to conduct the last judgement, and establishing the everlasting Jewish Kingdom. (Found in Daniel and the Book of Enoch).

1st Century, B.C. - a supernatural being, surrounded by myriad saints, an almighty moral judge, establishing the kingdom of righteousness on earth for all people. (Found only among Essenic documents and the Gospel Jesus)

In Isaiah is described a virgin who is to bear a child when Assyrians take Damascus and Samaria. The child is then to become the almighty God, the Prince of Peace, who ascends to the throne of David. When Judah and Jerusalem are conquered, He will bring together all the people of Israel who will rise and conquer the world. Elijah will herald His coming, so that false prophets and messiahs will be forewarned; and whosoever claims to be the messiah, and foists such a deception upon the people, will be put to death by stoning (Leviticus).

The Jews did not envision a Son of God who would bring redemption from the plight of human suffering; rather, theirs was one who would rule the earth in a Messianic Kingdom— a messenger sent by Yahweh. "Christ," from the Greek word "Christos" translating the Hebrew word "Messiah," was the title of an office, an "Anointed One." The King of Israel or Judah was ceremoniously inaugurated in anointing with oil. The significance of the word "Messiah" was thus to be a sacred appointee, Yahweh's elect. Saul was a Messiah, whom David had refused to kill because he was Yahweh's Anointed. The term around the 1st century, B.C., however, had come to mean an Agent of God who would appear at the ending of days to judge all men and establish a new order. Gentiles would follow the religion of Yahweh, because the empire of the Jews would embrace the world under a Jewish theocracy. The plight of the Jews was largely in their identity. They had been downtrodden, defeated and behumbled for centuries. Thus, did they dream of grandeur in power and might, with high-spoken and threatening words, all portending and pledging a comeuppance from the lowly status and defiling subservience of their people. It was out of this that, in their wildest dreams, they would rise and rule over all the world. These were the images, the visions they saw in a savior, a leader, a Messiah, who would raise them once and for all above all others.

In the Book of Isaiah, the Messianic image was of one who must symbolically suffer as they had suffered at the hands of the enemy and of the rich.

" . . . despised and rejected of man, and acquainted with grief . . . we did not esteem him; smitten of God and afflicted, the Lord placed on him the inequity of us all . . . it pleased the Lord to put him to grief when his soul is made an offering of sin . . . and the pleasure of the Lord shall prosper in his hand . . . and he bore the sin of many and made intercession for the transgressors." (Isaiah 53) " . . . The Messiah shall bring judgment upon the Gentiles and they shall become slaves (of the Jews) " (54) .

In Chapters 55-66, the Zoroasthrian impact is evident. The Savior is no longer a man, but a supernatural God idea. " . . . I create new heavens and a new earth . . . "

In a blessed new Jerusalem would be universal peace, with God the light and glory of the holy city. "I form the light and create darkness. I make peace and create evil. I have made the earth and created man upon it. Even my hands have stretched out the heavens, and all their hosts have I commanded . . . " (These latter elements were clearly based on Persian theology) .

In the face of competing religious beliefs the scribes of Isaiah vehemently rejected and decried any intrusion by other deities or soters. Of Ishtar they wrote " . . . Oh virgin daughter of Babylon....thou art given to pleasures that dwelleth carelessly; there is no throne, oh, daughter of the Chaldeans, for thou shalt no more be called tender and delicate....thou shalt no more be called the Lady of Kingdoms....for our redeemer is the Lord of Hosts, the Holy One of Israel."

In Daniel is found symbolic prophecy that Babylonia, the Median-Persian Empire, the Greek and the Seleucid-Ptolemiac empires are to be supernaturally destroyed. The Messianic Kingdom of Israel is to become as a great mountain, a stone cut without hands, that will destroy and replace these great secular empires. The Son of Man (cf., Zoroastrian-Soshan theology) , who was a divinely generated personage to appear 3,000 years after Zoroaster and establish a universal kingdom of righteousness, was to appear in the second century, B.C., according to such prophecy as given in Daniel and the Book of Enoch. Such universal age-old Jewish prophecy all essentially heralded the coming of a human Messiah, who would revivify their nation, that they might rise again and be respected, even feared, by those who oppressed them. Later Mediterranean influences modified the Messianic expectancy which, in the form of the Gospel Jesus, became a Parousia—a natural and supernatural final kingdom of the Jews. These later formulations were a conglomeration of Zoroastrian, Buddhistic, Osirian, Pythagorean, and Ishtarian precepts, and based not solely on Jewish materialistic aspirations, but as well on pagan beliefs absorbed from Eastern religions, and an emerging moral-ethical system influenced in large part by the Greek philosophers, Socrates, Plato, Aristotle and Pythagoras.

Until recently, the Greek, Latin, German and English versions of the bible have been the primary classical expositions on the character of the Messiah, as well as that of Jesus. These had been subjected to extensive revisions and expedient theological interpretations calculated to promote the dogma. Both the Catholic and Protestant texts carry essentially the same classical tradition and narrative, with the exception of minor points of theology peculiar to respective religio-politico views. Jesus as the Messiah has remained a man of mystery, as may well have been intended to inspire awe and build a basis for faith. Recent Dead Sea Scroll findings, however, have enlarged the fund of background information upon which biographical descriptions of the man Jesus might be based. He lived in a land of sects and prophets, but the most closely akin sect emphatically influeencing or determining his doctrine (or that of the chroniclers) was the Essenic. Jewish historians, Josephus and Philo, had described the Essenes, and similarities to the Gospel Jesus have often been noted by scholars. With the scrolls, however, we have been taken directly into the sect, even as outsiders to experience vicariously the discipline, ethics and dogma. It is now possible that, through these data, the Jesus story, whether he were man, tradition, myth, or superstition, may be pieced together to give a new narration. Two versions are presented in the present text. The first is the classical version, in which much of Jesus' life has been obscured. The second version is a parsimonious step-by-step analysis of bits and pieces of information from Essenic and other sources, that serve as a more fundamental basis for fabrication of a theory concerning the man Jesus.

Certainly a contemporary individual, one whom we might observe, and today subject to batteries of personality tests, is of such complexity, frequently, as to defy description, particularly if aberrant, evidencing neurotic or psychotic trends, being changeable, moody and unpredictable. The religious leaders were likely of such a nature, being radical and rebellious, if not clearly neurotic. (cf., Luther against Roman Catholicism, Augustine against the Manichaens, Guatama against the Hindus, or Orpheus against the cult of Dionysus). Such religious reformers as these were erratic, and, because rebelliously in conflict, necessarily neurotic by definition. For this reason, any very detailed character and personality description of such "historical" figures is presumptuous, and descriptions may become hazardously inaccurate. It is with such misgiving that these narrations about the life of Jesus must be treated.

Chapter 12

The Christ Story — Classical

The early beginnings of Christianity have been documented in stories of the Hebrews in the Old Testament, upon which is based the geneology of Christ in the legend of the tribe of the Israelites found in the Book of Genesis. In the Old Testament [1] we find the story of the creation of man in the image of the gods, and of his tale of woe in being cast from the Garden of Eden for having knowledge, because his woman had cavorted with a snake. From there man went out and toiled, and begat children. The God Yahweh, or Jehovah, came to favor certain of the sons of Adam. Abraham was told to reproduce, and thenceforth to build a nation of select people. So Abraham reproduced, and there was a son Isaac, who fathered Jacob. Jehovah called Jacob, "Israel" which means "contender of God," because Jacob pleased Him. Israel, as Jacob was then called, sired twelve sons, who each in turn fathered many children. These, and further generations of the children's children, formed the Twelve Tribes of the Israelites.

The Tribe of the Israelites among the Hebrews prospered, and moved about seeking and finding rich grazing land for their herds. Then came a great famine. They moved out of Canaan or Palestine, a land that was paradise, to other lands such as Egypt.

---

[1] Perhaps the story of creation, and the subsequent history of the Hebrews, can be read in a cryptic way, and in fact contain insights that parallel the knowledge of our time; and the myth of the trees and fruit, the serpent, and God speaking to man, may be regarded as unconscious symbolism truly saying, in a different way, much of what modern man says about evolution and world social order. On the other hand, they may be simple interpretations and primitive explanations of the beginning of life, born of the same superstition that created gods of the Greeks, and of the Egyptians—crocodile gods, jackal gods, hawk gods, gods of the sun and moon, of thunder, and rain, and of love. The question of the real meaning of these writings may be a proper subject for debate among theology students or religious scholars.

In Egypt they did not worship the idols of the Egyptians. The Egyptians, too, feared the Hebrews because of their growing numbers. Because they were different and feared, the Egyptians made them captive and enslaved. Then it was hoped they would become as their masters and believe as the Egyptians. This occured. But yet the Hebrews remained one among themselves. The Egyptians still feared the threat of a possible Hebrew uprising within their land. In order that the Hebrew outlander would intermarry and become absorbed within the nation of Egypt, it was decreed that all male Hebrew babies be drowned. This was the story of Moses, whose Hebrew mother could not bring herself to drown him. She set him afloat in a basket on the Nile. Moses was found by the daughter of the King of Egypt, and adopted as her own. He grew up to become an Egyptian prince.

When Moses learned of his Hebrew origin, he became the leader of the Hebrew people. He refuted the power of the King of Egypt, and, with the magic given to him by Yahweh, he obtained the freedom of the Hebrews and they escaped from Egypt in the first Exodus.

Moses first brought his people to Mount Sinai, where they would come to know their God. Yahweh was unlike any God of the Egyptians. He spoke through Moses, and commanded that those of the Hebrew tribes should know no other gods, have no idols, take not his name in vain, rest on the seventh day, honor parents, never murder, nor to take the wife of another, nor to steal, nor testify nor swear falsely, nor to envy others, or covet theirs. Yahweh was the God of the Israelites. His commandments were for among themselves. With the faith of Jehovah in their hearts, they went on to conquer the rich land of Palestine in battle, with the Moabites, the Amorites, and the Kingdom of Bashan. They were always victorious under Yahweh and took the rich fertile land of Canaan, or Palestine, the promised land of Jehovah.

The land of the Israelites in Palestine grew and prospered. In its history, there were three great kings, Saul, David and Soloman. It was King Soloman who had built the Temple of God, the Holy of Holies in Jerusalem where Yahweh dwelt. It was later in this Temple in Jerusalem, after it had been destroyed by the Babylonians and rebuilt during Persian rule, that Jesus was chagrined when He found the Temple of God being used as a market place.

After the last king, Solomon, the people of the North and South sections of Palestine split into separate kingdoms; they became so weakened within themselves that they fell prey to their enemies. The Assyrians attacked and conquered from the North; later the Kingdom of the South, called Judah, (named as a tribe after a son of Jacob) fell to the Babylonians. The Babylonians were later taken in war by the Persians, and the Persians called the people of Judah, "Jehudis," from which the word "Jew" comes. The religion was called Judaism.

From the Persians, the Jews learned of the beliefs of the prophet Zoroaster—of life after death, and Heaven and Hell. These beliefs were to become part of their religion. It was from Zoroastrianism that the belief grew of the coming of a Messiah, a redeemer of Palestine, a descendant from the House of David, to restore the Jewish Kingdom as it had once been under David and Solomon. After the Persian captivity, the belief in Yahweh changed. He ruled over not only Palestine, but the entire world, as Lord and Ruler of the Universe. The Jews, it was believed, had become a weakened and broken people because of their sins for which Yahweh was punishing them. The Persians finally released the Jews to return to their homeland under the rule of the Persian king, Cyrus. They were never to recover the strength they had once known as a nation under David and Solomon. Persian power fell, and the Greeks conquered, and later, from the west came Rome. In the continuing oppression by foreign powers the Jewish belief in the coming of the Messiah grew. A century before the conquest of the "Holy Land" by the Romans, the Book of Daniel was written. In it he told of dreams of grave foreboding, of frightening animals with claws, horns and fangs, issuing horrendous cries. He dreamed of a ram with powerful sharp horns, that swung to the South, West and North, which no animal dared oppose; then a powerful he-goat appeared having only one horn between his eyes, and it attacked and trampled the ram to death. These dreams were strange to Daniel until an angel came, and explained their meaning that a time was at hand when a redeemer, a Son of Man from the House of David, would bring the Kingdom of Heaven on earth. Happiness and peace would reign; but before the coming of the Messiah, there would be a time of trouble as never before known to the Jews. Under Roman rule, they thought surely the time was at hand. The promise and expectations of the coming Messiah grew ever more important. Many Jews became so convinced of his imminent arrival, they gave up their homes and families to fast and pray in preparation for the great day. In synagogues, and market places, and in homes throughout Palestine His coming was told: "The Messiah! His day is near. Blessed be the name of the Lord!" Some called Him "Christ," the Anointed One; some called Him the "Son of Man," others, "the Son of David," and some, the "Son of God." They talked of how he would appear; whether as a man or a women, he would come directly from heaven in a fiery chariot. The learned said the "Son of David" would appear on a mountain top with a crown of glory upon His head, and be surrounded by a host of angels. Some said He would appear in the North, others, the South. Some said He would appear from the clouds of Heaven, and descend upon the roof of the Holy Temple in Jerusalem. On such matters they disagreed, but all were agreed that He would come soon.

At that time Augustus Caesar was the emperor of the Roman Empire, under whom served King Herod who was neither Jew nor Roman. Herod ruled as king of the Jews, and he feared the talk of the people about the coming of a Messiah, who would displace him. This was treason and threat to his rule. When Herod was seventy years old, a report came to his palace of three Persians who had come to Jerusalem carrying precious gifts in search of the child who was to become king of the Jews. He ordered these Persians to be brought before him. Herod asked how they knew of this child who was to be born King of the Jews. "It was a star that moved from the East," replied the Persian Magi.

"Bring me word when the child has been found, so that I too might worship him," said Herod.

The Persians continued their search, and followed a purple star that moved out of Jerusalem, and finally stopped over a dwelling in Bethlehem. The house was that of a carpenter named Joseph (cf., a stable at an inn). According to the book of St. Matthew, Joseph's wife, Mary, had a newly born son called Jesus. The Persians laid gifts before the infant Jesus and heralded Him as the new King. The Persians did not return to Herod for they suspected him of treachery; Joseph dreamed of Herod's treachery, that his young son would be killed by Herod's soldiers; he fled with his family to Egypt. Herod waited but the wise men had deceived him and left Judea. Herod, in fear and anger, ordered all male children under two years of age in the city of Bethlehem to be killed.

When Herod died, Joseph returned from Egypt to Judea, and settled in the town of Nazareth in the Province of Galilee. Nazareth was a small town, hidden in a valley of rolling hills. Houses were of white stone cut from nearby quarries, and the town appeared as a dazzling white in the sunlight. Thus, Nazareth was known as the "White City." It was remote, some fifty-five miles from Jerusalem and a quiet and peaceful out-of-the-way community, where Joseph spent his days as a carpenter.

Those who could afford it sent their children to be educated under the Rabbis in Jerusalem. Joseph could not provide his children with this. Rather, Joseph and Mary taught their children themselves in the ways of their people. The children memorized the Holy Commandments. Mary taught them the morning and evening prayers. In the synagogue on Sabbaths and holidays, the children heard readings from the Bible, and learned the holy law. The children[2] of Joseph and Mary played about the streets of Nazareth and in surrounding hills. Jesus was a serious child who preferred the company of adults. He listened to the talk about the synagogue, to such stories as that of a Rab-

[2] Controversy is found among theologians as to whether or not Jesus had siblings. In the story of the virgin birth, and in the exaltation of the Virgin Mary, such theological interpretations will not allow for carnal relations with Joseph. In Matthew she was first thought by Joseph to have been unfaithful, and with child; this was a virgin pregnancy, with penetration by the Holy Ghost, with Christ becoming the long-awaited Son of God. Theological interpretations differ, but, save for theological exaltation of Mary, they seem of little importance historically to what is known about the life of Jesus.

bi Hillel. A heathen asked the Rabbi to tell him the holy law while he stood on one leg, and the Rabbi curtly replied, "What is hateful to you do not do unto others—this is the whole of the Holy Law."

Jesus heard these stories and He heard also the whispered talk about the coming of the Messiah and everlasting joy. At the age of twelve, He was confirmed. In that year He traveled with His parents to the city of Jerusalem, capital of Palestine, for the annual Passover. The Passover was a devotion service that dated back to the period of the Hebrews in Egypt, when Yahweh spared the first born of the Hebrews, and smote those of the Egyptians. On the pilgrimage to Jerusalem, the numbers swelled entering the gates from all over the land of Palestine to serve Yahweh in His Temple. It is easy to imagine a young Jesus as His party approached the thrice-conquered city of Jerusalem; He had visualized the splendor of the city, the proud City of God. It must certainly have been different from what He had dreamed, for there was a crude mixture of foreign people in strange garb. Everywhere, Roman soldiers mixed with the crowds; and in the Temple, the House of God, the great Rabbis assembled and spoke long and wordy explanations that young Jesus could not understand. About the Temple was the sacrilege of the market place, herds of bleating sheep and oxen, offered for sale as necessary sacrifices, with noisy cattle dealers haggling with the pilgrims. Money changers shouted for those from other parts of the land to exchange their currency into silver used in Jerusalem. After returning to Nazareth, the dreams of young Jesus of the glory of the City of God crumbled. He began reading the Book of Daniel foretelling the coming of the Messiah, and He became moody, thinking more and more about the coming of this expected Redeemer of Mankind.

From his twelfth year, little is written about Jesus; Joseph had died; Mary moved from Nazareth to Cana, the place of her birth. In Cana, Jesus worked at carpentry, and helped support his mother and brothers and sisters. On the Sabbath He went to the synagogue for prayer and discussion of the Holy Law. In the custom at the synagogue, those who felt so moved arose before the congregation to interpret whatever parts of the Laws to which they had given thought. When Jesus stood before them, His words were simple and appealing, and they listened. He became a teacher, and the congregation began to discuss His teachings.

The prophetic teachings of John the Baptist were also widespread throughout the land of Palestine. For centuries in Asia, people believed in the mystical power of flowing water. In India, the water of the Ganges is believed to wash away sins. This is what John believed as he baptised his followers in the River Jordan before he preached. He preached, and believed deeply that the Messiah was soon to appear.

Mary told Jesus that John was a third cousin; so Jesus traveled to see John the Baptist of whom He had heard so much; and John, when he saw Jesus approach, spoke: "There cometh one mightier than I after me, the latchet of whose shoes I am not worthy to stoop down and unloose!"

Jesus was baptised by John, and listened to his prophecy that the Redeemer was soon to come. After meeting with John, Jesus went off by Himself in the desert for several weeks alone to think and meditate. He thought of the Brotherhood of Man, of Justice and Peace, and of the Messiah who would bring these. After Jesus returned to Galilee, He left for the annual pilgrimage to Jerusalem. In the Holy City, chagrined by what had disillusioned and angered Him in times past, He looked up at the Holy Temple glorifying Yahweh and back at the desecration of the bound cattle, with the eager merchants, dealers, and money changers. With sudden impulse of indignation, He grabbed the whip of a cattle dealer, and beat the cattle from the court, tipping over coin tables. "Take these things hence! Make not God's House a market place!"

Priests and religious leaders throughout Jerusalem condoned these merchants in the Temple. In this demostration, Jesus aroused their wrath; but many admired the Man who had defied the authorities in their desecration of the Holy Temple.

Jesus went on to preach in the Province of Galilee, in Nazareth and Cana. He told of a religion that should come from within, in truth and sincerity. Many who had known Jesus as a child, mocked Him. He left Cana without honor among those who thought Him unwise. He went then to live in Capernaum, a fisherman's village, with Peter and Andrew, two brothers, who already believed Him to be the Messiah. Jesus preached in Capernaum among the fishermen. His wisdom seemed profound, and His fame spread throughout Palestine. Many came from all parts of the land to hear Him. On a hillside outside Capernaum, Jesus delivered the famous sermon that has since become known as the Sermon on the Mount. " . . . Blessed are the poor in spirit, for theirs is the Kingdom of Heaven....blessed are the meek, for they shall inherit the earth....blessed are they which do hunger and search after righteousness, for they shall be filled ....blessed are the merciful, for they shall obtain mercy....blessed are the pure in heart, for they shall see God....blessed are the peacemakers, for they shall be called the children of God...." In this sermon, He made clear how His teachings differed from those of the priests and the rabbis: He had not come to destroy the Law, nor refute the teaching of the prophets, but to fulfill these. The old law said "....whosoever shall kill shall be in danger of judgment." He said "....whosoever is angry with his brother without cause shall be in danger of judgment." It had been said "....an eye for an eye and a tooth for a tooth." Jesus held the Buddhistic doctrine "....that ye should resist not evil, but whosoever shall smite thee on thy right cheek, turn to him also the other." The law stated "....Love thy neighbor and hate thine enemy." Jesus told His followers to "....Love enemies, bless them that curse you, do good to them that hate you, and pray for them that despitefully use you....for if you forgive men their trespasses, your Heavenly Father will forgive you, and if you do not forgive, neither will He you."[3]

There is inconsistency in the sayings of Jesus. He denied the truth of the doctrine, 'an eye for an eye, and a tooth for a tooth;" yet He held: "Judge not that ye be not judged, for with what judgment ye judge ye shall be judged; and what measure ye mete, it shall be measured against you." But Jesus was a simple man. His teachings were not those of a learned, disciplined

---

[3] Much of what Jesus preached seems to parallel that of other prophets. For example, Lao-tse, a prophet of the Orient some six centuries earlier, wrote that to know Tao was to know peace. Lao-tze wrote ". . . to those who are good to me, I am good; to those who are not good to me, I am good; thus, all get to be good; as with sincerity, I am sincere with all."

scholar, and He spoke on matters that all could understand. His basic doctrine differed somewhat from the conventional laws of Judaism. Conventional Jews leaned more toward the God, Yahweh, of pre-Egyptian days, while Jesus sought to establish a new institution: "Therefore, whosoever heareth these sayings of mine, and doeth them, I will liken him unto a wise man, which built his house upon a rock: And the rain descended and the floods came, and the winds blew, and beat upon that house; and it fell not, for it was founded upon a rock."

John the Baptist had been put to death for speaking against Antipas, King of Galilee. At the news of John's death, Jesus went to Judea to teach. To the religious leaders, the Pharisees, Jesus was known as a heretic. The Pharisees strove to maintain the old religion of days before the Babylonian captivity. They did not believe in heaven and hell, and life after death; nor did they tolerate claims of Messiahship, beliefs that had all come from the Persians. They rather required strict adherence to the old Mosaic Laws, and the teachings of the early prophets. Jesus espoused all these former views, for which He came later to be heralded as the Messiah in direct conflict with the Pharisees.

In the days of Jesus, under Roman rule, freedom of religion prevailed. No man could be forbidden to preach what he believed unless he spoke against the Roman government in Palestine, or unless he mocked God. Jesus could only be charged with treason or blasphemy. The Pharisees searched for signs of blasphemy: Which was the first commandment. "Hear, O Israel, the Lord our God is one God! Thou shalt love thy neighbor as thyself. No other commandment is greater than these," replied Jesus. Pharisees and priests argued with Jesus for hours, holding that Holy Law should be followed to the letter. Jesus always countered that religion is meaningless unless it comes from the heart. He denounced the Pharisees and their scribes, and talked against them in public, and He became increasingly in conflict with Judaism.

On the third year after His confrontation in the Holy Temple, Christ went again to attend the annual Passover Feast. He was then known throughout the land of Palestine. Crowds followed Him through the streets of Jerusalem, and cried, "Hosanna! Blessed is He that comes in the name of the Lord!"

Those who did not know whose praise they shouted asked, "Who is this Jesus of the Province of Galilee?"

They were told that He was Jesus, the Prophet from the town of Nazareth; and whenever He walked through the streets of Jerusalem, people followed. Again in the Temple Court, He saw the desecration He had seen three years earlier, and again drove the dealers in cattle and money from the House of the Lord.

The Pharisees and Head Priests now looked emphatically at Jesus as a threat. He brought crowds of followers. His influence was widespread and growing. These religious leaders conferred in secrecy. This man must be stopped.

Jesus knew. He told those close to Him of a foreboding that His antagonists were determined to see Him dead. This was nonsense, His friends replied, for He would surely announce Himself as the Redeemer during the Passover, and remove all doubt. His power and glory were mightier than all His enemies put together.

Jesus watched the pilgrims pour into Jerusalem from a hillside near the city. The crowds swelled at the gates, and a high pitch of excitement prevailed wherever they gathered in joyful anticipation of the feast to the Lord God Yahweh. But Jesus was morose. He and twelve close followers, called the apostles, dined at the house of a friend on the night before the Passover day. The apostles quarreled about who should sit next to their master, Jesus, who would reveal His Glory during the Passover to become the long-awaited Messiah. Jesus demonstratively left His place at the head of the table. Taking wash basin in hand, He stooped to wash the feet of each man present.

The apostles were perplexed. They could not understand that their beloved chief would reduce Himself to washing their feet. Then He spoke, in the ostentation of the act, "You strive for a seat of honor next to Me. You should do as I have just done, and remember, the servant is not greater than his Lord; neither is he that is sent greater than he that sent him."

The spirit of the supper was dampened; the disciples had been rebuked, even as unruly children, and they drank and ate of the wine and meat not as heartily as they might have otherwise on this occasion. Then Jesus spoke again: "There is one among you who will turn from me to mine enemies." The disciples eyed one another suspiciously, and suspected even themselves. "Is it I, Master, who would do this?" some asked.

It would be one among the twelve of them, said Jesus, who, after he had done the dastardly deed, would be sorry he were ever born. They ate in silence, were glum and depressed; nor did they enjoy their meal. Then Jesus spoke again, now in tenderness and affection. "I shall not be with you long, but do not seek me, for you cannot come where I go. A new commandment do I give you: Love one another as I have loved you, and by this all shall know that you are my disciples."

After supper they left the city to go to a nearby park called Gethsemane for prayer and meditation. All the disciples went save one, called Judas, who had left earlier in the evening. It was a long walk to the park, and they rested in the garden. Some fell asleep. It was after midnight when the torches of Roman soldiers lighted the garden.

"Who among you is Jesus of Nazareth?" asked a Roman officer.

"I am He," replied Jesus. The sleeping apostles awakened; upon seeing the Roman soldiers, they scrambled off to hide themselves.

Jesus was bound and taken to the house of the High Priest, with whom Judas had consorted. Jesus was accused and insulted. In the morning He was taken to the Judgment Hall before the Roman Governor of Jerusalem, Pontius Pilate. The charges were read—blasphemy and sedition.

Pontius Pilate had little interest in the religious bickering of the Jews. He, however, questioned Jesus to learn if He were one of the many Jewish leaders who spoke against Roman rule in Palestine.

"Give to Caesar what belongs to Caesar and to God what is God's," replied Jesus tersely.

This answer was evasive, but there seemed to be no treason. Pontius decided to free Jesus, but the Pharisees reiterated: "He stirs up the people against the Law!"

"He is a Galilean. He should be tried before the Governor of Galilee, Herod Antipas, not me," insisted Pontius.

Antipas, in Jerusalem for the Passover, would not hear Jesus, nor the charges, but returned Him to Pilate. Pontius Pilate, to pacify the Pharisees, decreed that Jesus was guilty as charged, to be put to death by crucifixion, by the slow torturous method of driving spikes into the hands and feet on cross wood members. Before the Governor feasted, it was the custom to pardon one of the death-condemned prisoners. By coincidence another man named Jesus had been convicted of treason and rebellion against the Roman Empire and condemned to die. This Jesus Bar-Abbas stood beside Jesus of Nazareth. One would be pardoned. "Which of these do you wish to pardon," Pontius Pilate asked the leaders in the Judgment Hall. Bar-Abbas was pardoned. Bar-Abbas had agitated the people in Jerusalem to riot against the Roman soldiers. Several of the rioters were killed, among whom was the son of a carpenter who worked in Jerusalem. Prisoners condemned to die carried their own crosses to a hill top. The father of the boy who was killed was bitter, and asked that he be permitted to make the cross for Jesus Bar-Abbas. The carpenter built the cross, in retribution, of such a weight that Bar-Abbas would suffer in pain and anguish in the final moments of life as he struggled with the heavy weight to the top of the hill. This was the cross that Jesus of Nazareth was given. He fell and stumbled with it in the climb until the Roman soldiers finally called upon a passerby, Simon the Cyrene, to assist Jesus to a hilltop called Golgotha.

Name and crime: in mockery, "Jesus of Nazareth, King of the Jews" was inscribed on the cross. Spikes were driven through His hands and feet. His cross was raised beside two fellow sufferers convicted of thievery. A woman offered drink of frankincense, myrrh and vinegar to relieve His pain. He refused. He was derided by the crowd, and taunted, but He said, "Forgive them, God, for they know not what they do." But in long hours of suffering, His pain became unbearable. He cried out in spite of Himself, "My God, My God, why have you let them do this to me?" and He died.

Chapter 13

The Christ Story — Reconstructed

a. The Essenic Training of Jesus

On a date in history not certain among historians, a male child was born to a woman named Mary and a man called Joseph.[1] It was in the small country of Palestine, on the eastern shores of the Mediterranean Sea at a city ten miles south of Jerusalem called Bethlehem.[2] (See Figures 4 and 5)

In Rome, Gaius Augustus of the Caesars yet reigned as the first emperor, while Tiberius soldiered and studied to ascend to the head of the empire; in Northern Palestine, Herod the Great was King.

Mary was young, not yet sixteen, while Joseph had lived his life fully having already fourteen children, and they with children. His first wife, with whom he had lived for sixty years, had died several years earlier before he had taken Mary to wife. Joseph was now feeble, brittle and imbued with the caution that comes with old age lest the body meet irreparable damage.[3] There were many among his neighbors in Bethlehem who suspected Joseph was no longer capable of producing, and the blasphemous sin of adultery was Mary's. Yet during the years of co-habitation

---

[1] Genealogies have been discounted since, as is known in ethnic propagandizing practices, these documents were written by Jewish Christians wishing to perpetuate the ethnic tradition.

[2] Birthplace is confounded in the Gospels. Mathew has them living in Bethlehem, Mark neglects this detail, and Luke has them journeying to Bethlehem to meet Roman tax obligations. Both, however, have them living in Galilee. For some reason they later moved north, even though Joseph was old and feeble.

[3] According to the Pseudepigrapha, Joseph was a man of 99 years at the time of Jesus' birth, while Mary was but sixteen.

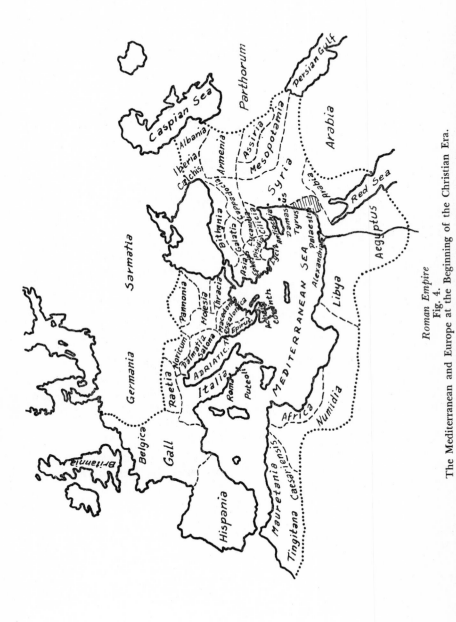

Roman Empire
Fig. 4.
The Mediterranean and Europe at the Beginning of the Christian Era.

with Joseph it was said she bore him other children and they were of his flesh.

The son, called Jesus,[4] was as a doll to Mary, and she showered upon him the affection that was hers, yet as a child herself, to give, and received from Jesus the infant response of a growing love that was lacking in the marriage of patriarchal convenience with Joseph.

As Jesus grew he worked with his father Joseph, even when only four years old. He brought the hammers and wood chisels from among the tools of Joseph, as Joseph hacked and whittled with the tremoring hand of old age. The benches and tables of Joseph's handiwork as a carpenter were of rough-hewn wood, crude and unsmooth, though marked with the skill of 90 years in carpentry; and as Jesus grew, he steadied his father's hand. By the time he was ten, Jesus finished benches with inordinate skill, that Joseph might rest, and yet they might receive Roman coins for food and drink.

When Jesus was five years old Herod Archelaus became King of Judea following the death of his father, Herod the Great. For years this half-breed Jew, Herod the Great, had dictated his demands upon the people of Judea, and the nation of the Jews had suffered by his indifference to their plight in his consuming loyalty to Rome, while Jews were burdened by the heavy taxes imposed; for the masses were of small means, without political influence nor recourse. Shortly after the death of Herod the Great, Joseph was approached to join an organized resistance, to enlist his sympathies, while a band of younger men of Pharisaic religious-political views were planning an attack on the palace. They would be rid forever of the Herods, that they might select a leader of their own choice.[5]

---

[4] The name smacks of apocalyptical revelation in Judaic tradition, since it means "Salvation of God."

[5] Mary and Joseph must nominally have been Pharisees, practicing sacrificial ritual (Luke 1). Joseph appears to have been a marginal Pharisee, being a "Nazarene" in sympathy. This group, as indicated by the derivation of the word, believed that an "offshoot" of Jessie, father of David, would come again i.e., the Messiah. The sect may have been Essenic in nature, devout, but marrying, unlike those in the celibate colonies. The fact that there is no evidence that a city of Nazareth existed at the time also supports this surmise.

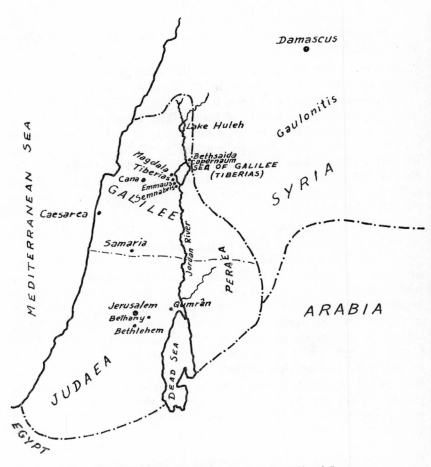

Fig. 5. Palaestin (Palestine) During the Life of Jesus.

Joseph wished to live in peace in the few remaining years of his life. Such insurrection[6] would mean making a battleground of the very streets before his house, and even bring Roman soldiers into his home again, making overtures to his pretty wife, Mary; and he could do nothing. For so, was it not promised that a new Jewish king would come in due course? Ninety miles to the north there were those among his friends and relatives who believed this, and risked neither their lives nor the lives of their families, for the Lord God would bring His will to the people, and destroy the aliens when the people were ready.

Joseph made his decision. Then he called his wife Mary to him, and told her that they would leave Bethlehem to join their friends to the north of Samaria, who, while not seeking a place for the Jews in his time, held the promise of bringing Yahweh's will, in whose grace they lived in accordance with His laws, and were at peace within themselves and among others, for no man was an enemy. Joseph sold what he did not need, and bought two donkeys. On one Mary loaded her pots and dishes and blankets, and she tied about the donkey the tools of Joseph's trade that he could work among his friends, and his family might eat. On the other donkey Joseph rode. Mary took the hand of young Jesus, and they walked at the side of Joseph. They walked for three days, sleeping by the roadside at night and ate bread and honey. In the evening of the third day, after traveling 95 miles to the north (See Figure 5), Joseph met his friends among the Nazarenes, and they were given shelter.

At a place near the Sea of Galilee Joseph, with Mary and Jesus, began a new life. He found a house, opened, but protected from the sun, and worked at carpentry among the Nazarenes. They lived now in strict obedience to the laws of Yahweh; but this was not strange to Joseph who had abided by the laws of scripture since his childhood.

Jesus grew in body, and Mary taught the laws of the people; but the patriarch, Joseph, was overly weary from the work of

[6] Herod Archelaus succeeded his father in One A.D. He was able to maintain his position against the Pharisees, who incited insurrection. Mary and Joseph, either returning from Egypt, or not having gone, were in Bethlehem. They could hardly have remained untouched by the insurrection and, being Pharisees, would have been expected to support the action.

the day. Jesus could not learn, as he might, from the wisdom of Joseph. Joseph, dutiful in his obligations to train the child in the strict discipline of his people, in the laws of Moses, the code and practices of the sect which he had recently joined, pondered with Mary the training of Jesus.

"The child must come to know the ways of the Lord, and what is expected, that our place among Jews and men will be fulfilled."

"Yes, Joseph, but a child of ten...."

"I am old and weary and must work. I cannot give the child what he needs. He must live among them who have been taught by the great prophets. There will be other children. It will be good, and he will learn much."[7]

Jesus was taken as a child to live with the sect called Essenes. There were many other children in the camps by the Sea of Galilee. There were men without women, and the few women who were there were not looked upon; many of the children stayed, while others returned to their parents, some left when grown to marry, and took their women not in lust, as in concubines, but to procreate. All worked at the camp; the children watched flocks of sheep, or seeded wheat and barley, or made wine. They shaped and baked clay pottery, or wove rope and blankets for sale in Cana. They ate in the company of an elder, who broke the bread and passed the wine; they were clean and washed, and raised their arms in the thanksgiving at each meal. They became as one with their great prophet who had spoken and died for the Lord, as they partook of each meal. The elders went daily to the banks of the Jordan River to be immersed for the sake of their souls.

Jesus sat in the evening and on the Sabbath with other children. The laymen of the village spoke of the great deeds of a righteous prophet[8] who had died for Yahweh, and for all men, and who would return to teach all men to follow the path of righteousness and worship the Lord of Hosts. This great prophet

---

[7] The Essenes have been described by Josephus as taking in the children of others while pliable and fit for learning. The children were esteemed as their own, and they formed them according to the manners of the Essenes.

[8] The "Teacher of Righteousness" as translated from the Dead Sea Scrolls.

had lived at Qumran—a place of holy worship near the Dead Sea. He bore the wisdom of the ages. He had brought to the monastary, and the people of the sect, the secrets of Holy Worship from the East in Media and Persia, and from the South in Egypt. He had learned that grain could become the flesh, and liquid the blood of God infused in man. The Great Prophet foretold of the Soshan of whom he had learned in Persia, who would come to establish a land of equality and justice for all men as a messenger of the Lord.

He had learned from the East in India that lust was born of evil, and women carried the darkness of temptation in their bodies (In India, impoverishment then as now was due to over-population coming from sexual congress and multiplying beyond the means of support and equity). He learned that those who lived in truth and righteousness would find a place in God's Land, but those who followed the ways of the devil would burn forever in a hole of fire.

Jesus studied and learned. There was an Essene called Milay[9] among the laymen who took Jesus as his own, whom he called "my son," and Jesus called Milay his father.

"By what grace to you live?" asked Milay.

"I live in the house of my father, who is wise in the ways of God Who has made us all," replied Jesus.

"By what virtue must you live?"

"I shall live to suffer for others, for as they are pained, I am pained."

"And to whom must you be obedient?"

"I obey my father and my God, and I do not go against men who rule the land and the cities that we might live together as God wishes us to," recited Jesus.

"Why must you never marry?"

"It is evil to marry and live with women, for they make man's body dirty to lay on them, and man must be clean in the eyes of God."

"Why must you not own things of men?"

---

[9] A fictitious name, but likely a man of the sect did take special interest in Jesus as his tutor, and became a nominal kinfolk. This was a common practice of the sect.

"We own only what belongs to all that each might live."

"You are learning well, my son, and you have come to be with me only these few months."

"Why are you not a priest, my father? You are as wise as they. I hear their talk, but they speak only what you know so well and have taught me."

"Many would like to be priests. Few can. The community does not see me as you do, Jesus. I see but through a pinhole compared to the vastness that they see of God. They speak to him and know well that He will be with us soon, and that He shall come to make us free. He will show Himself through the Great Prophet who will return to life, or another will be sent by God to bring the light to shine upon all the earth. This He will do when we are ready in the cleanliness of our ways, for we are among the children of light and by living according to God's Law we will dwell forever with Him in Heaven."

"My father, you see brightly. I have heard no priest speak as you. Their light is dim, for all they do is dunk the brothers in the Jordan, and break the bread before each meal. I have heard no wisdom."

"Speak of wisdom, my son, only when your beard grows long, and bear respect for the holy priests—then take the truth to all men that they might see too, that the Lord will come when we are worthy. Whenever you are in the company of men who are not of us, go easy. They do not treat kindly our words of truth. It was in treachery that the Great Prophet died for us, when he tried to show the Pharisees the error of their tribute to Yahweh. Our Lord does not want the blood of animals spewn about. He wants us to prove ourselves worthy by right living. Then will He come; but go easy when you leave from among us. Nor should you reveal to others not of us, as casting pearls before swine, the Sadducees, the Pharisees, who believe wrongly."

"Why should they not know the truth? Can they not see as God has shown you?"

"You leave with your parents for Jerusalem on the Passover in the Spring, do you not, Jesus?"

"Yes, father. They come for me before the harvest."

"Do not speak of what we teach of the holy days. Nor would your parents understand. They have long followed the Pharisaic festival days."

b. Early Conflict with the Pharisees

At the First Passover in Harvest, Joseph, Mary, Jesus and his young brothers, James and Joses[10] traveled the mud-clogged roads in the 90-mile pilgrimage to Jerusalem. This they had done each year since first going to live among the Nazarenes. They arrived in Jerusalem weary and mud-covered on the morning of the third day, and went to the house of Joseph's son to bathe and eat.

Celebrants swarmed about the streets. On every corner were gathered crowds who listened to the prophecies of itinerant preachers. Some cried that God would not tolerate the evil of those in the big houses, who made their own people slave for them and gave only a pittance in return. Was this equality, for were not all the chosen people the same in the eyes of Yahweh? It was wicked! The Jews would suffer, and only too late would they learn. In ignorance, through the centuries, they had defied the Lord God. He had surrendered them to humility before the heathen of Babylon and Persia, the Macedonians and Greeks, and then the Romans. Would they never learn? God's Law, through Moses, must be obeyed—to treat your neighbor as yourself....

As Jesus walked through the wet streets of Jerusalem during the First Passover of the year, the cries of prophets echoed within the walls of the city and from the stone and mortar of the shabby, deteriorated buildings of the back streets.

" . . . Elijah is come . . . "

" . . . I bring word from God . . . ."

" . . . the city of David will rise again . . . "

"I am the Messiah, and I say the time is here when the Lord will help us throw off the yoke of the tyrants!"

" . . . for does not God wish us to show others the way? We

---

[10] James, Joses, Simon and Judas were his brothers. He also had sisters who were among the Nazarenes. (Mathew 13-56, King James version.)

are His people, of his flock. We have lost our way, we must work for Him to show His way . . . "

" . . . Let the Romans in. Show them the Lord's way . . . "

Roman soldiers stood nearby each group, in twos and threes, hands resting on swords lest they must be hastily drawn to control an outbreak,

Jesus walked near the temple, and saw there, as he had each year that the family had attended the Passover, merchants of the Temple selling live pigeons, doves, lambs, and oils, to those who would enter and place their bleeding, seared sacrifices before the shrine of Yahweh. Now Jesus questioned all this. His parents, Joseph and Mary, bought something as they had done every year, to take to the altar for sacrifice. Yet Milay, his Essene father, taught this was not God's will. He wanted His people only to be good and live in His ways, even as the men in the street seemed to be crying.

Jesus saw a merchant make the sale of a pigeon to a scraggly old man who drew the strings closed on his empty purse, and carried the pigeon forward to the Temple for slaughter. Suddenly what he had seen many times before now became repulsive to Jesus. The merchant appeared to take on an ugliness and a darkened countenance. This both sickened and angered Jesus. Surely this was desecration of the Holy Temple. Jesus entered the Temple and fell to His knees.

"Dear God: Forgive them for the terrible crimes they do against You. They do not know what You will, and feed you these bleeding carcasses. They think You want this. My father, Milay, has told me of Your ways, and Your people distress You. Help me to show them of . . . "

A large hand lay heavily on Jesus' shoulder as he knelt and spoke silently. A crowned, berobed and bearded Pharisee peered down at Jesus. "Where is your cap? Where are your parents, boy?"

"I am praying to God. My parents are preparing to leave the city."

"You had best find them. Have they paid their homage?"

"God does not want all this—the killing of animals for His sake."

"He will come to us when He is ready. We must show the Lord in tribute how we care, and beseech of Him His help in uniting His people. You go now, boy."

The family of Joseph returned north, with Jesus walking at the side of his father's donkey, and thinking in despair of the false notions of the Pharisees who could never know God in their blind ways.

c. Jesus is Called To His Mother's House

In the twelfth to fifteenth year of Jesus' life he lived with the Essenes, and learned more of their doctrine from Milay, his Essenic father. But Milay, as many had done, left the northern camp to travel and teach elsewhere.

Jesus learned more of the carpentry his blood father had taught him, and built lattice work for grape vines and fences for cattle compounds within the Essenic camp. In the evenings and on the Sabbath, he read scriptures and heard the priests speak. All this he tried to understand. Of girls he saw none—only older women whom all the men ignored. Yet Jesus felt an uncomfortable excitement when he saw them when their breasts hung loose bending to lift water jugs. He began then to understand the evil in women, and how one could become unclean with them.

Beyond the camp, at the Passovers in Jerusalem, in Cana, Magdalene, and Emmaus, he saw the sins of man—the wealthy in their chariots and walled houses. He heard Sadducees revile God, and they exploited man by playing Roman against Jew for personal profit, demanding taxes even of those who could not pay. He saw the Pharisees in their Temples and houses and heard them speak false words about the Lord's will. They were kept priests who let others labor while they took what they needed, and who knew scriptures only by rote. Yet even among the Essene priests and their assistants, the Levites, he saw this—holding high their office while preaching that all men are equal.

Among the Nazarenes, where his mother and father, Mary and Joseph, lived, there was ever the cry, "He will come"—a king like David of old, anointed and to be commissioned by the Lord to unite the Holy Land and rule over the people in peace and triumph. Then would Jew and Roman alike come together under the Law and worship the Lord.

Among the Essenes the one it was believed would come was the Great Prophet who had been persecuted by Jews even before the Romans had come to Jerusalem. He would appear as the Son of Man, and of God, to bring the wicked to justice, with their flesh, bone, and spirit sizzling in eternal fire and pain, and the righteous would acquire all the wealth; for this was the sine qua non of the Essenic Order—only in righteous living were they the servants of the Lord. Only when they proved their righteousness would He come. When the seeds of Truth were planted, there would grow a tree of righteousness, a Holy House of Israel, the most holy institution of Aaron, to make atonement for the earth, and decree the condemnation of wickedness, that there would be no longer perversity. It was in this, not in the empty, vain, offensive rituals of the Pharisee, that the Lord would fulfill His promise to the righteous. Man could become righteous only by proving and heeding God's Law, and by baptismal purification. When the righteous were of sufficient number, then would the Great Prophet be born again. Then would he send the wicked wailing, and bring the attainment of heaven to righteous men, Jew and Gentile alike, over all the earth.

In his fifteenth year, Jesus was called home, for he was the eldest of the children. Joseph had died. Jesus took his place as the head of the household, as he had done at the head of the family table in times past.[11] He became a patriarchal surrogate, who assumed the role of Joseph in all but wedlock. He left the Essenes, the Holy Order, never having attained the status of novitiate, nor in the code of the order had he become righteous. Yet, he knew the will of God as no one among the Nazarenes would.

The house of his parents had never presented a firm view to Jesus, nor to the other children. Joseph had been a Pharisee, and for the many years of his life had practiced their ritual, and paid tribute with sacrifices. Jesus, as had all his brothers, had been bled in the penis as an infant in such a sacrifice. Yet Joseph would turn from these Pharisees and their rituals, even as an old

---

[11] According to the Gospel of Pseudo Mathew, Jesus had supplanted his father at the head of the family even before Joseph died. In the Apocrypha, Joseph is written to have died at the age of 111.

man, when his life was threatened, and join his friends who believed more strongly than the Pharisees in the coming of a new king. They believed strongly in divine intervention, that God would send one who would bring all Jews together, as at one time had Jesse's son, David, done. Though ostensibly devout Pharisees, Joseph and Mary had also taught this strong doctrine of the Nazarenes, that Yahweh would send another to bring council and strength to the Jews, and unite all men to live under the Law.

As the new family patriarch, Jesus was now responsible for the religious instruction of the younger children. His own Essenic learning was confused, for he could not understand why they taught, on the one hand, that righteous living of man according to the Law alone would bring the favor of Yahweh, while on the other hand they practiced a ritualistic caste system of priests and demanded veneration for their office. In this, they seemed like the Pharisees whose office in turn the Essenes held in contempt.

Jesus pondered these disparities. He knew the holy doctrine to be true, and taught his brother James and John, as he had himself learned from Milay, in the way of right living.

As He grew to maturity Jesus' carpentry skill continued to improve, and he earned farthings and shekels and Roman aureus. The family ate and lived well, for Jesus worked hard and long through the day. He thought often of the camp at which he had spent five years, and learned so much. Sometimes, on the Sabbath, he took leave of the family and journeyed the ten miles to camp. There he was received as one would a close relative and was fed, and in the afternoon they talked about the scriptures which he still read daily.

Jesus had no time for the young women of the community in which he lived among the Nazarenes, though he had grown to manhood. He remembered the teaching of Milay, that the impurity of carnal relations made one unclean before God[12]; he

---

[12] The Essenes, as the Pythagoreans and the original Buddhists, taught abstinence to be the most sacred state. The origin of this principle with the Indian Buddhists was, of course, in the scourge of overpopulation among the lower castes. Unfamiliar with birth control, as even today, the impoverished people of India were kept in abject submission in a hand-to-mouth existence, even in massive

instead grew in increasing fondness for his mother who was yet a women of beauty at 36.

Sometimes on the Sabbath, when the Nazarenes gathered in meetings in a synagogue, Jesus stood before the congregation and spoke of what he had learned among the Essenes.

"You who are called Nazarenes would have the Lord send another, as was King David, but you think not of what God wishes. Rather, you are so wrapped up in your own woes, truly you must enjoy the oppression brought upon you—crushed under the Roman heel—for you heed not the commandments of the Lord. Make it right with God. It is not enough that you desire not what belongs to your neighbor, but that you suffer also compassion in your neighbor's needs. It is not enough that you beseech of the Lord to bring together His people of Israel, that He would send to us a leader in His name that was like David. Hear, oh you Nazarenes, the words of the Great Holy Prophet. If you would have God make whole the people of Israel, live then in purity. Cast out the demons of greed and avarice. Be washed in the Holy Water. Turn from the pleasure of your organ, and spewing seed into woman. Give all your energies to God! Show God we are worthy to be His people. Look to the scripture of the prophet Isaiah. Has it not been written that the Lord will come when we are ready? Make ready, you people, you Nazarenes and He will come!"

Jesus developed rhetorically. He spoke loudly and clearly, and the people listened. But he was young. His beard was neither long nor gray, and his skin was smooth unlike that of the wise old patriarchs of the community, tanned and wrinkled from decades of squinting in the glow and heat of the Syrian sun.

"This Jesus is the son of Joseph who died five summers ago, is he not?" spoke a Nazarene centennarian. "He has learned

starvation. In the wisdom of such sages as Guatama, overpopulation or uncontrolled birth, was seen as a source of such subjugation; thus the religion encompassed the dominating principle of celibacy, the veneer of which obtains even today among Roman Catholic clergy. (See Sheen's writing, for example). Why such emphasis operated among the Essenes is speculative—perhaps it occurred merely as a random influence, or perhaps it was based functionally upon similar socio-economic circumstances among the Jews, as among the Indians, or perhaps it was a reaction to the orgy cults (cf., Ishtarism) that violated private property rights to own women among the Jews.

well from the Holy Ones, but they, as others, create new fables of God. Life goes on, and there are those who say to bring the Lord we must suffer for our transgressions and some tell us tribute to the Lord is the only way. The Lord God will come when He sees we are ready—not in the mistaken blundering of His people to please Him. Let young Jesus find his way. He will be good for the people."

Jesus heard such comments by the elder laymembers of the Nazarene group. He realized his inadequacy. He read scriptures and studied, but his day was long at the carpentry bench. He alone was responsible to keep the house of his father. But each day he grew more restive. His life lacked the goals of one who would marry, and his increasing devotion to Essenic ideals held him firm. He must return to the camp, but he could not. He was torn between devotion in his patriarchal duty in the house of his dead father, Joseph, and the urgency among his people to hasten Yahweh's intervention. The Lord must come and show the Gentiles His way, and make judgment on the wicked, but how would He come, and by what precedence? Perhaps only the Essenes knew. Jesus lived a disquieted life and the conflict heightened as he entered his 22nd year, for he knew the rules of the Essenic order, to forsake all family and worship the Lord in complete devotion. James and Joses were nearly grown, he reasoned. His mother would not be destitute.

d. Return to the Essenes

Jesus left his family and friends among the Nazarenes to join, once again, the Essenic order in which he had been indoctrinated as a child. Now he would be accepted as an advanced novitiate. The council members knew him. He was accustomed to the discipline, but he must be screened.

"This was the child Jesus who studied under Milay," spoke a Levite to a priest, as Jesus stood before the group of Essenic priests who were to pass on his status. "He learned well from Milay. He has been with his mother, but now renounces all family to join us again."

"Have you had women?" asked the priest at the center of the table. "Will you forever leave them in their carnal ways?"

"I have never had woman, nor shall I," replied Jesus.

"Do you know the scriptures?"

"I study them constantly," replied Jesus, "and have preached them to my people at my home."

"Have you ever spoken of our Holy Prophet who was among us as the Lord to return again?"

"No. That I could not tell for I know it is heresy among the Pharisees, and the people of my land await a Messiah whom they do not know."

"Do you have property for the community?"

"I have none," replied Jesus.

"You work as a carpenter. This work you may continue among us or in Semnabris where, if you receive coin, it will be paid to our community treasurer. You will eat with the novitiates and find bed among them as you have in the past."

Jesus was humble as he worked and lived among the Essenes. He studied and wrote, and thought long about the teachings of the Great Holy Prophet; but he was not ready to be admitted, in the eyes of the priests, to the sacrament; nor to become a brother, or go out and speak in the comunity at large that the people of Israel might see that God would come again, and would raise His people above all others of the world. During the first half year of his probation, Jesus again became impatient. He must speak to others to show them that the Kingdom of God was at hand, and waited only for the people of Israel to come among the righteous.

Jesus left the northern Essene camp, and journeyed south through Samaria. He traveled among Essenic communities in Judea. The priests at the southern camps permitted him to stay, but questioned his meanderings. His novitiate, they admonished, should be completed where he had been accepted; but Jesus worked and gave of himself in devotion and study, and was admired by the laymen of the community. Many even then would have welcomed him as brother, for he exclaimed, even as the priests, that the glory of God would shine upon the righteous.

e. Jesus and John

At a camp adjoining a monastary near the Dead Sea, Jesus met John among the novitiates.[13] John was in many ways as impatient as Jesus to show the people of Israel the way—a way that the Essenes were reticent to show, for theirs was a slow proselytizing. There were indeed few who joined the Essenes, while the wicked Pharisees and the heathen Sadducees continued to win converts to the error of their ways. John, as Jesus, was an advanced novitiate. He worked long hours in the scriptorium writing on thin copper sheets and leather as a scribe, to provide additional copies of the great books of the prophets. As he read the words of the prophets his breast heaved heavily, for he knew the Kingdom of Heaven was at hand. The people of Israel would not heed the word. Nor was his sect concerned with expediting the process. In his assigned tasks he copied and wrote diligently. Yet, brother clung only to brother to share the belief only among themselves, as they shared their food and raiment. Their gospel and ethics were also only for among themselves—to love God above all else and a brother as the self, and to cringe before enemies and verily love them for their sins.

"God's way must be followed!" exclaimed John to Jesus. "And yet the brothers, and our holy priests, live only within themselves and let the rest of the people of Israel go their own way."

"Take heart, John," replied Jesus. "The great and righteous prophet shall come again. He may even now be among us. It is written that he will suffer as have his people, even at their own hands—for great are the powers of evil, and fight we must to overcome them."

"Yes, and our holy masters of the sect see the only salvation to be within the sect. Each must wait to prove his purity of intent for many seasons. I have not yet even been baptized, though I wish for righteousness, and the Lord's coming with every fibre of my being!"

"Oh, John, you carry high hope. Veritably you sound as might Elijah, who would call for all to open their eyes and hearts that the Lord will come."

---

[18] John the Baptist may not have been an Essene, though he evidenced marked similarities in characteristic doctrine and practice (cf., Josephus' Essenic father in the wilderness eating wild uncooked food, etc.) He obviously renounced principles of the other parties, Pharisaic and Sadducean, thus taking the position of the Essenes, emphasizing their purification through baptism in the extensive proselytizing that he later carried out.

"Let not the brothers hear what I say, Jesus, but the Lord will not come from within the sect, for they restrict too much the pure and righteous. All men must see the light and overcome the wicked. This forte that is the sect of the Lord should bring light to all."

"I know, John. We must not let these utterances be heard, or we shall be castigated, but man must speak. The sect holds the truth, but they set up an order of precedence almost as the Pharisees, and we sit most lowly—we, who are most knowing in God's way. Surely, before God in Heaven, all are equals. Surely we cannot remain passive, John, and wait out our turn to become— what? Merely brothers; and without appeal to our people, the sect diminishes. Never would the Lord give his chosen their due while they sin. Though we of the sect rise to Heaven, our people would remain always beneath the heel of the heathen. Let us raise our voices, John, and be heard, that the Kingdom of God is near if we all but heed the way of the Lord. Let he who is inspired speak, for he may be the Messiah; and who knows but that you yourself, John, are Elijah who has come to prepare his way?"

"I feel it, Jesus. I grow restless in our time. Oh, there is strength and hope in what you say. Who might be among us who is He, who will combat the evil and bring light to all the people?"

"Let the light to shine upon all. I will soon return to Galilee, John, but here in the monastary, in this wilderness, in the stench of the sea and the barren ugliness of rock and parched earth, you will see cool streams to flow and flowers to bloom when the Lord is come, for they are the righteous even among the righteous, and as it is written, so be it. But take up the cry, as you must, John, and I will join you when the time is right, when I have met my obligations as a brother.

f. Jesus Becomes an Essene Brother

Jesus, in the last months of his novitiate year, returned to the Essene camp near the Sea of Galilee and was welcomed as a brother. His fame as a devotee and teacher of the scriptures had spread among all the camps. The priests and the Levites, whose good grace he must yet seek for official sanction, were those who most dubiously regarded his intent, though among his peers he was most highly regarded. They had heard of his impatience, and of John's. True enthusiasm and evangelism were welcome, but criticism of the sect could not be tolerated. However, Jesus did not stand accused—only suspect, and his popularity dictated his acceptance into the brotherhood.

Jesus truly knew scriptures and the law, for as he stood before the priests in final examination they were themselves confounded as he quoted profusely from Isaiah, Proverbs, The Twelve Patriarchs, Genesis, and the Essene manual.

In quiet, solemn respect, the chief Essene priest said merely, "You are one of us."

Jesus partook of his first sacred meal during the second Spring after he had rejoined the Essenes. Unlike other Essenic camps or communities in the cities, the Galilean camp had no building in which an upper room was customarily prepared each day for the feast. In this camp, a large tent was used. Jesus sat cross-legged, garbed in a freshly-washed white robe, among the other brothers, as Levites passed among them carrying trays and distributing bread, fish, and a chalice of wine to each.

"We break this bread, oh Lord, and eat of the flesh of the Great Prophet whom You will send again....and of the wine we drink, for it is His blood, and we become as He to enter into Your Kingdom, which is in Heaven."

Jesus was baptized in the waters of the Jordan and this became, with the other Brothers, a daily occurrence. The priests performed the immersion as did the ancient Persians of the prophet Zoroaster.

" . . . by this water I cleanse you of the evil that resides in you, and the power of darkness is subdued . . . "

Each day in the Brotherhood Jesus journeyed to Semnabris and worked at a carpentry bench, and he returned twice daily for his rations in the eucharistic meal, and in the evening he was purified in baptism.

Each day that passed made Jesus more anxious, for the glory of God swelled in his bosom and he felt clean and worthy, while all about the creatures of darkness dwelt, blind to the light that upon him shone so brightly.

"I must leave the camp to teach," he said as he sought council with the chief priest.

"You are pure, Brother Jesus, and wise. You will enter the Kingdom of Heaven. Do not go among those who would corrupt you. The Great Prophet will be sent to us to destroy the people of darkness and bring Heaven on Earth. Stay among us. You can do no good."

"The prophet may even yet be among you," replied Jesus, exasperated by the priest's passive indulgence. "It it written that His way must be prepared."

g. Jesus' Ministry

In the early days of Jesus' ministry, the son of Herod the Great, Antipas, reigned in Galilee and Peraea. The Herod family were of Edomite descent, but of Jewish religion, and the Pharisees predominated, through Antipas, in Galilee. When Jesus undertook to teach in Galilee, he remembered the words of his old Essenic teacher, Milay, who warned of the treachery that had taken the life of the Great Prophet who, during the Asmonean reign, had flaunted his knowledge of God before the priests. The Asmoneans, of whom the Pharisees were offshoots, in the ways of darkness had persecuted Him who was the very incarnation of God. In Judea, to the south, Roman procurators governed. There, Jesus knew that greater freedom prevailed, but while in Galilee and Peraea he must exercise the greatest caution when speaking among the Pharisaic rulers and their people.

The Messiah would come. Everyone knew this. Some even thought that He had come in the figure of Herod. But this was only in their ignorance, for Jesus knew that only in purity would God evidence Himself, and Herod was truly a child of darkness. Jesus first preached to his people among the Nazarenes who believed in the coming of a great king in the tradition of David. He later preached in the towns and villages about the Sea of Galilee and Lake Huleh, in Magdala, Tiberius, Cana, Emmaus, and in Gaulonitis. He did not go among the people of Samaria, for they were not of God's chosen. When Jesus spoke, he was

profound. He told the gatherings of God's intention to send a
holy one, who would come to perform miracles among them.
They would know when He came. Only by devotion of the people of Israel would it be fulfilled.

" . . . go and leave the wickedness of your lives behind, and
worship the Lord your God, for the glory of God will be upon
you, and He will crush the enemies of Israel; and the pleasures and joys of Heaven will be yours. Give up your women
and your lust and surfeit. Go into the camps, and give yourself to the ways of the prophets and of God."

The words of Jesus spread throughout Galilee, in the camps
and in the cities of Judea. He spoke not as other evangelists of
the time, for he had begun to reveal certain notes of the Essenes,
sacred to the Brotherhood—the extremes and mysteries of chastity and common sharing for the good of all, were not meant
for others outside the Essenic community. But Jesus spoke of
these. The doctrines were different and the people listened as
if to heed the conscience within them that they knew so well;
for they suffered in guilt for the violation of the Law.

" . . . it is not enough to leave your neighbor's wife alone; if
you even think of her in lust, the wrath of God is upon you. If
you think of harming your brother, this is an act before the
deed, and punishable. To eat when others are hungry and have
nothing, will burn your soul, and keep you from Heaven . . . "

After his third year as an Essenic teacher at large Jesus had
traveled throughout all of Galilee,[14] and among Essenic communities in Judea. Because he told what was forbidden, though
with no serious repercussions among the Essenes, he was chas-
tised according to the rules. Many camps to which he sojourned
would not welcome him as was their custom, to provide food
and drink to itinerant Brothers. Yet others would, insomuch as
the chief priests at each camp differed in outlook. Some understood the qualifications and character of Jesus to bespeak of Messiahship—for when the Great Prophet returned He might not

---

[14] When Jesus called for disciples (cf., Mark 1) they followed straight away without
question, leaving jobs and families. This suggests that, as a religious leader, he
was not only known and respected, but obeyed.

come as one proclaimed, but only by signs would He be known, then to reveal Himself in all His power and glory.

Jesus journeyed south to Judea in his teaching, though he had intended conversion primarily among the people of Galilee who were directly under Herod and priestly rule. John, in the earlier days with whom he had been a novitiate, was preaching along the Jordan and baptizing. John had been expelled from the Essenes for speaking against the sect. He finally spoke publicly on what for years he felt privately—that the Essenes were impassive, without the fierce, angry insistence of the Lord—to call His people and prepare them for the coming. So John did as he had learned in the Essenes, and almost blasphemously flaunted their esoteric purification by baptizing freely, even among the heathen, that they, too, might experience the cleanliness and come to the light.

"Sing praise to the Lord! God shall send to us the Great prophet, who died at the hands of wicked hypocrites for they falsely spoke in the Lord's name. He shall come! Cleanse yourself and live for Him. I do not ask you to join the order for they demand long residence and suspect sincerity. Come! Feel in your heart that you are pure, and be ready, fast and and follow the Law! This is all that the Lord will ask of you. Salvation is yours this moment if you will believe and give of yourself . . . "

As Jesus approached the baptismal gathering on the banks of the Jordan, John recognized him immediately. "I have remembered you well, brother Jesus. Your words have echoed about the Jordan. You teach in wisdom almost as one inspired."

"I will be baptized, John."

"I am not of the order, Jesus."

"You do wonders, John, and your following grows. The sect would do well to see your work and bring in others. You will bring God's blessing the sooner."

"You are good, Jesus, and need no cleansing. The light shines already brightly upon you. The Lord is pleased with your work, though I will baptize you to keep the darkness from upon us."

After Jesus was baptized by John he went to the camp at the Qumran monastary near the Dead Sea.[15] There the priests refused to admit him as a Brother in good standing. He had been in the company of John; word had also come to them from the northern camps about Jesus, the Nazarene, who spoke as an Essene, but his message was to those who awaited only an anointed king. He had revealed the secret codes, as one casting pearls before swine. Jesus, without food, remained in the desolate country about the Dead Sea, sleeping in caves in the night, and meditating, and pondering his estrangement with the Essenes during the day. Their ways were those of God; yet they did not understand the urgency to bring God's light to His people. How could God work through his chosen people who were forever leaving the fold, failing to heed His call? They must be made to see. Jesus ached in his body from hunger as he sat amongst the rocks in the bleak, barren wasteland. He was wracked in the turmoil of his distress, in the tension of his chastity and years of forbearance, and then hunger gnawned his bones. He had given his very life to the sect, that they might please God, and bring about fulfillment of His final promise. But with so few of the good to do battle, with so many wicked . . . why were they in the order so insistent upon keeping out those who could be so easily converted? Truly, if the Great Prophet were to return, He would be among them now. Did not John prophesy this? Is John not the very prophecy of Elijah fulfilled? Could John not be Elijah, heralding the coming of this son of Man who is God's promise fulfilled—come to judge the wicked and the dead? In the pain of his struggle for realization, the anguish of his conflict, and the deadly loneliness of the barren rock-bound shores of the Dead Sea, Jesus began himself to answer these questions. God's light must shine upon the whole world and His laws be obeyed. The outcast status of Jesus was a denial of God, for God was within him. This Jesus knew, and his very strength

---

[15] Jesus, in the Synoptics, is described as having gone into the wilderness (cf., the wilderness of Qumran near the Dead Sea), fasting for 40 days in dire temptation. As an Essenic-Christian composition, the influence of Zoroastrian-Buddhistic tradition is evident. In both traditions Zoroaster and Guatama were tempted (cf., also the 40-day search of Isis for the dismembered body of Osiris). Assuming some basis for connecting Jesus with this tradition, such a sojourn is here described.

was that of God. He would but have God speak to him—"You are my messenger. My favorite of the holies . . . " even as He spoke to Jacob and commissioned David. "I have sent you! . . . "

He had come. He was the Great Prophet reincarnate. He was Jesus the Nazarene, a believer in the Kingdom of David, but who had come to convert the wicked, and cleanse, and, as the great Buddha, bring peace to the suffering, promise to the despaired, joy to the lonely, and light to the darkness.

h. Preaching as the Messiah

Jesus left the Dead Sea to return to his ministry. He journeyed north again to Galilee, and sought aid in his efforts, this time among those whom he had inspired—among the fishermen: Simon, Andrew, Zebedee and John " . . . if you believe that God will come, and would live a life of devotion, then come with me to teach . . . "

Jesus preached in Capernaum, entering among groups who had gathered to worship the Lord. As was his custom, He arose before the congregation and told of the Lord's emissary who was even then among them. "You are a Nazarene," spoke one of the congregation, "a believer in the Messiah. Let us worship as we choose and believe in our way."

Jesus stood and spoke long. Galilee was his home and they were all his people, whom he loved. He would and could not deceive them—for they must know, as it was written and told by all who were holy—that God would come and deliver His people from bondage, but they must heed His commandments and live in peace and humility. They must live the law twice again as it was written—to do no acts of evil, but more, not even to think them, to give double what was asked, and to be humble by again as much as the Romans asked (for theirs was pre-eminence in danger, and reaction formations—to love those hated was even to survive). When they had sinned against man and God, they must come to be cleansed and to sin no more....Surely He who spoke, they realized, was the son of man, and to the congregation before Him, He told about himself, Jesus the Nazarene who spoke for the people. They immediately felt love for Jesus. When He visited the house of Simon, whose mother-in-law lay sick, she was aroused by the spirit of this Man, Whose Name she had heard spoken in love.

The night of his first sojourn in Capernaum, the group to whom He had earlier spoken gathered about, and asked for more of his sage wisdom; for they knew the evil that prevailed in their souls, and would be cleansed in soul and body and relieved of their guilt (from which many had developed bodily symptoms). When Jesus told of the forgiving nature of God if they could mend their ways, many became cured of their guilt and of their symptoms, and, too, for their suffering, He promised a life everlasting in Heaven, of peace and joy.

Jesus, with his nucleus of followers, the erstwhile fishermen, moved and preached throughout Galilee. Those of the congregation who did not herald Him as the Messiah, praised His learning. He welcomed all and blessed them in the Name of the Lord, regardless of what they had to offer. In their deep gratitude, when some found in the words of Jesus relief from their anguish and soul suffering, they offered their lives in devotion to Him, but He asked only that they keep the Laws of Moses. In His ministries, the call became so great for Him to speak that He took respite living in a tent on the desert; yet they followed Him even there. Upon one occasion, in return to Capernaum, He sat in the house of scribes with whom He discussed the Law. A crowd gathered outside the house and called for Him to come out to show His curing power on one sick. When He failed to respond, they removed a piece from the roof and lowered the sick one who had palsy. Annoyed, yet flattered by their belief, He touched the one with palsy and said, "Let there be no more sin in you and relieve your soul, for I am forgiving you."

But the Pharisaic scribes, with whom He spoke on theological matters, denied His right and power to forgive even before them.

"I say this is within my power," He retorted, "and this man shall be relieved of his guilt and the devil that is within him. Leave from among us and follow the Law. You are well."

The one with palsy and immoveable limbs, looked up and moved, and cried like a baby. Then he arose and left from among them.

It was from among the pained and remorseful Galileans that Jesus drew his followers, the adulterers, those with hate and murderous intent, the thieves, the harlots, and the impoverished. He taught, as the Essenes, that deeds merely followed the intent in cleansing the thoughts of man. They sought Him, heavily ladened with their deeds of evil for which He forgave them, and required only that they heed the Law to the very core of their being. As the Buddha, Jesus did not demand more suffering and deprivation. He required no fasting—as new cloth sewn to old would rip the old, so would fasting bring more pain, and discourage those who had already suffered. So his doctrine and practice was made easy to follow. It was new and many could easily accept it to gain relief from their burdens.

"As new wine is poured into old bottles, the bottles break. New wine requires new bottles."

This was Jesus' innovation. The practices of the Essenes, the Pharisees, and even of John the Baptist, were not effective because of the severity of demands. The doctrine of Jesus was expedient and developed as He found in various practices that His following increased. The observances of the Sabbath was such a case. His disciples worked to bring food on this day. Man should not be denied his needs, whatever the day. The Sabbath was made for man. Thus he departed, in expediency, from rigid Essenic dogma, as well as that of the Pharisees. Bits of philosophical Buddhism had penetrated east and west of India in the centuries following the teaching of Guatama. In the first century A.D., it had been adopted by men in China, was revivified and reformulated by the librarian-philosopher, Lao Tze. In the West, the formulations of Pythagoras were developed eclectically from Buddhistic elements. In like manner, Jesus, as He preached under such philosophical influences, pacified and quieted the hatred and anguish in his people:

"Suffer not in ignorance. If you hold tightly to what you crave, you will surely lose this as you will your very soul. How does a man come to a profit if he acquires a super-abundance of wealth, but has not the heart to enjoy even the freedom of the air. Give yourself to God. Do not cling to wealth, to wife and child. You must give these up, as your very breath, that you might have them again. Unto yourself be true, and God will watch over you as He does the fowl of the air and the fish of the sea."

The new gospel, as espoused by Jesus, was made easy. Many had suffered under the severe code of the Pharisees. Only the important commands of God were to be heeded—to do good for others, to heal the sick, to repent, to regret and forever cease transgression against man as against God. Jesus seemed almost to flaunt these views before the Pharisees. He had long forgotten the admonition of Milay to beware of persecution. He had also turned from the Essenes after many of the camps had rejected Him. Now the threat in Galilee increased. Priests among the Pharisees, and those who espoused the deification of Herod, joined together against the Man Jesus, whose following grew. The appeal of Jesus' heretical doctrine was clearly a threat to their tradition. "How is He to be dealt with?" they asked.

Jesus continued preaching in Galilee, but kept his back to the sea, where His disciples had procured a boat. Word had spread throughout Galilee, in Jerusalem and through Judea, Syria, Tyre and Sidon, of the doctrine of forgiveness, and fell upon ears of hordes of the guilt-ridden Jews who failed the strict codes and rituals of the Pharisees, who were thoroughly pained by conscience, veritably suffering bodily hurt. They came to see Him to be cured, many proclaiming Him to be in the authority of God. Jesus saw His power grow in controlling the spirit of men, and to cure them of their mortal anguish. And He, too, believed that this was truly in the power and authority of God. "He is the Messiah!" exclaimed some, while Jesus at first discouraged such talk that smacked of blasphemy. Seeing the success of His ministry, and realizing how the following could grow beyond His highest expectations, Jesus sought evangelists from among His followers: Simon surnamed Peter, James of Zebedee and John his brother (who together were to become as thundering preachers), Andrew, Philip, Bartholomew, James of Alphaeus, Thaddaeus, Simon the Canaanite, and Judas Iscariot. They met together, and, in the midst of a swarming mass of followers who would hear more and worship Him as the Lord, Jesus spoke to His twelve evangelists (cf., "twelve", as the number of the tribes of Israel) :

"Take up the sermon, and preach and cure as I do that others will follow. Tell them that I have come—He has come to fulfill the promises of the Lord of Hosts who is my Father in heaven. I have come to deliver you, my people."

Word of the claims of Jesus to Messiahship reached His family, and friends. Scribes to the south, who dealt in Hebrew theology, also heard. He was, they claimed, working for the devil who bred flies. He was indeed able to rid the people of demons, because He was in league with Beelzebub, chief of the devils. But Jesus refuted these theologians. The devil in chief would never choose to work against himself. Their claims were ridiculous. The King of Darkness could only be subdued by someone stronger. Jesus performed in the name of the Almighty Lord, and He could forgive His people for anything if they would but follow Him. The friends and family of Jesus came to Him now, His mother Mary, and His Brothers. He was not well, they said. He spoke as one stricken of mind, thinking Himself the Messiah. He needed rest to let His reason return. But Jesus refused to see them. "If they will not follow me as do others, then I have no mother, nor brothers." (He had long since forsaken His family when joining the Essenes, but now He denied them, for they lent no credence to His claim, nor bearing to His prestige).

During the days that followed, as they moved about the northern shores of the Sea of Galilee, Jesus lived aboard a ship. His sermons were to the people who came down to the shore. There he lived with the twelve disciples and taught them in the ways He had learned among the Essenes. To those who thronged about the shore to hear Him speak, He spoke of riddles—of a sower who spread seed, some of which was eaten by birds, some that fell on rocks and dried in the hot sun, and others that took hold in fertile ground and grew into great tall fruit stalks.

"I speak to the masses in this fashion," He explained to his disciples, "for there are among them, those who could hear not what I said were it straightforward." (As the Essenes spoke of casting pearls before swine) "For those who would listen well, will understand, but many are steeped in the deceitfulness of this world and live in wealth and lust. They are not ready. There are those certainly who would go against you and what you say, even to punish you for the light you bring. For to speak straightforward would be to invite rebuke from the Pharisees and Herodians, where in the land of Galilee without Roman neutrality it may be dangerous even to our very lives. Here in Galilee we must bring the light; though we speak in parable and riddle, those who are of right mind will hear and heed."

They soon departed across the Sea of Galilee to visit other shores and preach. In one area of the wilderness where they touched the shore, a severely disturbed man came to them. In our time he would certainly have been institutionalized and bound in a strait jacket. When Jesus appeared to him, he became pacified and sound of mind. He wished to follow and pay homage, but Jesus told him only, to repay the Lord he should tell throughout the land of the deed, that He, Jesus, had done. On another shore Jesus cured a woman of a blood disease, and still another, returned a tribal chief's daughter to life.

Jesus later entered the land of His childhood, where His mother, Mary, and brothers, James, Joses, Juda and Simon, and His sisters yet lived. When He spoke before them, He tried this time to tell them of His divine mission—for he spoke in the Name of the Lord. But they were contemptous of the man who had mended their furniture, whose name, which among others brought such awe, was here laughable. "He is a fool to think of Himself so," they said.

Jesus left his old neighborhood, and called his disciples to Him. "Go out and preach in my name!" "Take nothing with you, and be completely itinerant. Show them in their faith they can be cured. Go into the camps of the Holy Ones when you are hungry, and seek shelter when you are tired. If they know you come in my name, and will not welcome you, then curse their place. For when the day of Judgment is here, in all the goodness of their holy rites, they will suffer more than it is written Sodom and Gomorrha did."

The disciples traveled and preached throughout the land of Galilee in the name of Jesus. In the faith of those who came to repent, many cures of body ills were bestowed. The name of Jesus became known widely among the sick, the poor, and lowly ones.

Alas, word came to Jesus that John, the Essene brother of Jesus, who had baptized all men for the sake of their souls, was dead. He had cried out against the inequity of Herod, who lived in lust against the Law of the people; for Herod had married his brother's wife. She sinned, John had claimed, and must be stoned as an adulteress. John's head was removed for espousing the righteousness of the Law of the Lord. When Jesus heard this He grieved heavily, for He realized the imminent danger to Him and His disciples in Galilee.

Jesus bade his disciples to rest in the desert from the weariness of their travels. They were never without throngs of people who came for cures, to repent and seek salvation. The numbers were great of those who needed solace,[16] in those days about the land of Palestine. The people craved, in their guilt for transgressing the Laws of Moses, the forgiveness of One Whose claim to Messiahship seemed real. The stories about Jesus seemed to make Him truly one anointed by the Lord, for many were cured of what today is recognized as psychoneurosis, who were hysterically crippled, pained and suffering manifold disorders for breaking tribal code in their conscience and in their hearts; when he forgave them if they promised repentance, and in joyful reunion with the tribe of the Hebrews, they were cured.[17]

Jesus worked his ministry; He became more involved in conflict with the Pharisees. The people among His converts—His disciples, and others who followed Him or came for cures, were not of the Pharisees. They had strayed from such tradition as washing of hands and feet, nor had they paid strict observance to the Sabbath. This was, in part, responsible for their guilt, from which Jesus absolved them. He, too, had even strayed from the strict ways of the Essenes, for it was expedient to bring flocks to God. Thus it was that many orthodox priests challenged Jesus

---

[16] The feeding of the 5,000 (Mark 6) has been omitted as folklore; also, the overtaking of His disciples across the sea enroute to Bethsaida as he walked on the water is plainly legendary. Such stories as these, assuming some historical basis for a man called Jesus, were evoked in hearsay in a superstitious age. The nature of folk legends that grow up about a legendary hero has been described by Bartlett.

[17] Modern Psychosomatic Medicine has thrown much light on the nature of such ostensible physical ills. Much blindness, deafness, skin ailments and various physical symptoms have recently come to be medically known to have a basis in the social adjustive interactions of the individual. "Hysterical" symptoms, subject to miracle cures, have been found most commonly among primitive peoples, or those moderns in the lower-socio and educational groups. (Refer to Kasanin, and Simeon for discussions.) Even today, who among us is without these, when lacking peace within and among ourselves?

for these transgressions. To such He replied with anger in a complete spirit of rebellion:

"You are hypocrites, who know nothing but what will profit yourselves! You demand that we conform to foolish tradition that has no meaning. As surely as you eat food, it will pass through you in stool, and means nothing. Look to the heart of man—not his belly. There you will find from whence sin and evil spring. Therein is adultery, fornication, murder, thievery, covetousness, wickedness, deceit, lasciviousness, curses, blasphemy, pride, foolishness!"

He traveled widely in Galilee, Sidon, Trye, DeCapolis, Dalmanutha, and spoke and ministered to whomever came to Him. It might have been a Greek of the Syrophenician nation, as well as any of the people of Galilee; He asked only that they believe in Him. It was later said that He made the deaf to hear, and the dumb to speak. In the presence of His disciples, He made the blind to see, and once spat in a blind man's eyes who was indeed awed by the very presence of Jesus and once again was able to see. Jesus knew the curative powers He possessed. "Tell no one what I have done for you," He admonished, knowing full well that tales would spread about these miracles in scope and magnitude.

On the way to Caesarea Phillippi, He asked the disciples, "How is it told about me as you have heard people speak?"

"Some say you are a prophet, others that you are John, who baptized, reincarnate," replied Peter.

"Who do you think I am?"

"You are truly an anointed one of God," said Peter.

Thus Jesus began to define His destiny. If He were the Christ, as Isaiah foretold, He must suffer at the hands of man and sinners to achieve His immortality.[18]

---

[18] The "suffering Son of Man" (Mark 9) is steeped in Hebrew tradition. The legendary Yeshu was born illegitimately of Marian, fulfilling the prophecy of Zachariah. Yeshu rode into Jerusalem on an ass, and was executed as a false prophet. The followers of Yeshu declared His body gone from the tomb and three days later He ascended into Heaven and sat on the right hand of God. So goes the tradition. (Refer to M. Goldstein's, "Jesus in Jewish Tradition"). John Robertson (refer to his *Christianity and Mythology* and *Pagan Christs*) has also seen the passion drama of the Hebrews to have origin in an ancient Palestinian rite in which an annual victim, known as Jesus (Joshua), Son of the Father, was actually sacrificed.

"I will die for my God to show them who I really am," said Jesus, half-aloud.

"Oh, master, I beg you not to speak like this. You do wonders as you preach and cure. Put this out of your mind," said Peter.

"You would miss me. Peter, when I am gone, but I must know death that others might have life everlasting. Let all our people follow me, and give their very lives up to God, and forsake all things of this treacherous, sinful world. Come to me, as others have to the Holy Ones (Essenes) and the glory of God shall be upon them and they shall reign in Heaven and Earth; this I promise will happen, that God will bring His will on earth even before others of us die."

Near Caesarea, Jesus led Peter, James and John of his disciples away from the teeming masses in solitude high in surrounding hills. They sat in silence, and meditated, and Jesus, in His intended self-sacrifice, suffered hallucination, and pain, as he had felt it once before, alone in rejection by the Essenes, in the wilderness at Qumran.

"Moses is here," he cried, "and tells me that the Lord speaks again! Oh, hear Elijah! Oh, hear him who tells of the Son of Man who is to come! He is here!"

Peter tried to quiet Jesus. "Yes, oh master, He is here and we shall worship all three of you."

Yet, Peter, as the others, in following Jesus through His turmoil of spirit and anguish and hallucinatory experience, heard voices among themselves, each crying differently, yet speaking together.

"The prophecy is fulfilled. Elijah is here!" blurted Jesus.

"Why is he here?" asked James of Peter.

"It is written in the scriptures."

Some among the poor and down-trodden seeking solace, had followed them to the hills. And Jesus came down and found his disciples at work. Among them was a man with a child. The man wept, for the child was siezed with a frightening tension, with foaming mouth and gnashing teeth, and eyes rolled up.[19] His disciples had tried to bring the child about in vain, and the man beseeched Jesus, "Oh, Master, do something for my boy!"

"Why must I always be subjected to this foolishness?" murmured Jesus. "You could do it with your own faith. Bring the boy here."

As the people gathered about, Jesus looked at the boy writhing upon the dust. He noted skepticism in some among the crowd in their silent sneers. Then He spoke: "Come out, you accursed demons of the dark. Leave the boy!"

He charged them long to depart from the child, and held His face upward in prayer. After many minutes the boy lay quiet. Then Jesus lifted him and the child stood, pale and weak; and the crowd marveled.

i. The Expectancy of Martyrdom

In later days about Galilee, Jesus told those close to Him again, as though depressed, "I must die for all to see, at the hands of the sinners that they might suffer guilt and see, and repent before God, My Father."

The disciples knew of what He spoke. The Kingdom of God was truly at hand, and Jesus was He who had come. They vied for His favor.

"You fools! There is to be no hierarchy among you. There is to be no chief among you like the priests in the Holy Ones.[20] We will be done with that."

He spoke again to the disciples, "I ask only that you bring before God such believers as are children."

"What of those who cure in your name but do not belong among us?" asked John.

"They who are not against me are with me, and whoever speaks in my name will be duly rewarded in Heaven; but they who deny me will burn in hell fire....Keep yourself ever pure

---

[19] Here is described a case of grand mal epilepsy, even today awesome in its manifestations. The attack, as Jesus tended the child, may have subsided, giving the appearance of cure. Among these superstitious people, the child was thought to be infested with demons.

[20] This was the Essenic structure to which He referred. This suggests resentment of Jesus toward the Essenic priestly hierarchy where chief priests, scribes, laymen, and novitiates fell into a rigid order of caste.

before me and the Lord. Whoever would sexually violate a child, he would be better drowned. If you handle your sexual organ and it becomes hard, it is even better that you should cut off your hands than to enter into eternal hell for teasing your organ. If you are stimulated by women, or other things that you see, it is better that you should poke out your eyes than suffer hell fires—for truly, it is the purity and goodness within yourself that shall save you, and as you live at peace among yourselves."[21]

Jesus and his disciples sailed down the Jordan River, along the coast of Peraea, finally landing on the northern shores of Judea. As Jesus preached on these shores, Pharisees came suspiciously to hear Him and examine His doctrine for heresy.

"Is it all right for a man to break up with his wife?" they asked.

"Why do you ask these things" replied Jesus evasively, "when you know what has been written?"

"Moses wrote reluctantly in favor of divorce."

"Yes," answered Jesus, "for those of you who are without compassion he wrote this, but God has made man and woman, as it has always been, and meant that they should leave their parents and be together as one. He has ordained that they be joined and by no man be separated."

He said later to his disciples, "Any man or wife who leaves the other, and takes another commits the sin of adultery."

There came children whom, lest they pester Jesus, His disciples told to go away. "No!" said Jesus. "These are the prototypes of God's pure. When men come to care, as a little child, to accept what I say on faith, then shall they enter His Kingdom."

There once came a man following Jesus who had heard of his wisdom. "Please, Good Master, tell me how I might enter the After Kingdom."

"Call me not Good," replied Jesus. "There is no one good but God. If you would be with Him, follow the commandments,

---

[21] Celibacy was demanded, as in the Essenic discipline, to which Jesus had been subject. (Also see Footnote #12.)

do not be adulterous, nor kill, steal, talk against your neighbor, or cheat."

"These I have followed."

"Then more—give up your worldly possessions. Give them away to those who are without anything. Then become my disciple."

But the man could not bring himself to do this for he enjoyed much of this world's wealth. Jesus watched the potential proselyte leave, and said, "Such as he, with their riches and luxury, will never enter God's Kingdom. It is impossible, when they weigh so heavily their wealth against God's wishes."

"All men have property, except the Holy Ones (Essenes). How can any possibly go into God's Kingdom then?" asked John. who had never been among the Holy Ones.

Jesus paused; then He answered. "It is possible if God wills it".

"We have given up all these things, Jesus," said Peter. "What is for us?"

"You will be rewarded a hundredfold, for all you have given up in this life, by eternal life in Heaven. Those who were first among the Holy Brothers will fall out, and many will succeed them, especially those who would not receive me."

James and John, sons of Zebedee, who were among Jesus' disciples, came before Jesus. John spoke, "Master, we ask that you would give us a share in the glory that will be yours. Let us be your second in command."

"You can share with me whatever you will," replied Jesus, "and come into the Kingdom of Heaven, but to ask to be a leader among us is presumptuous." He noticed others of the disciples look in anger upon James and John for attempting to gain His favor. "Look at the Romans—the Gentiles," he began again. "They are given authority to rule over others and receive high and mighty status, and make the people their servants. Not so among us. He who takes the leadership will be himself a servant of all."

j. The Passion Drama

It was the season of the Passover Festival in Jerusalem, the great city in which stood the Temple of God first built by Solomon. The small band of Arabic, religiously devout nomads began the journey under the leadership of Jesus.

To Jerusalem would come thousands from over all the land, in celebration. Near Jericho, crowds gathered about Jesus. "You are Jesus the Nazarene!" shouted one. "You have come to free us, as even King David, and to cure the sick, oh, Great One."

"Hold your tongue!" said a disciple. "To speak such is treason here in Judea."

But they spoke the more: "Have mercy, oh Son of David."

As they camped outside Jerusalem, on a hill called the Mount of Olives, Jesus called two of the disciples to him who had themselves been erstwhile Essenes. "Go into the city by your Gate (that of the Essenes) and you will find a young ass tied near the Gate. Untie him and bring him here. If the owner questions you, tell him that Jesus, the Nazarene, wants to use him."

This his disciples did, and brought the ass back to the camp. There Jesus mounted the animal. "Let us enter Jerusalem as it is told.[22] They all gathered about him, shouted and sang, and carried wreaths, spreading out leaves and branches as they moved along the way. Entering the city, the disciples shouted out his name: "There is Jesus, the Nazarene. He is come—the son of God, the Lord's own. The Lord has anointed this one (The Christ)....This is the Great One incarnate....our leader, whom God has sent...."

It was late in the day, but there were still other bands of Arabs from the north and throughout Palestine, and even those who practiced ministries in Jerusalem, who made similar claims, and their prophets preached about street corners. Jesus' band of followers, however, became formidable, as they collected, streaming for several hundred feet, young and old, crippled and sound, all shouting enthusiastically. Roman soldiers, walking in pairs, paused momentarily, and eyed Jesus atop the ass suspiciously. As they approached the Temple, the group broke up. Jesus dismounted and gave the ass to a disciple to return to his Essene friend near the Gate. Jesus then walked about the Temple and the city, and saw and felt the excitement among the

---

[22] Compare again to the Yeshu tradition. (Refer to Goldstein.)

great throngs arriving for the Passover celebration. Late in the evening he returned with his disciples to camp at the Mount of Olives.

Jesus arose the next morning irritable, for they were without food. On the way to Jerusalem that morning he spat and grumbled. Coming upon a fig tree, He sought to eat off it but it was not yet fruit-bearing. Jesus, irritable and angry, cursed the tree.

They entered the city and others joined them as they walked the street. "Here is Jesus!" one cried. "We will follow him even to death. He brings the promise of liberation from the tyrant. God is with us."

More joined in as they proceeded to the Temple. There, as Jesus had seen each year even as a child in exasperation, were merchants selling the fowl for burnt offerings, and those who changed the various coinage used throughout Palestine for the Roman money used in Jerusalem. Now Jesus was incensed. He cried out at them, "You foul contemptible blasphemers! Get out of this, the House of God, with your sickening commercial ways—making profit on His name." He pushed coinage off tables with coins rolling and scattering throughout the yard. "Your filthy beasts are laid before the altar of our Lord who turns His head lest he vomit!"

Jesus shouted in scorn and admonition while a mob of Zealots, who had joined him along the way, were caught up in his fury. In the way of mobs, they tipped over tables and set fowl free, and thrashed out at the merchants, who cowered and fled for their very lives.

When they were gone Jesus stood upon the stairs and addressed a gathering crowd of hundreds. He told of the Lord's will, and he spoke in most familiar terms, as one would of his beloved deceased father. He spoke of the strength of faith in believing that all things are possible, to believe in prayer and the power of forgiveness.

Jesus later sat silently in the Temple and prayed, as He had done before even as a child. Then there came in angry step several Essene chief priests and scribes, many of those whom Jesus had known as his teachers.

"Are you mad? By what right do you come into this sacred house and incite riot?"

"Did you believe that John who baptized was without right and not sanctified by the Lord?" asked Jesus as a defensive play.

Furtively the priests glanced at the mass of people who had joined Jesus in prayer. All had revered John as a great Holy man of God, even now as they followed Jesus.

"We do not know about John," said one defensively. "We can not tell of what he was inspired, but he left the Order."

"Then do not ask me what inspires me," replied Jesus. ".... this Temple, and the sacred rites of God that you in the camp practice, is like that of a man who owned a large plot in which he planted grapes; then he left the land to be cared for and harvested by those he trusted, and went to live in another place. When the grapes were harvested he sent a servant to collect his money from the harvest. Those he had trusted beat the servant he sent and gave nothing. Another time the man sent still another servant whom they stoned and severely wounded, and yet other servants, each of whom they killed and wounded, and gave nothing to the man of his right deserts. Then the man finally sent his son whom surely they would not violate. But, sure enough, the son of this man they killed also, and expected they would get the land now that the man was without heirs. But the man would come to these men in whose trust he had placed his vineyard and destroy them for their wrongdoing. You who are Holy Priests and Scribes are supposed to know. Don't you read the books that you are supposed to venerate? See Psalms 1-8, the stone rejected by the builders (the Essenes) now becomes the very headstone, because it is the Lord's doing. Do not ask me what inspires me."

Jesus, in arrogance, a man of lowliest stature, challenged the very Essenic office that they held. His affront was even to their sacred Essenic codes, and they themselves, who were holy men of God. As an Essene, death would have been his punishment; but he had left them. They were infuriated by this lowly-born peasant who had failed as an Essene, and now who momentarily flaunted before them His power over the mob.

These chief priests among Essenes went then to those they knew among the Pharisees and Sadducees and even the Herodians. Jesus must be destroyed before he destroyed the very Order that was sacred before God. "The man is dangerous to us all," they said. "We can persuade him in no way, even though he once was one of us."

A clever Pharisaic priest sought to trap Jesus, that he might indict himself before witnesses in treason under the Roman rule in Jerusalem. "We know that you sincerely believe in yourself as the Son of God. This makes you invulnerable, does it not, even here among the Romans? You surely do not cower before the dictates of the Caesars?"

"You tell me then," replied Jesus, "who rules here."

"The Romans, of course," replied the Pharisee.

"Then follow the rule of the Romans, but give up to God what is His."

A Sadducee then confronted Jesus on fine theological points, though he himself believed nothing of what was taught. He questioned Jesus, almost as if in poking fun at his beliefs, for among Sadducees these prophets were all considered to be fanatics.

"What if a man dies and leaves his wife, and a brother takes her, then the brother dies and another brother takes her, and so on for seven brothers? In your kingdom, then of these, whose wife shall she be?"

"Your question is foolish," replied Jesus. "In heaven, all men are angels. They neither marry nor are given in marriage. As God was the God of Abraham, Isaac, and Jacob, He is not the God of the Dead but of the Living.[23]

Then an Essene scribe, who had been listening to the arguments of Jesus, asked, "What is the most important of the commandments?"

And Jesus answered, "For the people of Israel it is that God is one, to be respected, revered and obeyed above all else. Then, as within the brotherhood, to love and hold a brother above the self."

The scribe was touched, for as an Essene this is what he, too, had taught and had himself written. Jesus was yet among them in thought and principle.

---

[23] Cf., in the Egyptian Osirian belief system, Osiris made judgment of the dead.

"What you have said," replied the scribe, "means more than all the burnt offerings and sacrifices."

Jesus smiled at the sympathetic scribe. "You are, yourself, closer to God than you know."

When Jesus heard the talk about Himself as the Son of David, He wished to clarify His position as he desired it. "How can the scribes say that one anointed (Christ) by the Lord is merely the Son of David—for did not David himself say that He who is anointed (Christ) would be his Lord also? How, then, do the scribes say that one anointed is merely the Son of David. Be wary of these scribes, for all their gawdy ostentation and show of friendliness, who take the chief seats at meetings and sit first in the upper rooms for communion, who cheat widows of their property, and hypocritically pray—theirs is a destiny of hell fire."

As Jesus sat in the Temple He observed those who came to make offering to the treasury. Some came who were wealthy, and dropped into the coffer large sums of money; but there was one who, he learned, was a widow of poor means, who threw in a pittance. Jesus called over a disciple, "Did you see that poor woman? The rich can give much and feel it little, but that poor woman gave all that she had. The light of God will shine brightly upon her."

In the evening when Jesus and His disciples sat together at the Mount of Olives, He spoke of the city of Jerusalem—that magnificent and holy city of Judea where the Temple of the Lord stood amidst sin and corruption.

"Mark my words. There will be destruction of this city; but before it happens you will hear many come again in false prophecy claiming to be the Messiah. But you now have your Messiah. I am He. Let no man deceive you. I say to you, there will be much strife before the Lord will come. Here will be earthquakes, famines and war, and terrible grief. As my disciples, you must expect to be treated badly. The councils will judge you, and before gatherings you will be beaten. Yet you will stand before heathen kings and not worship them, for you go in My name, and the gospel will be published in all lands. You will suffer much, but speak up, as the spirit of the Lord would have you, even in that time when nothing is left, when brothers and fathers become filled with fear and animosity for one another. There will be a time when all must flee from Judea in haste to the mountains, even leaving all properties behind, or leave directly from the field and they with children to drag will perish. It will be a time of travail, unlike any since God first created the earth—all will perish, but those who have been chosen to deliver the gospel.[24] There will still come those with false claims to Messiahship, and even tempt you to believe in them but keep your faith in Me. After these trials will come tempest and darkness, then cataclyism, when the sun and moon will die and the stars will drop. Then will I come—on the clouds with a band of angels. I will call you to me, and all others in Heaven and on Earth. As the leaves of the tree precede the Summer, know these signs, for then will I come to fulfill. You here will yet live to see these things happen, and the glory of God upon the Earth. But be wary, for it may happen when you least expect it, for only our Father in Heaven knows. Watch always and pray. For this I will leave you, and I will return to bring these things. Do not be sleeping when I come, but praise always the glory of God."

Jesus knew He had antagonized the chief Essenic priests and Scribes, and the Pharisees, and even the unbelieving Sadducees in Jerusalem. They surely would not let Him live. How they would contrive His death in Jerusalem, under Roman rule, He did not know, for He had incited no insurrection, a capital offense to Romans; even as the Essenes, He respected the civil law, nor had violated none, save in subtlely promising a Kingdom in Heaven and on Earth to the people of Israel. Yet, He knew His life would end, for He would make no compromise with the Lord's will. There were rumors of plots to kill Jesus. The Pharisees wished not to make Him a martyr such as the Great Prophet had become with the Essenes—though for the highest among the Essenes He was only contemptuous and must suffer death for His very betrayal of the Order. The danger

---

[24] In Mark 13 is evident the practice of apocalyptic revelation, in writing common to both the old and new testament. The author (or the one who redacted) wrote in hindsight, while attributing foresight to his characters who lived centuries earlier. It is thus here indicated to have been written sometime after the destruction of Jerusalem in 70 A.D.

lay in the appeal He held for the poor not of the Order, and for those few in the Order who had been deceived by His claims.

As Jesus sat at supper with His old friends among the Essenes in a house near Jerusalem, a woman entered carrying a white opaque box of fragrant oil. She went directly to Jesus and poured it over His head. "This is to consecrate you, Jesus, for some say you have spoken too freely and will die."

"Why do you waste the stuff like that?" asked an Essene layman. "That could have been sold, and brought a handsome sum to the treasury."

"Do not speak against what she has done. You will have much time to fill the treasury, but I will not always be with you. The woman has done me good, for she has anointed me before I die. What this woman has done for me should be told and praised."

On the first day of the Passover feast, Jesus called for two of his disciples to find an upper room in the city for their communion, as was the practice of the Essenes.

"In the city follow any man you see carrying a water jug," he told them. "He will be from a community of the Holy Ones. In the house to which he goes, see the layman there. Tell him that a Holy priest wishes to have the Passover meal in the upper room; and prepare the leavened bread and wine there for us this evening."

In the evening they sat at the table together in the upper room. Now Jesus grew disquieted for He knew His death was near. "There is one of you who has done the dastardly deed that will mean My death." He glanced about the table, and saw Judas sitting quietly, while others spoke protestingly.

"Let us be quiet in these final hours." He took leavened bread of the eucharist and, as He had witnessed Essene priests do many times before, for the body and blood of the Great Prophet, He blessed it, and broke it.

"Eat of this. It is my body."

He filled a cup of wine from the flask and held it to the Heavens. Then all sipped it as the cup was passed from one to another. "This is my blood."

When the meal was finished in the Essenic format, Jesus and his disciples returned to the camp at the Mount of Olives outside of Jerusalem. "When I am taken, you must all deny having known me. For they will think your leader is gone and so will be the inspiration. If you linger, you will surely die. You must continue the gospel in my name."

"We will be with you until death, even after, Jesus, for you are our Lord," spoke Peter.

"I will meet you in Galilee."

He left with Peter, James, and John, and went to a place called Gethsemane.[25] Of the twelve disciples, Judas Iscariot had left the group upon hearing Jesus speak of His death, and sought out those among the Essenes and Pharisees who wished Him dead. [26] Jesus must be apprehended while away from the crowds that customarily enshrouded Him that He might be easily and surely taken. As they rested in the Garden of Gethsemane, Jesus grew apprehensive, for He knew they would come to take Him. "I feel sorrowful. My spirit weighs heavily for I know I am to die. Stay near and watch." He fell to the ground in deep grief as the moment approached. "Father, most graceful and merciful, do not make me do this."

While the disciples slept, not knowing the imminence of Jesus' demise, Jesus prayed. "All things are possible to you, oh Heavenly Father. Make it different in your divine plan that they should not want my life."[27]

But as he prayed there came a large band of men of the priests, carrying torches, swords, and bludgeons.

"This is He," said Judas. Two grabbed Jesus, one about each arm.

---

[25] Gethsemane was likely the place of rendezvous, where Judas was to bring the priests for the arrest, i.e., no other mention is made of the place as one frequented by the group. Thus Judas would not otherwise have known where they had gone, had it not been pre-arranged.

[26] Such a "betrayal," if historically authentic, may have been pre-arranged. To accomplish His martyrdom (if this is not, as written, merely the revivification of Jewish tradition) a definite plan was necessary, e.g., to fulfill the prophecy of Isaiah as Jesus interpreted it.

[27] The prophecy of Isaiah was to be fulfilled by Jesus (or the author of Mark). ". . . The arm of the Lord is (not) revealed . . . despised and rejected of men . . . He hath borne our grief and carried our sorrow . . . The Lord has laid on Him the inequity of us all . . . He opened not His mouth . . ."
   Also, refer to Psalms 22 (David's Prayer) "My God! My God! Why has thou forsaken me . . . I am a worm despised of the people . . ."

The disciples, outnumbered in men, stole away, but some among those with the priests turned against the mob. "It is He who was in the Temple. Let Him go! He brings Truth among us." They raised swords against the others but were themselves dropped by many swords.

"Why do you come like this? You could have taken me when I was in the Temple teaching."

He was led away to Jerusalem and taken before the priests and the scribes, to be condemned of blasphemy.

"Come forward any one who has evidence against this blasphemer," said a chief priest.

"He said he would destroy the Temple with His own hands and build another for himself," testified one.

"I heard him say that the people of Israel should worship Him as God," said another, and several more.

"What is your defense against these accusations?" asked the chief of the council.

Jesus said nothing.

"Then let me ask, are you the Son of the Blessed?"

"I am!" cried Jesus. "You will see Me in all God's power in the clouds of Heaven!"

Such arrogance needed no further support of this man's guilt. He must die. Now they turned on Him and humiliated Him, tearing His clothing, spitting in His face, and striking Him.

The Roman Procurator, Pontius Pilate, was harried by the keeping of order during the Passover, and annoyed by the trifling and bickering of the people and priests of Judea. Now they brought a man before him for execution—a violation only of their own simple-minded religious precepts. "I am not concerned with these infernal conflicts. Can't you accept a man's religious views merely because they differ from yours?"

"This man does not merely have differing views," replied the chief priest. "He would incite the people to turn, not only from the religion of their fathers, but against Rome itself. He believes Himself to be the Son of David—the most esteemed and aggressive of all our Kings. Just follow through the implications of such a claim. He would become King and the people would follow him."

The procurator turned to Jesus. "Are you King of the Jews?"
"You said it, not I."

"His speech is that of a Galilean. He is not even from Judea.
How could he lead the Jews?"

"He has preached here in Judea. He belongs to a group called the Nazarenes who expect the rebirth of David, whom He
believes Himself to be."

"Why don't you defend yourself—what's His name—Jesus?"

But Jesus stood mute and impassive, almost as one in fatalistic resolve to die. "This man is harmless," insisted Pilate. "Why
don't you let him go? You have the right to release one condemned prisoner during the feast, you know. Let it be him."

"Ask the people," said the priestly spokesman, knowing full
well that the popularity of another condemned, named Barabbas,
would make the latter their choice.

"What would you have done to this man, Jesus the Nazarene?"
"Execute Him!" came the cry, and it seemed voiced as the
wish of the majority.

"I'll never understand these people," murmured Pilate to his
deputy. "The man seems completely harmless. Do as they wish,"
he ordered.

Jesus was given to the Roman Guards of the Praetorium.

In the days and lands of Roman rule, capital punishment was
accomplished by nailing wrists and feet to cross timbers, thus
called crucifixion or fixing to a cross—a slow bleeding that took
several hours, even a day, for death to come.[28] At Jerusalem the
place of execution was a hill called Golgotha where offenders
were impaled for all to witness and be deterred.

On the morning of the execution, the carts carried the heavy
timbers to the crest, and there workmen crossed the members.
On this day there were three to be executed, two for thievery,
and one for alleged sedition.

Then the procession came up the hill, the three condemned,
and sundry interested parties, both morbid and compassionate;

---

[28] Stoning, or throwing the victim over a cliff was a common means of execution
among Hebrews (cf., ". . They led Him onto the brow of a hill . . . that they
might cast Him down headlong," Luke 4-29). Such may very well have been the
fate of Jesus had he been convicted in the North. Phillip Wiley has also sug
gested that, in our time, the Christian symbol may have become an electric
chair rather than a cross.

the guards and executioners, girded with swords, pushed and lashed with whips to prod the prisoners. A ring of guards held back the crowd. Wine was given the prisoners, as humanitarian, to dull the pain, but Jesus took none. They were stripped and laid spread-eagle on the cross members with spikes driven through wrists and feet then crossed and spiked; blood came to smear the executioners' clothing when they placed the bleeding bodies, bound to the crosses, in the holes aligned upright.

The signs "For Thievery" were placed over two, and "Claimed Kingship over Jews," over one.

Jesus was the Nazarene who died believing himself inspired by God, that the promises to the people of Israel would be fulfilled in His name—in the name of Jesus, the Son of Man. Jesus was a laborer of low rank, aspiring to high station in God's Kingdom. (Unlike Guatama, the Buddha, who was born in royalty and had no craving for high places.) Jesus was an impatient Essene who wished his generation to see prophecy fulfilled. He wished for His beloved people of Israel to rise up in the power of the Lord, and conquer, and to bring God to all nations of the world. They had sinned, and strayed from the ways of righteousness, from the love of God. Jesus led them along the path of righteousness, and they slew Him. He carried on the cross the guilt, the burden of inequity of all men, not only those who took His life. Suffer He must for the sins of man. His was the symbol and the burden of guilt, the suffering and misery of the poor and the desperate, for the infamous crimes of man against his fellows. He suffered as the epitome of the living and dying, in the universal shame of man for transgressing the codes of society.

Jesus hung in pain, the flesh and bone torn from His arms and feet.

"I am a worm! Forgive Me, Father....Forgive them...." In pain He whimpered, "My God! My God! Why have you left me?"[29] Then he sobbed.

Before evening fell, a wealthy Pharisee named Joseph, who believed in Jesus, requested the body.

[29] Cf., David's cry in Psalms 22.

"Is the man dead already?" asked Pilate. The captain affirmed that He was, and the body was released to Joseph.[30]

Long after the crucifixion of Jesus, there were stories of his having returned to Galilee, and met His disciples again, as he said he would. Before them, it was told, He reiterated that they should go out and preach the gospel, and cast out devils in his name, in the name of Jesus Christ, the Lord and Savior.

Note: Mark, as others of the stories of Jesus, was written after the Book of Acts and the Epistles by several decades. Thus the hindsight apparent in the relation of the story, must be taken into account, e.g., temple destruction, hardship and persecution of the disciples, etc.

[30] In Mark is suggested that Jesus may not have been dead yet. There may have been contriving to nurse Him back to life as in resurrection, that He might make such appearances as were subsequently described among His disciples. This, however, implies a thoroughly pre-meditated deception. Yet, it may not have been contrived and Jesus, in shock, may well have appeared dead, or the Captain may have been bribed. In any case, if there had been a resurrection, it may well have been a medically feasible one.

Suggested Further Reading

1. Angus, S. *The Mystery Religions and Christianity* Charles Scribners and Sons, 1925
2. Barthelemy, D. and Milik, J. *Discoveries in the Judaean Desert, I, Qumran Cave* Oxford Univ. Press, 1955
3. Boker, Rabbi Ben Zion *Wisdom of the Talmud* The Citadel Press, N.Y., 1962
4. Burrows, M. *The Dead Sea Scrolls* Viking Press, 1955
5. Burrows, M. *More Light on the Dead Sea Scrolls* 1958
6. Carpenter. E. *Pagan and Christian Creeds* Harcourt, Brace and Co., 1921
7. Clemen, C. *Primitive Christianity, and its Non-Christian Sources* Edinburgh: T. and T. Clark 1912
8. Charles, H. *The Apocrypha and Pseudepigrapha of the Old Testament in English Supra* The Clarendon Press, Oxford 1913
9. Cross, F. "The Scrolls and The New Testament" in *Christian Century* Aug. 24, 1956

10. Davies, A. *The Meaning of the Dead Sea Scrolls* The New American Library 1961
11. Dupont-Sommer, A. *The Jewish Sect of Qumran and the Essenes* (trans. Barnett, R.) The Macmillan Co., 1955
12. Edershelm, A. *Life and Times of Jesus, the Messiah* Longmanns Green & Co. 1907
13. Foreign Technical Translation Section Electro-Optical Systems Inc. 300 N. Halstead, Pasadena, California (Write for discussion of difficulties in translation)
14. Ginsburg, C. *The Essenes* 1955
15. Goldstein, M. *Jesus in Jewish Tradition*
16. Josephus, F. *Wars of the Jews* T Nelson & Sons, London 1873
17. Milley, C. *The Prophets of Israel* Philosophical Library 1959
18. Mowray, L. *The Dead Sea Scrolls and the Early Church* 1962
19. Murray, G. *Five Stages of Greek Religion* The Beacon Press, 1952
20. Horowitz, D. "New Light on Jesus" *Fact* Vol. 1, No. 4, 1964 P. 60ff.
21. Howlett, D ."Faith and History" in the *Atlantic Monthly* April 1956
22. Howlett, D. *The Essenes and Christianity* 1957
23. Kasanin, J. "Developmental Roots of Schizophrenia" *American J. of Psychiatry* 1945 p. 770 f.
24. Kenyon, F. *The Bible and Archaeology* Harper & Brothers 1940
25. Knox, R.A. "On Englishing the Bible" Burns Oates and Washbourne, Ltd. published in the United States by Sheed and Ward as, *Trials of a Translator* 1949
26. Krech, D. *Individual in Society* 1962
27. Potter, C. *The Lost Years of Jesus* Univ. Books, Inc. New Hyde Park N. Y. 1963
28. Renan, E. *Life of Jesus* 1864
29. Schurer, E. *The Jewish People in the Time of Jesus Christ* Edinburgh: T & T Clark 1897
30. Unger, M. *Archaeology and the Old Testament* 1954
31. U. S. Government Printing Office "Inaugural Addresses of the Presidents of the United States" Washington, D. C.
32. Schweitzer, A. *The Quest of the Historical Jesus* The MacMillan Co., 1948

33. Sheen, F. *The Life of Christ*
34. Simeons, A. T. *Man's Presumptuous Brain* E. P. Dutton & Co., Inc. N. Y. 1961 .
35. Steinmann, J. *The Life of Jesus* Little Brown, Boston, 1963
36. Westcott, B. and Hort, F. *The New Testament in the Original Greek* Macmillan & Co., 1885
37. Wilson, E. *The Scrolls from the Dead Sea* Oxford Univ. Press, 1955
38. Wright, G. *Biblical Archaeology* 1957
39. Zander, A. (ed.) *Group Dynamics* 1960

IV

The Pagan World of Christian Conversion

Some years ago a former Roman Catholic priest, named Jo-
eph McCabe, strongly antagonistic to religious dogma, wrote
that social evolution clearly reveals a pattern of normal and universal development from "spirit belief" to "animism" to "polytheism" to "monotheism," and finally "atheism." This does not,
to me, seem clearly indicated, when today in civilized countries animism seems to predominate even among the educated,
when reverting to the demonology of absolutes, and never having
cast off ancient soul psychologies. Polytheism is also a major
belief of our time (cf., Catholic saints), and within the depths
and grains of our culture, there hardly seems to be any appreciable progressive ideal espousing atheism. The World of Christianity today, and the World from which it grew, are but little
different in socio-cultural belief. This we shall see in a brief
review of the converted prototypes.

Chapter 14

The Tribal Jesus

Jesus, the Nazarene, was Hebrew. In affiliation, we must assume that he embraced one of the three then contemporary and predominate religious ideologies of the tribes—Pharisaic, Sadducean, or Essenic. In the foregoing narration, it was assumed that he was Essenic, but he, as many others (e.g., Josephus), left the sect because of the austere life, and because of the schizoidal relinquishing of self demanded by the discipline. It was then in the cultural climate of the Mediterranean that Jesus preached and had his appeal. He was first a tribal Jew, but the Jewish culture was by no means unique. They had, in fact, usurped virtually every facet of their religion from other cultures: The first glimerings of monotheism from Egypt, the creation story from Babylon, hell fire and damnation from Persia, and philosophical ethics and mythology from Greece and India. There was, of course, the tribal ethnocentricism in the Gospel Jesus, viz., that the people of Israel would emerge rulers of the universe; but otherwise nothing, as narrated in the Synoptics nor in the Book of John, was unique.

The fact that Jewish folklore, that a Jewish tribal hero, could become successful among the pagans is of fundamental significance in itself. Sociologically there is no mistaking the process and the doctrine as it developed, as it became an accretion, integrated with the myths and folklore of other lands, to become the universal religion that it is today. The word "Christ" was used from a Greek word meaning "one anointed." Thus, the tribal significance of its meaning is almost completely obscured. Most Christians today have no idea that they identify with the practice of rubbing an ancient Jewish King with oil in an inauguration ceremony. Rather, they believe in a kind of superman who was sent down from above the clouds in celestial realms, by a supra-superman who is "God." This belief came from the pagans, not from the Tribal Jesus.

Insight into the pagan doctrines, before, during and after the period of Jesus, is virtually mandatory if any comprehension is to be had about how the Christian Church developed. The tribal Jesus is very largely obscured in contemporary Christian dogma, but so are Gilgamesh, Osiris, Isis, Ishtar, Demeter, Zeus or Jupiter, Orpheus, Zoroaster/Mithra, Guatama, and Pythagorus.

Chapter 15

Early Prototypes

The Jews developed self-consciousness as a people in the years before their exile to Babylon. Supernatural ordination, however, in the Babylonian period, lost its significance, and the demoralizing consequence obscured the Jew-centered heritage. Many Jews began, even as today, to follow their own personal inclination beyond the precepts of the tribal religion.

A vestige of the Yahweh priesthood in Babylon, toward the end of the exile period around the 5th century B.C., began an unholy crusade to reunite the people. It was then that the priestly code was formulated, and the priestly group in Babylon attemped to crystallize a tradition. It was then that an almost irresponsible fabrication of tribal history was perpetrated, when mythologies and ancient folklore, that were prevalent about the Mediterranean, were usurped and solidified into the religious doctrine we know in our Occidental heritage.

The Biblical versions themselves betray the veritable foisting of these documents on the people, (cf., II Chronicles xxxiv: "Hillah the priest found the book of the law of the Lord given by Moses . . . " Jeremiah viii, 8: " . . . How do we cry, we are wise and the law of the scribes has wrought falsely . . . ")

Then, midway in the 5th century B.C., a zealous priest named Ezra returned from Babylon to Jerusalem, succeeding Nehemiah. In the apocryphal Greek work, I Esdras xiv, 22, is found the statement that (Ezra) " . . . shall write all that hath been done in the world since the beginning and the things that were written in thy law . . . " Ezra, as a scribe, is believed by some to have written the whole of the Pentateuch. (cf., Moses, who is presumed to have authored these books 1,000 years earlier.)

The influence of then existing mythologies on both earlier forms of Judaism and on primitive Christianity becomes appar-

CHART I
THE GILGAMESH RELIGION, PRE-CHRISTIAN

Christian Time and Geographic Location	Chief Characters	Doctrine and Communicants
Iranian-Sumerian in the areas of Mesopotamia, Assyria, Babylonia, and east ca. 6,000 - 2,000 B. C. (See Figure 6)	Gilgamesh, 2/3rds god, King of Etruk and son of Ninmah; Arura, great mother goddess; Enkidu, creation of Arura (made to subdue Gilgamesh), with hind-quarters of a bull; Huwana, monster of evil; Ishtar, goddess of love; Ut-napishtim, King of Shuruppak and possessor of the secret of immortality	King Gilgamesh, being 1/3 mortal, lusted after women and took any whom he fancied. The people of Urak, fearful and desperate, beseeched the goddess Arura to give them someone as powerful as Gilgamesh to restrain him. Arura created Enkidu, whom she fashioned as a bull and gazelle, but from the waist up as a man; thus he had the speed and grace of a young colt and the strength of a god. Enkidu met Gilgamesh in a magnificent wrestling bout, but neither could subdue the other. They became life-long friends, and engaged common enemies in battle. They together met and annihilated the evil giant Huwana. When Gilgamesh and Enkidu made offerings to the gods after this great battle, Ishtar, the goddess of love, was besmitten with the charms of Gilgamesh who spurned her because of her treachery. In vengeance, she cursed the beloved friend of Gilgamesh, Enkidu, who died. Grief-stricken at the realization of the death and departure of his friend to the House of the Dead, Gilgamesh set out in search of the secret of immortality from Ut-napishtim. His journey took him over treacherous seas. Ut-napishtim, having won eternal life from surviving the great flood of the gods, was reluctant to yield, but finally permitted Gilgamesh to pluck the plant of eternal life from the depths of the sea. As he returned to Uruk, alas, Gilgamesh grew careless, and the plant of eternal life was stolen by a serpent.

ent from brief review of the extensive cults prevailing about the Mediterranean. The Babylonian myth of Creation was almost literally transposed to the Book of Genesis. Note Chart I, outlining the Gilgameshian religion. Here might be seen the interplay of the complex of Gods in that period and notions of immortality, of the soul psychology and a place for the dead. The great wrestling bout between Gilgamesh and Enkidu is reminiscent of the bout in which Jacob engaged. In Genesis 32, 24-32 is found:

" . . . And Jacob was left alone and there wrestled a man with him until the breaking of the day. And when he saw that he prevailed not against him he touched the hollow of his thigh. And the hollow of Jacob's thigh was out of joint as he wrestled with him. And he said, Let me go for the day breaketh. And he said I will not let thee go except thou bless me. And he said unto him, what is thy name? And he said Jacob. And he said, Thy name shall be called no more Jacob but Israel, for as a prince hast thou power with God and with men and hast prevailed. And Jacob asked him and said, Tell me, I pray thee thy name. And he said, wherefore is it that thou dost ask after my name? And he blessed him there. And Jacob called the name of the place Peniel: for I have seen God face to face and my life is preserved . . . "

Antedating this Jewish wrestling match by a few thousand years, we must assume that these elements of tradition were Gilgameshian.

Tribes such as the Moabites and Edomites occupied the desirable regions of Palestine. The late-settling Hebrews found left only the poor hilly lands of the South (later Judea). Some Hebrews may have looked farther south to Egypt, infringing on the rich Nile Delta and coming directly under the influence of Egyptian culture. In any case, Egyptian influence undoubtedly prevailed extant over the land in this period, as did its religious tradition. The monotheistic overtures in a brief period of Egyptian culture, (refer to Chart II) became evident in early formulations about Yahweh, viz., they should have no other God but Him.

The Egyptian god and goddess, Osiris and Isis, (refer to Charts III and IV) seemed not directly to influence old Judaism. Rath-

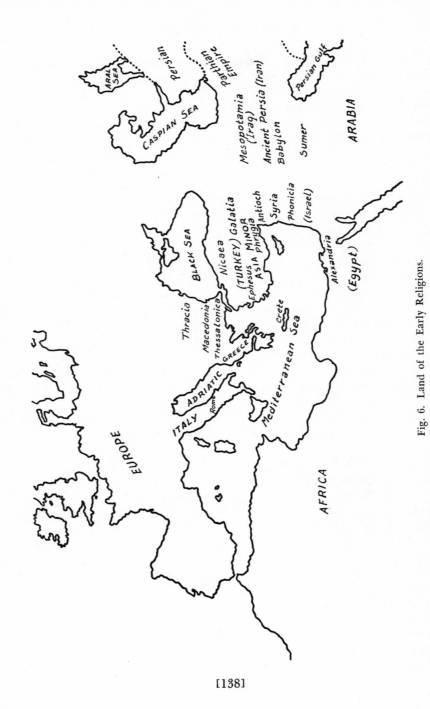

Fig. 6. Land of the Early Religions.

CHART II
THE RELIGION OF ATON, PRE-CHRISTIAN

Origin	Time and Geographic Location	Chief Characters	Imputed Supernatural Circumstances	Doctrine and Communicants
(Inspired by Pharaoh Amenhotep IV (Ikhnaton)) Atonianism prevailed during the reign of Amenhotep III in a brief revolutionary period.	ca. 1400 B.C., to 1300 B.C., in Egypt. In this period, Egypt had established a great and stable empire, and men thought in Universal terms. It was without force and popular following. The reaction of the Osirian-Amenate priests, and the populace, damped it out in less than a century.	Originally the Sun-god Aton. Amenhotep IV proclaimed himself the high priest of Aton, and Aton became the beneficent universal god, as figuratively the finger rays of the sun grasped all men.	Maker of all creatures, and actively concerned for all.	Aton was the benevolent father, creator of all mankind, and concerned for all. Convicts and slaves were released; landed estates of Amen priests were confiscated and given to peasant serfs. Schools were established. Egyptian armies were diminished, since such a loving god could not permit killing and oppression (the empire withered).

er, it was not until the later sects, such as the Essenes, and then the Christians, that such traditions as the Eucharist, and judgment in an afterlife, began to appear. Other pagan traditions, later to be grafted onto Christianity, were of course direct outgrowths of the Osirian-Isisian prototypes. (cf., Ishtarism, Dionysus, Demeter and Persephone). Also compare the "40-day search" traditions in Zoroastrianism and Christianity. The significance of the Cult of Isis is somewhat more apparent as a later extant influence on Christianity. The Gospel Jesus was at first devoid of a mother goddess in the tradition of Isis, Demeter, and Cybele. The Virgin Mary idea thus grew from the figure of a woman to whom Jesus would not at first even speak, into a replica of Isis, Queen of Heaven. Other Egyptian traditions influencing Judeo-Christian developments may have been Serapis, combining Osiris and Apis the Bull, assuming an evil stance as well as phallic aspects of the Dionysus and Aphroditic religion (cf., the serpent of Genesis.)

The impact of Zoroastrianism (refer to Chart V) on later Hebrew sects, particularly the Essenes and Christians, was quite fundamental. It was after this influence that a Parousia, or the final triumph of the God-Man idea, made its appearance (cf., Ahuramazda with the Messiah idea and with Jesus' Second Coming). The sacred nature of water, the eternal flame, and the dualism in Zoroastrianism are seen in the God-Devil idea, the burning of candles, holy water sprinkling and baptism in Christian practice. The utterances of John the Baptist are clear cut in this regard: " . . . I baptize with water but after me will come one who will baptize with fire and the holy spirit . . . "

Buddhistic influence (refer to Chart VI) also spread throughout the civilized world east and west, and made its appearance most emphatically in Essenic discipline and in the Gospel Jesus.

The wide-spread Grecian influence, leading to later Christian developments, is perhaps somewhat epitomized by Pythagoreanism (Chart VII). The religion of Pythagoras was truly a synthesis of the religions of the East. It was apparently that after which the Essenes modeled their organization, and the elements of which both early and later Christians engrafted to Christian dogma and practice.

CHART III
THE RELIGION OF OSIRIS, PRE-AND POST-CHRISTIAN

Time and Geographic Location	Chief Characters	Imputed Supernatural Circumstances	Doctrine and Communicants
ca. 3,000 B.C., to 550 A.D., in Egypt and Syria. In 380 A.D., the Edict of Theodosis, to destroy all pagan temples, was largely ignored; in 550 Justinian ordered his generals to destroy Osirian temples in Philae, where the cult, per se, finally died.	Osiris (likely an early Sumarian leader who was deified)* Tradition had Osiris born illegitimately of Nut; Isis, a sister whom he married; Set, his evil brother; Horus, son of Osiris and Isis. *Egyptologist Sir Flinders Petrie, has interpreted Osiris to have been a memory of an Asiatic invasion, repelled by a native king named Osiris.	Nut was wife of the Sun God, Ra. She bore five illegitimate children. Set, the evil one, destroyed Osiris, tearing his body into 14 pieces and hiding the pieces in different places throughout Egypt. Isis searched the kingdom for 40 days, found and assembled them, and resurrected Osiris, who went to live in the world of the immortals, while his son, Horus, slew Set and became identified with his father Osiris.	Immortality could be achieved and one could go to Elysium (Heaven) by being transfused into Osiris. At death, the heart-soul projected the body spirit, which lived on and took nourishment until it went to Elysium. Priests taught that the body must be intact and preserved.** To become Osiris, (resurrected) one needed to be clean and pure, and to be severely judged by Osiris and Horus in the Hall of Judgment for his deeds and debts. Priestly rites concerned the resurrection ceremony, making of models of the pieces into which Osiris had been torn by Set, and the making of a figure of Osiris. Eating of other human beings or gods was earlier believed to instill the eater with the virtues and powers of the eaten. In this later period bread was identified with the flesh of Osiris, and barley ale with his blood. Whosoever ate the flesh of Osiris, and drank his blood, had eternal life in the Osirian sacramental ritual. Sacred books: Papyruses of Nesi, Nu, Nebseni, Neheht, and Ari, and The Book of the Dead. **This perhaps became a social control device to discourage cannibalism common to this period and culture.

CHART IV
THE RELIGION OF ISIS, PRE-AND POST-CHRISTIAN

Origin	Time and Geographic Location	Chief Characters	Imputed Supernatural Circumstances	Doctrine and Communicants
(Independent cult diverging from the Osirian)	1500 B.C., in Egypt; 700 B.C., in Syria; 300 B.C., in Greece; in Italy from 200 B.C., to 550 A.D.	Same as Osirian, except for a shift in emphasis	Same as Osirian	A bread and milk sacrament was practiced. Also, there were two great festivals, Spring and Fall. Spring was the harvest in Egypt. Fall was a passion play depicting the search for Osiris, involving weeping and other signs of grief; then in the second two days he was found and reconstructed.

Just as Osiris regained life through Isis, all devotees were then reborn. On the 4th day there was unrestrained rejoicing, for the god had arisen to immortality. Those for whom Isis interceded, Osiris gave mercy in his judgment.

In Apuleus' "The Golden Ass", written about 200 A.D., the author was turned into an ass by a witch which could be reversed only by eating roses. Isis came to his aid. She was called the Blessed Queen of Heaven, the motherly nurse of all fruitful things, later becoming a synthesis of all the great goddesses of love, protection, creative life, and maternal nourishment; she was a sweet mother's love, giving light to the sun and trampling under foot the powers of hell. At her word, winds blew, clouds gave increased abundance, springing seeds to birth and buds.

Statues of the Mother Isis and her suckling son, Horus, were often mistaken for Mary and Jesus early in the Christian era. |

CHART V
THE RELIGION OF ZOROASTER, PRE-CHRISTIAN AND CONTEMPORARY

Christian Time and Geographic Location	Chief Characters	Imputed Supernatural Circumstances	Doctrine and Communicants
4,000 B.C. in Iran. In ascendancy, circa 500 B.C.; declined from 490 B.C. on; in the Parthian Empire and all the area between the Euphrates and the Indian Ocean. Approximately 100,000 presently live in the area of Bombay, India.	Ahuramazda, god of sun and fire; Zaratust (Zoroaster) a spiritual body, becoming a fleshy incarnation; Frahimwana-Zois, his wife; Dukdaub, virgin born and virgin mother of Zaratust conceived from a hom-juice mixture given cows of which she drank; Ahriman, the maker of the Evil world.	Zoroaster at the age of twenty began his search after the righteous, and journeyed as far as India. At the age of 30, he began his active ministry with baptism in the waters of the Daitih; Ahuramazda called him, and revealed secrets (in visions and conferences) of time and eternity, the duel nature of the cosmos, of Heaven and Hell, and the ultimate salvation of the universe. He was later assailed by the evil spirit, Angra Mainyu, with threat and promise, but Zoroaster's faith in Ahuramazda prevailed. He proselyted in travail and rebuff but won converts. The sacred book is: "Sikand Gumanik Vigar."	Water was essential; therefore, a sacred gift of Ahuramazda. A flame was kept always present, and the pure wind cooling the heat of the plains was the holy spirit of Ahuramazda. All things were sacred, in the proportion that they conferred life, comfort, and security. Ahuramazda sent comfort and security, and created the good and pleasant land of Iran; but Angra Mainyu sent pain and misery, and created the serpent of the sea, winter, grief, pride, heresy, and parasites, ants, locusts, drought, evil and false religions. The holy verbal formula was: "I confess myself the worshiper of Mazda, a follower of Zarathustra, one who hates the Daevas and obeys the laws of Ahura." To ward off the foul influence of Ahriman, priests proclaimed the prerogative of universal legislation. Fiendish possession of an individual could be dispelled only by priestly spiritual power. In this dualism, the God of Light, Ahuramazda, is at last to emerge victorious in the year 2400 A.D.

[143]

CHART VI
THE RELIGION OF GAUTAMA, THE BUDDHA, PRE-CHRISTIAN AND CONTEMPORARY

Origin	Christian Time and Geographic Location	Chief Characters	Imputed Supernatural Circumstances	Doctrine and Communicants
A Brahmanistic Reform, Buddhism treated all the despised, the poor, and ignorant, with equality. Sutras and outcasts accepted the doctrine to escape unrequited toil and social degradation. "Come unto me all ye that labor and are heavily laden, and I will give you rest," became the chief code.	500 B.C. to present. Beginning in India, missionaries penetrated every part of the known world, including Burma, China, Siam, Bankok, Japan, Tibet, Greece and Asia Minor. Original form is now found only in Siam, Ceylon, and Burma.	Mahavira pre-existing god, virgin born; Siddhartha Gautama, the Buddha—"Eye or light of the world, the Teacher, the awakened one," born miraculously of Owen Maya, wife of King Sakya of N. India.	Mahvira first entered the wife of a Brahman; then transferred to that of the Queen. Gautama was born; He entered his active ministry at the age of 30, and became an ascetic, renouncing his wealth, and status: "The wise renounce property, and become as animals who are provided for—individually man is born, dies, falls from a state of existence and rises to another." The Buddha observed weariness, poverty, and suffering; he abandoned his father, mother, wife, relatives, house and lands. He became an	Cast should be abolished. Social position should be based on moral excellence. The Vedas were discarded. Pacifism and non-violence were established as the holiest of all principles. Religious and civil codes should be entirely separate; the holy should abandon and repudiate worldly affairs. The social neutrality advocated was like that of the harlot, Bindumati, who treated all castes as equal when they paid for her with gold. First was a *repudiation of labor, then of home and family.* One should never marry, nor accept social responsibilities, since these were the instruments by which exploiters fastened slavery forever upon the necks of the poor, to keep the economic lords in luxury, struggling to feed, clothe, and house a domestic brood. Celibacy and idleness were the only solution to overpopulation. Workers were so exceedingly numerous that a sharp reduction in the available labor force was the only remedy. The evils of sexual consumation in human generation were portrayed as repulsive and unclean. Women were dreadfully dangerous; even the smallest love of man for woman must be destroyed. To dwell with a woman was worse than to have pins bore out the eyes. Rejection of parents and children was rewarded with knowledge, peace of

CHART VI (Continued)

Imputed Supernatural Circumstances	Doctrine and Communicants
ascetic, but gave this up too as unfruitful.	mind, cessation of desire, faith in the kingdom of righteousness, and eternal salvation. To support your mother and father as your duty in this world, is to be caught up in whirlpools that the wise avoid.
He suffered temptation to return to his family, but persisted, converting noble companions of earlier days.	Brahmanas ignored the ethics of the Upanishads, which Gainas and Buddhists embraced. The Buddhists also reversed the hell situation to condemn the rich. Do not bestow gifts, they contended, upon those who can reciprocate.
He did not reject humanity, only family, marriage, home and labor.	A six-spoked wheel of Law is the symbol of Buddhism, representing victory of the Arhat over the six deadly sins. Craving that arises from sight, taste, smell, touch, and hearing can lead to pain, torture, and misery. Salvation is an internal process, whereas priestly societies evolve forms of ritual and ceremonies which have nothing to do with man's moral regeneration "..as a man thinketh so is he ...," Hatred, etc, can only be replaced by tranquil love. Outward acts of religious ritual are without efficacy. None can purify a mortal.
When his soul passed at 80, there were great earthquakes and the sun and moon withdrew. No writing was done in India at the time of Buddha; thus, no sacred books are available.	Victory must be over the self "...if we possess two garments, we must give one to a needy Bhikhu .." No matter how unjustly one is attacked or abused we must never strike back. These are but a few of the principles in the placid doctrine of Buddhism.

CHART VII

THE RELIGION OF PYTHAGORAS, PRECURSOR OF ESSENIC-CHRISTIANS

Origin	Time and Geographic Location	Chief Characters	Imputed Supernatural Circumstances	Doctrine and Communicants
Pythagoras traveled widely among the Egyptians, the Chaldeans and Magi. He was a pupil of Zoroaster and a disciple of the Brahmanin. The movement became a reaction against economic exploitation to establish a strict communistic-disciplined community.	Circa 580 to 0 B.C. Greece and Southern Italy	Pythagoras-metaphysician, social revolutionary, and theologian, espousing metempsychosis and communism	Pythagoras descended into Hell and spent seven years. Emaciated and telling of his stay in Hades, his disciples wept and wailed.	The body imprisons the soul; sex and marriage must be repudiated as well as self aggrandizement, and exploitation of others. The essence of righteousness is in renouncing carnal and material things. Celibacy, communism, vegetarianism, equalitarianism, and non-violence were espoused. There was a perpetual Hell for the incorrigibly wicked. An industrious contributing brotherhood was necessary. Truly an eclecticism of the first order, it espoused: body-soul dualism, Hell, Heaven from Zoroastranism, original sin and metempsychosis from Brahmanism, suffering and renunciation and communal brotherhood to end the cycle of misery from Buddhism, eternal bliss through the sacramental initiation, and judgment after death from the religion of Osiris.

Chapter 16

The Superstructure of Christianity

It is sometimes argued that Christianity is unique in the figure of Jesus. He was the only begotten Son of God, who lived and walked on this Earth so that all men might know the path to salvation. All other preceding or contemporary religions, argue Christian proponents, are coincidental and independent. Coincidence, however, must be emphatically ruled out. Christianity, in truth, was only one among scores of religions in the pre and post Christian era dealing with almost identical patterns of abstract god men, and a host of similar dramas and pageantry.

The pagan sources are perhaps more significant to Church development than to the basic Gospel Jesus. For that reason it becomes necessary to examine the superstructure of the conglomerate religious ideologies from which Christianity (i.e., the Church) was built. The philosophers and thinkers of the Hellenic period, for example, were most directly responsible for the religious theology later to become that of Christianity. The Greek period of secularism, often referred to as the "Golden Age of Greece," produced those great moral-religious leaders who winked at the myriad of gods, yet whose religious heritage was still the provincial framework upon which their philosophical inquiry was based. Heraclitus, Empedocles, Plato, and Aristotle, were all body-soul dualists. Gods and men, they held, emanated from the same universal soul which was God or reason. The Pythagorian synthesis, as previously discussed, was also a fusion of myriad religious element of the time. Mendicant Pythagorian prophets, whom Plato decried, claimed the power to make atonement for man's own sins, and the sins of his ancestors, by sacrifices, through the use of charms, and in performing rituals for the redemption of the soul from the pain of Hell in releasing the individual from personal and original sin. This, too,

CHART VIII
THE RELIGION OF ATTIS, PRE-CHRISTIAN

Origin	Time and Geographic Location	Chief Characters	Imputed Supernatural Circumstances	Doctrine and Communicants
Compare with versions of the religions of Aphrodite, Adonis, and Isis and Osiris	Circa 1800 to 200 B.C. in Asia, and Phrygia. It was carried by Thracians into the Isle of Samothrace and Phrygia	Cybele, mother of the gods; Adcestis, son of a stone fathered by Jupiter; Nara, mother of Attis	Acdestis was conceived in lust by Jupiter and castrated by Dionysus. From the blood of the castration there grew a pomegranate tree, fruit from which Nara took to her bosom and bore Attis. The beauty of Attis brought the attention of the castrated Acdestis, who forced a homosexual relation on Attis. The mother goddess, Cybele, put burning passion in him. In his passion, Attis, under a pine tree, cut off his own sex organs and threw them at Acdestis. Cybele mourned Attis, burying his genitals, from whence violets grew. She carried the pine tree to her cave and there mutilated her breasts.	In early rites, a high priest was annually impaled on a pine tree. A thousand such emasculated saviors were crucified in Phrygia to die and arise so that others might have eternal life. On the 22nd of March the trunk of a pine tree was carried ceremoniously into the temple. An effigy of Attis was affixed. Mourners followed statues of the Mother goddess Cybele through the streets, crying and screaming, and cutting themselves with cutlery. Novices sacrificed their virility and flung their excised organs against a statue of Acdestis so they, too, might share in the resurrection. Priests removed the image of Attis from the tree and placed it in a tomb while initiates fasted through the night. In the morning the image was gone from the tomb. This was followed by rejoicing, gaity, and public licentiousness, celebrating the empty tomb and the resurrection. The Eucharistic sacrament consisted of a meal eaten from a drum and cymbal, and the Taurobolium (baptismal blood bath), in which castrated initiates stood in a pit beneath a freshly-slain bull to be washed in its blood. Auto emasculation was widely practiced.

was a superstructure for Christianity that catered to widespread and diverse proclivities of vast numbers in the population.

The religions of Attis (Chart VIII), and of Dionysus (Chart IX) also encompassed vast numbers. The Eucharistic rites were prominent in each of the latter; in the religion of Attis, a primitive form of the crucifixion drama was the forerunner of the same rites later to develop in Christianity. Christian conversion of Attis believers was an easy transition. Christian converts mourned and watched through the night, as they had done earlier for Attis. Likewise, effigies of Jesus were hung on a tree/ cross, and all were joyful at the apparently empty tomb. Auto-emasculation was practiced in the early Catholic Church; this also originated with the Attis cult. The crucifixion date, established at the First Ecumenical Council at Nicaea, was first celebrated by the Eastern Church in April, the time of the Passover. A later council adopted March 23rd as the crucifixion date, with resurrection on the 25th, to accord with similar Attis observances.

Dionysusians were easy converts, particularly following the Orphean reformation. (Chart X) The Dionysus eucharistic communion consisted of symbolic consumption of the god's blood and flesh. This transformed communicants to become as one with their god, to be resurrected to immortality. The Orphean reform had earlier changed the practice from one of eating actual flesh and blood, to the symbolic flesh of grain and blood of wine. This practice was adopted by the Christian Church (even as in the Gospel Jesus), and remains so today.

Many aspects of Brahmanism (Chart XI) were similarly adapted to Christian dogma and practice. The similarities here, however, do not appear to have been cogent to the winning of converts, except to where they may have been instrumental in converting followers of Pythagorianism. Rather, those facets of Brahmanism that were adopted seemed to have been more pragmatically based on socio-religious control—a precedent that Christian Church founders were wont to recognize as being essential to church organization. The church organization developed many principles that are similar to those of Brahmanism. The Law of Karma, also a Pythagorian precept, in which we are

CHART IX
THE RELIGION OF DIONYSUS, PRE and POST CHRISTIAN

Time and Geographic Location	Chief Characters	Imputed Supernatural Circumstances	Doctrine and Communicants
ca. 800 B.C., to 300 A.D. in Greece	Dionysus; Chaos (Earth) Uranus (Heaven) daughter of Chaos; Rhae, daughter of Uranus; Cronus, son of Uranus; Zeus, son of Rhae.	Rhae bore children by Cronus who ate the first five. She fled to Crete and later gave birth to Zeus. When he became a man, Zeus battled his father to become king of the gods. Zeus fathered Dionysus in a mortal woman, Cadmus (Semele of Thebes) Dionysus then assumed the archetype tradition of Osiris.	Festivals of Dionysus honored the phallus as a member (also esteemed by Isis). Celebrants were predominantly women, eating the flesh of a bovine, an enemy or of a new born, in wild feasts. The women worshiped the male generative organ, at the same time rebelling against the extreme domination of the Grecian husband, yet expressive of the need for pregnancy. The Eucharist was in actual eating, as a primitive form. In variations, grain, bread, grape wine, etc., were identified with flesh and blood; in these transformation rites, they then became as their god to be resurrected to immortality.

CHART X

THE RELIGION OF ORPHEUS, DIONYSUS REFORM

Time and Geographic Location	Chief Characters	Imputed Supernatural Circumstances	Doctrine and Communicants
See Dionysusian (Chart IX) Osiris could not penetrate Greece under his own name. He did so many times under the guise of Dionysus.	Orpheus; Eurydice, his wife; Calliope, his mother; Persephone, a goddess.	Orpheus passionately loved Eurydice who died and descended into Hades. He petitioned Persephone to permit him to bring her back. Persephone consented on condition that upon leaving Hades he would not look. As they ascended, he stole a glance and Eurydice was gone in an instant. He deeply mourned her loss and foreswore woman-kind, turning to a life of celibacy. This brought the wrath of the Bacchantes, who lynched him, tearing him into bloody remnants.	Divinity was never achieved, though Orpheus was attributed with all the prerequisite experiences. Orpheus arrived among the Hellenes after they had become sophisticated. He was thus recognized only as a great poet, musician, and prophet. Dionysus had developed as a savior god. Orpheus reformed the Dionysusian religion to make it acceptable among the Hellenes. The Orpheans refuted the eating of raw bovine flesh and the flesh of human enemies and infants. Under Orpheus, wine became the blood of Dionysus, as grain became his body. Thus did the symbolic Eucharist replace the more physical and primitive practices.

CHART XI

THE RELIGION OF BRAHMAN, (HINDU SECTS) PRE and POST CHRISTIAN

Christian time and Geographic Location	Chief Characters	Imputed Supernatural Characteristics	Doctrine and Communicants
4,000 B.C., to the present in India	Brahman, an abstract man; the world soul called also "God" or "Self Existent;" Manu, the Second Progenitor of the human race; Vishnu, Creator	In the beginning, the universe existed only as darkness in deep sleep. Then God placed a golden egg in the waters from which Brahman himself was born. Thence was mankind made from his own body. Manu was the first being; then came mankind; but not all were of equal nature. From Brahman's head were made the priests (called Brahmanas); from the hands and arms were made the warriors (Kshatriyas); from the thighs came the craftsmen (Vaisyas); and from the feet came the workers (Sudras). Only the highest castes could be priests.	There is a body and a soul. The soul is most important in the three upper classes, for from them it goes into a new infant at death. If a good life was lived, the soul rises, and, in rebirth, moves to a higher caste. If an evil life were led, the soul migrates to a lower caste, or even to animal forms, such as fleas or mosquitos. This is the Law of Karma, of the rewarding of good and punishment of evil. The Brahmans, or priests, are the microcosms of the Brahman, "Fathers." The final authority is in the Vedas as interpreted by the priests. Salvation is exclusively through the Brahmanic codes of unalterable and irrefragable authority. Penance involves elaborate formularies devised by the priests for sin by which one might be freed. Hell is awesome and described in terms of pain, while Heaven is vague. Most simply pass into a reincarnate life. Works of holiness are not in labors nor in charity, but in ceremony and in reciting of the Vedas, or bathing in holy water. The priest controls a communicant's punishment by excommunication—cutting the individual off, not only from religion but human contact. The priest demands heavy tribute; none are permitted to live their own lives, nor to reason. Anyone not performing his religious duties is deprived of caste. Heretics or those arguing against the Vedas must be treated as outcastes. The soul of the universe is Brahman, and it is manifest in plant, man, fish, insect, and bird. (pantheism) Nirvana is the union of the finite with the infinite soul of the universe.

held responsible for the sins of our ancestors, is contained in the "original sin" dogma of Christianity. The final priestly authority, designating priests as "Fathers," is given precedence in Brahmanism, as well as in the secular Roman patronage system of Patricians, Penance, the grotesqueness of "Hell," excommunication, emphasis on "holy" ritual and ceremony, the use of water in baptism and the strong antagonism toward dissention and intolerance for heretics, also form a common base with Brahmanism. These are emphatic similarities, whether emulated by Christians, or independently developed by early Church Fathers as a means of social control.

Chapter 17

Socio-Religious Penetration of Christianity

In order to understand how the tradition has been built up in Christianity, and the forms that it took, it perhaps first becomes necessary to know the societies and religions prevailing within those lands in which Christianity gained its original impetus. Early Christian inroads among the Gentiles were made first among the Greeks, particularly those residing in and about Palestine, then on the mainland of Greece, spreading thence to Rome.

Greece was a nation ruled by a select few. Its economy was based on slavery. Family and property rights were straight forward affairs. Women were primarily valued in the procreative function; romantic attachments were largely between males. Sound male children were most highly esteemed and frequently groomed to serve in state functions. By temperament the Greek was quiet and reserved, cultivating a sense of humor, a contemplative nature, and enjoying aesthetic detail. He was vigorous and disciplined for physical endurance.

The Romans, on the other hand, were people of action and acquisition. Their literature and art, as well as religion, were largely assimilated from the people of their lands of conquest and occupation. Theirs, too, was a slave economy, with patriarchal dominance; the domain of the woman was restricted to housewifery skills. Soldiers enjoyed the greatest privileges and esteem, and were frequently found to be arrogant and bulldozing (cf., references to Roman soldiers in the Gospel Jesus). Roman temperament, by our standards, was severe and brutal. Their pleasure was found in unbridled sadism. The Roman government indulged the people in extravagant expenditures on circuses and raw arena combat among men, animals, and women. The Colosseum, constructed for this purpose, held over 80,000 people, and the Circus Maximus arena had a capacity of over ¼ million, that all might view such spectacles. Ruling tradition of the Romans was at first oligarchical, i.e., a group of senators were succeeded by birthright, whose responsibility it was to chose an emperor, who was in turn responsible to the Senate. After Julius Caesar, however, the emperor assumed increasing power. Some emperors later were proclaimed to be god. More will be said of these aspects of cultural conversion to Christianity later.

The ideological influence of Greece, and the administrative sovereignty of Rome, encompassed the whole of the civilized world at the time of conversion to Christianity. It was from within these two great cultures that Christianity developed, and that compromises were instituted with the prevalent pagan beliefs. It was from these cultures that Christianity was to multiply its following beyond even that of the nearest rival (cf., Mithraism). The religion of Ishtarism, (refer to Chart XII), popular in the Empire at the turn of the Christian era, also portrayed the common resurrection cycle. Many other elements of these pagan religions were to be assumed by the Christians. The same pattern of death and resurrection operated in the religions of Aphrodite and Adonis, and of Demeter and Persephone. These latter cults, however, had never been completely accepted by the Greeks, since they smacked of promiscuity. The Greeks were monogamous and property owners. Aphrodite had become for the Greeks only a symbol of abstract love and beauty. Ishtar had many faces, though, as had Isis. In Christianity she became "Easter," celebrating the traditional passion of Christ. After the seeds of the new Christian faith had been planted in this old stock of paganism, many elements were merged. The Easter celebration of the dead and risen Christ grew out of the annual celebration of the dead and risen Adonis. Greek paintings of the sorrowful goddess, with her dying lover in her arms, became the model for the famous Pieta in Christian art (i.e., the Virgin Mary with the dead body of her divine Son on her lap, as sculpted for St. Peter's Bassilica by Michelangelo.)

Such evidences of the roots of Christian beliefs and practices in Greco-Roman paganism are many. The mass, which is at the heart of contemporary church ritual, may even have had

CHART XII
THE RELIGION OF ISHTAR, PRE and POST CHRISTIAN

Time and Geographic Location	Chief Characters	Imputed Supernatural Circumstance	Doctrine and Communicants
Circa 6,000 B.C. to 350 A.D., Babylonia, Syria, Antioch, Alexandria and Egypt	Ishtar (also known as Ashtoreth, Astarte, Mylitta, Cybele, Anaitis, Cindymene, Aphrodite and Venus.)	Consumed with a passionate love for the dead Tammuz, Ishtar was led to the underworld of the dead. There Allatu siezed her and made her captive. Ishtar's departure from Earth caused great	The passion of Ishtar was celebrated annually; women wept for Tammuz. At the Temples of Ishtar women gave themselves in sacred prostitution before marriage. (Babylonians had formerly sold their daughters into slavery or wifehood.)
	Tammuz, her lover.	tragedy and sorrow. Green was gone from the fields and sexual love ceased among	In Egypt, the festival of Adonis was in mid-summer when the anemones bloom in Syria. The women lamented and
	Allatu, mistress of the Nether regions.	animals. A council of the gods forced Allatu to release Ishtar. In her passion, though, Ishtar	mourned for Adonis; coffins lined the streets, figure-bearing couches with the lovers, Adonis and Aphrodite, were car-
	Astarte later became the goddess Aphrodite; with King Cenyras of Syria; his daughter, Myrrha; Adonis son of Myrrha born of an incestuous relationship with her father; Zeus, King of the Greek gods; Persephone, mistress of Hades.	returned to the underworld every six months to be with Tammuz. When she returned she brought life and growth, birds and flowers, and love. In the Aphrodite version, the Goddess Aphrodite inflamed Myrrha with passion for her father and she stole her mother's place in bed. She was made pregnant by her father who then tried to kill her; but the gods made her into a myrrh tree. The tree then gave forth Adon (lord),	ried through the streets; altars were laden with fruits and cakes. The time of the festival was Spring or when the sowing began in Egypt. Then the star of Venus appeared, which was the goddess coming to rescue and resurrect him. Each female initiate became a member of the cult through intimacy with sacred temple personnel simulating Aphrodite and Adonis. The men consorted with sacred prostitutes.

CHART XII (Continued)

who grew into a beautiful
youth. Aphrodite herself fell
in love with him.
Adonis was later killed in a
hunting accident. He departed
for Hades. There Persephone
fell in love with him.
Aphrodite followed Adonis to
Hades and beseeched Zeus to
aid in his release. Zeus
arbitrated and permitted
Aphrodite to have Adonis
only half the year. Adonis
thus ascended each Spring
when the earth was reborn.

its sole origin in these pagan traditions (with the Gospels later redacted for it to appear in the Last Supper). The tradition of Christian nuns becoming virgin brides of Christ harks back to the Demeter tradition of the "Greater" mystery. (Chart XIII) Here initiates became bridegrooms of the mother goddess. The festival of Saturnalia (Chart XIV) is a direct predecessor of the Christmas celebration that had been dated to accord with the birthdate of Mithra (Chart XV). Likewise, the indulgence of Saturnalia was followed by an abstinence similar to that of Lent. Here, the 40-day tradition is panoplied with Zoroastrian and Persephone-Demeter tradition, as well as that of Saturn. The tradition of Mithra is clearly indicative of early Christian ecclesiastical compromises with existing pagan beliefs and celebrations. Mithra was born, in the Julian calendar, on December 21st when the sun began its symbolic ascent. This was directly transferred to the birth of Christ, which later became December 25th in the revised calendar of Pope Gregory. In Luke the tradition of shepherds bearing gifts at the birth of Christ (2:8-20) is a direct transference of Mithraic tradition. (Chart XV)

The phenomenal growth of Christianity becomes more clearly understood when the elements of faith and practice are traced to their origin in these Grecian and Roman pagan myths and festivals. Such compromises, the engrafting of pagan faith components to the body of Christian dogma, facilitated conversion of the pagans. When those of Northern Europe were later swept up by the Christian tide several centuries later, their motley superstitions (Chart XVI) were also readily transferrable to the more systematized Christian pattern. Likewise, the firmly structured Christianity of Spain encysted similar elements in pagan creeds of the Aztecs (Chart XVII) following the Cortes conquests; similarly, the traditions of South American people (Chart XVIII) were easily converted to the Christian Code. Compare these easy conversions to the failure of the Jesuits in 16th-century Japan, who had only Buddhism and Shintoism with which to work. In the raw forms of Buddhism, Shintoism, and even Brahmanism, there is nothing comparable to the Christian afterlife nor to a resurrected god-man.

Along the Mediterranean throughout Greco-Roman cultures, titular Christianity evolved through exceedingly clever manipulation of embedded pagan beliefs. Christian authorities wove and spun the vast web of dogma that was to catch up virtually all the people of the Occident. Christianity was then to become, for a time, the state, imbued with the divine power of an angry, jealous God, who tolerated neither heresy, skepticism, nor rational discord.

CHART XIII

THE RELIGION OF DEMETER AND PERSEPHONE, PRE and POST CHRISTIAN

Time and Geographic Location	Chief Characters	Imputed Supernatural Circumstances	Doctrine and Communicants
Circa 1400 B.C. to 400 A.D. in Greece and Rome.	Demeter, goddess of law, seasons and grain, and mother of Persephone; Zeus, god and father of Persephone (Kore), a virgin goddess; Hades, brother of Zeus.	Persephone was promised in marriage by Zeus to his brother Hades. Hades came upon her in a garden in Nysia. (Sicilian version was in the Vale of Enna near Syracuse which was also the home of Isis and Osiris.) Hades carried her away protesting to the depths of the sea. Demeter was griefstricken (this became symbolic in the primitive mind of the depression of winter.) She searched in vain over land and sea, holding torch high, for 9 days. In her grief she came to the people of Eleusis and demanded that they build a temple and altar to her. Yet, she would not permit grain to grow imperiling mortal life. Zeus beseeched her to permit corn to grow and sent Hermes to the underworld to persuade Hades to release Persephone.	Communicants, by initiation into the great mysteries, were given hope of immortality. There was no creed nor theology. The mysteries were "Lesser" and "Greater." The Lesser came on the 21st of March and were open to all; the Greater were open only to Athenians. Both were supposed to make the initiate just, noble, and happy. The "Greater" required a celibate character. Those who achieved a good life through the "Lesser" mysteries, might look to being admitted to the "Greater" ones. Achieving both, initiates were to live forever in heaven with the good deities and by becoming the bridegroom of the savior goddess, Demeter. Frescoes found in the ruins of Pompeii show initiates taking the veil, while a priest reads, and the sacramental meal was taken. A kid received milk from a virgin satyr; the initiate viewed a phallus in symbolic marriage. The Great Mysteries were celebrated in Autumn. (September) The mystae purified themselves, to be accepted, by lustrations or baptisms in the sea. A great soteriological sacrifice also took place, in which a holy bull or heifer was ceremoniously slain. The mystagogues carried torches and, crowned with myrtle leaves, stopped at stations commemorating the various incidents in the passion of Demeter. The sacred drama was presented in devotion to events in the Demeter-Persephone Passion. Then initiates were given the Great sacrament. The Athenian senate frequently met in extra-ordinary session to ascertain if any were in profanation in connection with the ceremony. This was the case of Alcibiades who was tried and condemned to death for impiety.
Hades consented but gave her a pomegranate seed which, upon eating, compelled her to spend 4 to 6 months annually in the underworld.			

CHART XIV
THE RELIGION OF SATURN, PRE and POST CHRISTIAN

Christian Time and Geographic Location	Chief Characters	Imputed Supernatural Circumstances	Doctrine and Communicants
From antiquity to the 4th century A.D. in Italy.	Saturn (Gr. Cronus) husband of Ops, father of Jupiter, Juno, Ceres, Pluto and Neptune	After the fall of the Titans, Saturn fled to Italy. There he civilized the people, and taught them the art of agriculture and husbandry. He thus became god of agriculture and husbandry.	A mock king was chosen and dressed in regal attire. He was granted license to indulge his passions and enjoy complete sensuality for thirty days. At Saturnalia he cut his own throat on the altar of Saturn. Saturnalia, a winter festival lasting seven days beginning December 17th, was observed by feasting and revelry, exchanging of gifts, exaggerated charity (e.g., changing places with slaves) closing of schools and courts, to commemorate the reign of King Saturn, the righteous and beneficent god and king of Italy. A period of abstinence and temperance followed the surfeit in magical preparation for sowing and planting.

CHART XV
THE RELIGION OF MITHRA, PRE and POST CHRISTIAN

Origin	Time and Geographic Location	Chief Characters	Imputed Supernatural Circumstances	Doctrine and Communicants
In Zoroastrian precepts, panoplied with the mystery cults	Circa 2,000 B.C. originally in Persia and India, thence to Africa, Italy, Gaul, Spain, Germany, and Britain. Mithraeums were found along the trading routes from Africa to Brittany	Mithra, invincible god of battle, lord of heavenly light (i.e., the sun), god of truth, cattle, and agriculture; Ahriman, king of darkness (Many characters by name were the same as those found in Zoroastrianism)	Mithra was born on December 25 (Gregorian calendar) in a cave, witnessed only by giftbearing shepherds. As he grew he set off to make the world his subject, granting benefit to the righteous and visiting with condign punishment the wicked. He smote adversaries, the creatures of Ahriman. Mithra made the sun subject to his will; he slew the bull, from which sprang celestial spheres and life on earth. Herbs and wheat came from the carcass, and from the blood came grapes and seminal fluids of animals.	The material world is the domain of Ahriman. Man's body comes from darkness, but his soul comes from the celestial sphere. There is a constant battle between these two forces, for only by subduing the Ahrimanic nature in us, through the sacraments, lustrations, baptism and communion, can victory of light over darkness be achieved. The "Taurobulium" was an initiation rite, in bull slaying and drenching the initiate in its blood. The priesthood consisted of Peres, Helidromus, and Paters or fathers. The hierarchy was a function of degrees, of branding on the forehead, fire rites, and finally receiving the sacrament of bread and wine. The world consisted of (1) the wicked to be destroyed in the final holocaust, (2) the essentially good who, however, had not participated in communion and (3) the elect who were admitted immediately into heaven.

CHART XVI

THE RELIGION OF THE NORSEMEN AND TEUTONS, PRE and POST CHRISTIAN

Christian Time and Geographic Location	Characters Chief	Imputed Supernatural Circumstances	Doctrine and Communicants
From pre-historic times, throughout Europe, England, Germany, and Scandinavia among the Goths, Vandals, Visigoths, Franks and Ostrogoths. Continued until Christian conversion of Goths in the 4th century, and of the Saxons in the 8th century. Remnants in Norway and Sweden found as late as the 11th century. The spirit of such gods—in hero worship—was revived in Hitler's time.	Balder, the sun god; His wife, Nanna, the moon goddess; Loki, a giant and god of fire as a destroyer; Hela, queen of the underworld and the dead.	Balder dreamed of evil early in his life; so Nanna went to all things on earth and made them promise never to harm Balder; but she missed the lonely mistletoe. Loki discovered this weakness and, in a sport of the gods in throwing things at Balder to prove his invulnerability, Loki introduced a dart of mistletoe that killed Balder. Balder descended to Hela's realm. She would surrender him only on condition that the whole world wept. Loki, in disguise, refused to weep and Balder could never be freed.	The world was considered to be a vast plain, with man living at the edge. Black magic and wizardry, such as hysteria, hypnotism and juggling were feared and abhored; while the white magic of dream readers and weather prophets was welcomed and esteemed. Heroes were thought to spend eternity in Valhalla heaven (cf., Olympus). Other souls remained in the grave. Giants and gods were believed to live, the giants being evil. The gods lived in a place called Asgard, as did the Greek gods at Mt. Olympus. Neither a carefully organized theological system, nor a priesthood seemed to prevail among these people.

CHART XVII

THE RELIGION OF THE AZTECS, PRE and POST CHRISTIAN

Religion	Christian Time and Geographic Location	Chief Characters	Imputed Supernatural Circumstances	Doctrine and Communicants
Polytheism with Tezcatlipocay sun god as chief deity	Pre-historic times to 16th century among the Aztecs of Mexico	Tezcatli-poca, sun god; Huitzilo-potchli, war god; Quetzal-coatl, god of the air; Xiuhtecutl, god of fire; Cioacoatl, goddess of water; her husband, Tlaloc, god of rain.	Mythology did not seem well developed, nor did drama	A single male individual was sacrificed to Tezcatlipoca annually. He was chosen one year in advance and paid high honors for his sacrifice to the highest of deities, given ease and luxury, attended by beautiful maidens who gratified his every need. He was promised to pass immediately to a land in the sun in pleasure, song and luxury. On the day of the sacrifice, he was led through the streets to the grand pyramid-like temple, and up the stairs to the altar. He was stretched in a convex sacrificial altar by priests dressed in black. With the razor-sharp sacrificial knife, a priest cut open his chest cavity, ceremoniously removing the heart, and placing it before the idol. The flesh of the body was then prepared for feasting by the populace. (Perhaps harking back to earlier cannibalism.) Huitzilopotchli worship was also in human sacrifice, requiring large numbers. A battle was arranged with neighboring tribes (mutually) to obtain captives for sacrifice. Quetzalcoatl, a regenerative god, left man the art of government and crafts and was to return. Described as white-skinned, tall, with black hair, the Spanish Cortez was likely thought by many Aztecs to have been Quetzalcoatl resurrected.

CHART XVII (Continued)

Doctrine and Communicants

Xiuhtecutl was worshiped in symbolic sacrifice, with a dough image of the god raised on a cross, with young men climbing for it, to pass it down to the worshipers for the sacrament.

Cioacoatl was honored in the festival of infant baptism.

A priestly hierarchy conducted all ceremonies, performing civil functions. They practiced asceticism under strict rules of penance, ablutions, fasting, and prayer. They were charged with education of the young. Sacrifices were of young males and females, suckling human infants and symbolic dough images. Confession of sin and absolution were also practiced.

CHART XVIII

THE RELIGION OF THE PERUVIANS, PRE and POST CHRISTIAN

Religion	Christian Time and Geographic Location	Chief Characters	Imputed Supernatural Circumstances	Doctrine and Communicants
The Great Sun Father	Pre-historic times to 16th century in Peru among the South American and Inca Indians.	The Sun God Pachacanac creator of Heat; Viracocha, creator of moisture	The great Sun God* sent two of his children with a golden wedge, to teach the arts and civilization to his people. Where the wedge was found to sink into the ground without effort was to be the center of the nation. The children of the Sun married, and their descendants became the Incas. *Some evidence exists in their records that a few Incas may have been free thinkers, for they observed that even the sun was regulated in its course. Thus, some greater supernatural god must be the supreme authority.	At the death of a ruler, (as in Egypt) his body was preserved, with servants and concubines immolated. Infant baptism and confession were practiced, as well as communion with a sacred bread sprinkled with sheep's blood.

Suggested Further Reading

1. Budge, E. (Ed.) *Egyptian Literature: The Book of the Dead*
2. Burnet, J. *Greek Philosophy* 1960
3. Ceram, C. W. *Gods, Graves and Scholars* 1963
4. Chantepie de la Saussaye, P. *The Religion of the Teutons* 1902
5. Cumont, F. *The Mysteries of Mithra* 1956
6. Flornoy, B. *The World of the Inca* 1956
7. Frazer, J. *Adonis, Attis, Osiris* 1961
8. Frazer, J. *The New Golden Bough* 1961
9. Goodrich, N. *The Ancient Myths* 1960
10. Guthrie, W. *Orpheus and Greek Religion* 1953
11. Henderson, J., and Oakes, M. *The Wisdom of the Serpent. The Myths of Death, Rebirth and Resurrection* 1963
12. King, W. I. *Introduction to Religion* 1955
13. Landon, K. *Southeast Asia, Crossroads of Religion* 1949
14. Larson, M. *The Religion of the Occident*
15. Magnus, O. *Norse Mythology* 1926
16. McCabe, J. *The Forgery of the Old Testament*
17. Menchen, H. *Treatise on the Gods* 1930
18. Muller, M. *Sacred Books of the East*
19. Murphy, J. *The Origin and History of Religion* 1952
20. Reinach, S. *Orpheus. A History of Religion.* 1960
21. Sejourne, L. *Burning Water: Thought and Religion in Ancient Mexico* 1961
22. Toynbee. A. *An Historian's Approach to Religion* 1956
23. Weber, M. *The Sociology of Religion* 1963
24. Zaehner, R. *The Dawn and Twilight of Zoroastrianism* 1961
25. Zaehner, R. *Hinduism* 1962
26. Zurcher, E. *Buddhism* 1962

V

The Phenomenal Christian Growth

Modern Christianity makes up about one-third of the world's population, or one billion people, the largest of all the great religions. The Roman Catholic Church, in turn, claims two-thirds of all Christians.

Of most compelling interest is how a relatively small group of Arabs, with exotic customs and peculiar ethnocentric tribal laws, could so influence the whole of the Western Mediterranean as to adopt their sectarian views. Here is attempted an historical explanation, lacking the customary zealous Christian partisanship, but hopefully to achieve some insight into how the small Judeo-Essenic-Christian sect could grow and spread throughout the Mediterranean, infiltrating the Roman Empire to usurp the throne and power of Rome in replacing the emperor with a pope.

Chapter 18

The Eclectic Nature of Christianity

Any individual tends to be selective in what he sees and hears. He tends to moralize according to his own standards, to have blind spots about some areas in which he is completely accepting, or extreme sensitivity in areas where he is completely intolerant. The arguments he accepts are in keeping with the persuasion in which he has been indoctrinated. A laboring man might be expected to be a Democrat or a member of a Labor Party. If a Democrat, he can be seen to hold views favoring governmental aid as contrasted with the Republican or Conservative. If he is Orthodox, or Roman Catholic, he may also be seen to hold to conventional ideas on birth control, marriage, and attitudes towards the Church, all of which are largely predictable.

Consistency in personality, the backgrounds of individuals, provide the basis for their views. Societies, in a similar manner, may be seen to be receptive to elements of innovation common to their background. This is evident in the development of Christianity. The Gospel of Jesus, as developed by the early people of the Occident, was composed of a soteriology, or god-man, a system of ethics, and an eschatology, or final rule of the god-man. The soteriology came from such mystery cults as that of Attis. The ethics were derived from the system of Pythagoras and Buddhism. The eschatology developed from Zoroastrianism. It was from followers of the religions of Osiris, Dionysus, Attis, Adonis, and Mithra, that Jesus was originally accepted. Similar traditions of a god-man creator were lacking in Persia, India, Arabia, Iran, Japan, and China. Christianity is found largely to be strange and Christ is seen only as a prophet by many people of these latter cultures.

THE CHRISTIAN PAGAN

Common bases in human nature and circumstances, and in human societies, whether agrarian, industrial, or military, make up the universal elements in religious practices and personifications. Compare the following:

1. The depression of winter. (e.g., winter festivals of Mithra, Saturn, and Christ)
2. Birth and rebirth in spring. (e.g., spring festivals of the goddess Astarte and the Christian Easter.)
3. Food deprivation, following crop failure or over-population, and the attendant economic and class discrimination.
4. Physical and mental pain.
5. Death of loved ones.
6. Control of primitive anger resulting from frustration.
7. Desire for what others have.

Such elements as these were evident in religions operating about the Mediterranean during Christian development. That a synthesis of early religions took place in the development of such sects as the Pythagonian-Essenic, as well as in the Gospel Jesus, has been evident to theologians and religious scholars alike. The religion of the Israelites, Judaism, was a conglomeration of many pagan elements. Components of Judaistic theology were selected by Hebrew priests and scribes from cultures of the conquering powers that swept over and engulfed Israel, as well as those territories in which the tribes moved. A synopsis of the conquests follows chronologically:

1. Assyrian Empire over Asia Minor from 1200 to 612 B.C.
2. Egyptian Empire 612 to 605 B.C.
3. Babylonian Empire stretching from the African Desert to the Persian Gulf and Caspian Sea, from 605 to 538 B.C. Nebuchadnazzar's mythological formulations during the Babylonian reign were incorporated into the Hebrew book of Genesis.
4. Persian conquest of Babylon under Cyrus the Great, 538-508 B.C. Cyrus introduced a policy of religious conciliation. All exiles captive in Babylon were returned to their native lands and religious freedom was permitted throughout the empire. The Jews, in gratitude, proclaimed Cyrus to be the "Christ" (anointed of Yahweh).

5. Persian rule under Darius, 508-330 B.C.
6. Greek Conquest in 330 B.C., after which Hellenic influence dominated. The spoken and written language evolved as a hybrid of Greek and Arabian, in their commercial transactions. This was the language in which the New Testament was written.
7. Political maneuvering and minor wars among Greeks and Persians persisted until the Roman conquest.

Intermingling of peoples, and the cross-cultural exchange resulted in the supernatural ideology that was finally shaped into Judaism. It was from this Judaistic theology that the marginally rebellious Gospel of Jesus emerged. Table 1 outlines pagan elements found in the Gospel Jesus. The Persian Zoroastrian religion, the Buddhistic, and other religions from India were also evident in the Greek Pythagorian formulations and Jewish Essenes, the latter of which predominate in the Gospel Jesus.

The ministries of such men as Paul of Tarsus largely affected the merger with immediate pagan beliefs. It was said of Paul, for example, that he was all things to all men. Such compromising diplomacy gave Christianity its initial impetus. The inherent Jewish tradition of Christianity otherwise presented emphatic conflictual interest with Gentile practices and beliefs.

In the history of religious and world movements may be seen two general types of institutional changes: (1) spontaneous or those arising from conditions harassing the common man. These occur as a reaction against tyranny, labor surpluses, or violation of personal and group standards, and (2) carefully planned and calculated formulations to foster control. Of the former type, four great spontaneous revolutions in religion are evident to religious scholars:

(1) Orpheus against the Dionysian cult.
(2) Guatama in his Buddhistic formulations against Brahmanism.
(3) Jesus thrashing out against Roman-Hebrew oppression and Essenic practices.
(4) Martin Luther denouncing the Roman Catholic papacy.

Each of these brought major reforms. Had there been no Orpheus, Guatama, Jesus, nor Luther, reforms may still have come about, for the times and conditions bore the seeds.

The growth of the Christian Church, however, seemed to have come about largely through the calculated type of revolution. There was no great spontaneity likely in the highly-organized administration of Rome. The politically-oriented see of that day was composed of various councils of priests aspiring to the widespread dispersion of nominal Christianity. They hesitated but little in transferring inherent pagan doctrine to Christian dogma. Table 1 outlines the various doctrines compromised/assumed by Christian priests to become cornerstones of Christian theology.

The dogma of the Virgin Mary was incorporated after the second century. This was quite obviously of pagan origin. Early religious practices and myths evidence ignorance of the process of sexual reproduction. In ancient Babylon maidens were required to meet a stranger at the Temple of Ishtar and lie with him for an hour in sexual congress in order to overcome sterility, i.e., birth was thought to be otherwise spontaneous. Athena was conceived in the brain of Zeus. A myrrh tree gave forth Adonis. Acdestis was born of a stone on which Jupiter had spent his lust. Dukdaub bore Zaratrust (Zoroaster) after she had been made pregnant by drinking hom juice. Later mythologies evidenced doubt about parentage. Understanding of the reproductive process is apparent, but there then seemed to be general misgiving about common phallic-worship practices, and promiscuity in sexual orgies in the groves and temples of Ishtar, Isis, Astarte, Cybele, Venus, and Aphrodite. Out of the pagan complex and confusion about the reproductive process grew such legends as the virgin birth of Attis, Mohammed, and Jesus. Popularity of the Virgin Mary seems also to operate as a function of an historical pattern. Goddess popularity seems most common in societies of a matriarchal nature. Ishtar became the chief national deity in a matrarchal period among the Babylonians. Previously she had been merely the mistress of Tammuz, but then became the first great Earth-Mother goddess. She was followed about the Mediterranean by Isis, Cybele, Astarte, Ashtoreth, Aphrodite, Venus, and the Virgin Mary. Such goddess popularity was never found in the patriarchal Judaistic society. In Isaiah, Ishtar, daughter of Babylon, is considered a maiden of immorality. To-

TABLE 1. ECLECTIC CHRISTIAN MATERIAL

Doctrine Found in Christian Tradition	Likely Source of Christian Inception
Zoroastrian	
— personal vivid hell and heaven	Gospel according to the errant Jesus' chroniclers
— water in baptism and spiritual purification	"
— demons that must be exorcised	"
— a messiah of moral justice	"
— universal judgment on good and evil works	"
— personal immortality	"
— final tribulation before the Parousia	"
— Purgatory	5th to 7th century Christian Priests
— Millennium Kingdom	"
— Armageddon, final conflagration	"
— defeat of Satan	"
— intolerance toward other religions	"

TABLE 1. ECLECTIC CHRISTIAN MATERIAL (Continued)

Doctrine Found in Christian Tradition	Likely Source of Christian Inception
Buddhism	
— brotherhood, charity and communism among the elect	Gospel according to errant Jesus' chroniclers
— equality of all men before God	" " " " " "
— wealth equated with wickedness and salvation possible only by giving to the poor	" " " " " "
— only indigent are righteous	" " " " " "
— divest self of world and its works	" " " " " "
— renunciation of sex and family	" " " " " "
— returning love for hate, kindness for abuse, rid mind and heart of anger and resentment	" " " " " "
— sin is in the heart as much as it is in overt acts	" " " " " "
— conversion is a moral transformation, conquering the indwelling evil	" " " " " "
— religion dictates to inner conscience and is separate from civil law	" " " " " "

TABLE 1. ECLECTIC CHRISTIAN MATERIAL (Continued)

Doctrine Found in Christian Tradition	Likely Source of Christian Inception
Mithraism	
—sacramental ritual became those of the Christian rites rather than the Judaistic sacrificial practices	Pauline compromise with Gentiles
—claims to being the Way, the Truth, the Light, the Son of God, and the Word, were assumed for Christ	" " "
—Sunday became the Christian holy day, rather than the Sabbath of the Jews	" " "
—Mithraic birth date was December 25th (Gregorian calendar) when the sun god was reborn, the days grew longer and living things revived. Mithraists kept vigil and at dawn it was announced that God was reborn (also traditional in the Saturn festival).	Chrysostom compromise, 6th Century
Hellenic — Paganism	
—absolute metaphysical dualism	Pauline compromise with Gentiles
—Logos or divinity of words	" " "
—transformation into celestial spirit	" " "
—celestial city lowered to become heaven on earth	" " "
—the Egyptian Persephone-Dionysus cult celebrated January 6th as the date that Persephone gave birth to Dionysus. This became the date of Christmas up until 6th century.	" " "

[177]

TABLE 1. ECLECTIC CHRISTIAN MATERIAL (Continued)

Doctrine Found in Christian Tradition	Likely Source of Christian Inception
Brahmanism	
—vows of obedience, poverty, and chastity	Nicene council in middle of 4th century
—intricate system of venial and mortal sins	" " " " "
—confession and penance to expiate sin	" " " " "
—priestly monopoly over training of youth	" " " " "
—denial of sacred scriptures to lower order of laity	" " " " "
—use of spells and incantations (prayer and blessings)	" " " " "
—reverence for sacred things	" " " " "
—excommunication	" " " " "
—discussion with heretics forbidden	" " " " "
—pilgrimages to alters and shrines	" " " " "
—degrees of legality in marriage	" " " " "
—honors bestowed upon ascetics (saints)	" " " " "
—ultimate authority in traditions	" " " " "
—Brahmanas (father-creator) were direct representatives of God who themselves were gods, lesser Brahmanas, or "Fathers." Christian priests assumed the title of "Holy Fathers."	Nicene council in middle of 4th century
—Brahman Vedas (Holy Books) can be interpreted only by priests or Holy Fathers	" " " "

[178]

day's societies tending toward a matriarchy, as in America, also evidence goddess popularity. The mother of Jesus, Mary, assumes an almost equal deistic status to that of her Son. Traditional matriarchy was recognized by early Church fathers, who incorporated the goddess into Roman Catholic dogma. Yet, in the 1964-1966 Ecumenical Council, some theologians sought to check growing excesses in Mariolatry lest the chief male deity be reduced to lesser status.

The theological nature of Jesus and many of His holy days were adopted directly from pagan doctrines. The Attis-Cybele cult in Rome was typical. Attis was god of ever-reviving vegetation, born of a virgin and reborn annually. His festival was a day of blood on Black Friday. Three days later it culminated in resurrection and rejoicing. The Attis festival was centered on Vatican Hill, and was marked by blood guzzling, self-mutilation, and dancing. The Christian Church at the Vatican Center, where Attis was popular, adopted the celebration of the death and the three-days-later resurrection. The Roman pagan celebration of Saturnalia, as held in December, was the happiest of all festivals, as a time of dancing, feasting, candle-making and gift giving. This tradition continued into the Christian era as Christmas. A perpetual fire was kept in the Roman Temple of Vesta. This became a Christian practice in the lighting of candles before the image of saints on the altars. Such typical pagan elements are found in Christianity on ad infinitum.

Perhaps mysteries that continue even today in eclectic Christianity are still legitimate. Even in an age of increasingly widespread education and insightful knowledge on the history of man's social origin and nature, there may still be room for such mysticism. On the other hand, such myths may be intellectually offensive to sophisticated intelligentsia even when interpreted as unconscious symbolism. Yet, the enigma of the universe is still with us and we still yet become perplexed and bereaved at the death of a loved one. As a culture, we are still steeped in the tradition of romanticism, even as the ancient Greeks, as in the ideal love relationship espoused in our popular love songs. The biological nature of man has also changed little in the half-million years of his fossil traces. His ability to handle abstractions is limited by prefabricated symbols and images of the culture. He is exceedingly slow to identify conditions and circumstances that would indeed obviate the ancient mysteries inherent in Christianity. But without further digression, let us again note how far we have come, rather than by compromising with mysteries, by understanding and controlling them. If man is further to regulate his destiny, he must come to know his origin in the light of natural history, and to see eclectic Christianity as a motley of pagan and other religious creeds spun into modern ecclesiastical cloth.

Chapter 19

Merging Theologies

Two major historical events mark the shift from pagan cults to Christianity, giving the latter its titular religious impetus:
 (1) Paul's conversion and zealous radical conflict with Jewish Christians.
 (2) Emperor Constantine's decision to convert to Christianity, seeing it as the strongest religious force in the empire.

Then, at Nicaea, the Council of Christian priests crystallized and formalized an eclectic theology that was collectively compromised with the pagan cults of Attis, Aphrodite, Astarte, Isis, Mithra, and Osiris. During the first century the Christian movement had reached out to embrace pagans or Gentiles. As a Judaistic sect, it may well have died the natural death of those other diverse Jewish sects that ran contrary to Jewish Law or priestly precept. But Christianity grew, with its impetus coming chiefly from those taking exception to the Jewish code. There was Stephen who was martyred. Peter compromised the law to admit the Roman Cornelius. Barnabas, Mark, Philip, and most notably Saul (St. Paul) systematically infiltrated the pagan cults. Paul's intense drive and compromising tactics, from which the Hellenic gnostic gospel issued, were directed to the promotion and development of the Gentile Christian Church. As a movement, Gentile Christianity became like a massive tidal wave that swept the pagan nations of the Mediterranean.

Paul's doctrine was essentially Zoroastrian. It contrasted with the Gospel Jesus on several points as in his regard of women: "God is to Christ as Christ is to man, as man is to woman . . ." Jesus honored women. He found devoted followers among them. Paul disdained them. Slaves, Paul contended, should be honest

[181]

and faithful to their masters. Jesus espoused equality. Such communistic elements found in the Gospel Jesus of Buddhistic origin: " . . . as the birds of the air are provided for, so shall ye . . . ", were reversed by the Hellenizing Paul, who held that . . . " . . . those who do not work shall not eat . . . " Paul's doctrine, found in Zoroastrianism, expounded on two antithetical natures: a spiritual one in redemption, and a material one, subject to forces of light and darkness.* An unrelenting struggle prevailed between the two: " . . . They that are Christ's have crucified the body with the affections and lusts . . . " Frail and sinful man, according to Paul, was hopelessly lost without divine intervention. Paul, like Jesus, believed the Parousia to be near. Jesus would be revealed from heaven with his mighty angels. He would come enshrouded in flames to take vengeance upon those who did not know God and failed to obey the Gospel. These would be punished everlastingly. The Parousia would be preceded by general backsliding and appearance of the Anti-Christ, a wicked man who claimed to be God.

Strongly Jewish Christian gospels in conflict with Paul, and later, the Gentiles, were suppressed. The Gospel according to the Ebionites contained the disputed dogma: " . . . Thou art my son; this day I have begotten thee . . . " After 400 A.D., the Ebionitic Gospel was eliminated permitting development of the virgin-birth story. The Epistle of James was strongly Judaistic. Addressed to the twelve tribes scattered abroad, it was written to refute the Pauline doctrine: " . . . faith, if it has not works (Mosaic Law) is dead . . . " Likewise the Petrine Epistles were also Judaistic. In this the eucharist is seen as based on Mosaic ritual as it is in the Book of Exodus. The new Christians were considered simply as a chosen generation, a royal priesthood of a holy nation to be called out of darkness into light, as the Israelites were called out of Egypt. Written later, when the Parousia had still not occurred, a thousand years was considered as but a single day. Christ would come when least expected. In the book of Revelation, Paul is the anti-Christ. Written by the Asian or Jewish Christian churches, Paul is seen as preaching doctrine contrary to Judaism. Paul tells that Jesus is to reappear

*See meaning of "heathen" as an unenlightened or irreligious person.

not as Messiah of the Jews but as a universal savior to transfigure saints of all nations, providing them with celestial bodies and immediate translation into heavenly mansions. These doctrinal conflicts in the Synoptics are also explainable by conflictual Judaizing and Hellenizing interests. Geneologies are Jewish. The virgin birth was a Hellenistic adoption making Jesus Christ compatible with pagan doctrine.

The present-day books of the New Testament are largely of composite partisanship. They had already become widespread before Gentile redaction was possible. Judaizers treated of the birth of Jesus in a traditional Jewish lineage back to King David, thence to Adam. Jesus was the Messiah who would deliver His people from bondage and fulfill prophecy. Frequently Gentile proponents introduced redactions, as did the author of Luke, but interpolations were hasty and poorly integrated. Hellenizers, for example. superimposed Mathew 1:18-25 and Luke 1 describing the virgin birth of Jesus. This presented Him as a savior similar to the Grecian prototype of Dionysus. Though then making Jesus acceptable to pagans, the narrations lacked consistency. In Luke, Chapter One, the Angel Gabriel had come to Mary before she conceived by the Holy Ghost. He told her of the things to happen in her virgin birth and the greatness of Jesus. Yet, in Chapter Two, she marvels at the things about Jesus' great future. The author carelessly overlooked such inconsistencies. In the Book of Mark, it is implied that Mary even thought that Jesus had lost His mind in claiming Messiahship. (3, 21-31) Thus discrepancies between the books vividly portray Judaistic-Hellenistic disparities.

The Book of Revelation is of Judaistic-Persian partisanship. Jesus is presented as a human being of Davidic descent. Christ was conjoined as the word, the power and the wisdom of the Supreme God. Rome was denouced, not for persecution of Gentile Christians by Nero, but for the attack on Judea and assaults on Jewish communities throughout the Middle East. Paul is condemned in terse criticism for his blasphemy: " . . . of them who say they are Jews but are of the synagogue of Satan . . . " Jesus was first a Jew, but of a Zoroastrian Saoshyant nature. He was the King of Kings, the Davidic ruler, the Star of Jacob, the

Christ Who would conquer the Gentiles to rule them with a rod of iron.

Paul's thrust into the Gentile pagan world became essentially a militant departure from Jewish source dogmas, heralding the eclectic Christian theology existent today.

Chapter 20

The Jewish Church

The historical bases of Christianity may well account, in part, for its development and survival. As societies grow in sophistication, skepticism emerges. Methods of inquiry and investigation evolve and institutions become increasingly subject to scrutiny. Without a basis in fact, or at least a semblence of historical authenticity, Christianity might easily have failed to survive. A progressively evolving society develops a cultural accretion of critical attitudes as a necessary by-product of progress. More and more it questions and rejects elements of belief, sifts and sorts out what is useful, stabilizing its institutions with meaningful fact. Lacking factual foundation the Greek gods began to tumble; so did Osiris in antiquity; Mithraism, as the chief competitor of Christianity, failed, having no historical basis nor realistic personification. This Jesus had.

At the time of Jesus, the pattern of the soter, or the god-man, was firmly established about the Mediterranean in the prototype Egyptian god, Osiris. Osiris was transformed again and again to provincial soter images such as Adonis, Dionysus, Attis and Mithra. The eastern religions, too, were absorbed and synthesized into Greek philosophies and religions. Pythagoreanism incorporated elements of Buddhism and Zoroastrianism. The profound influence of these great religions was also apparent in the Jewish sect of the Essenes. Jesus, perhaps having left the sect, adopted the liberal elements of Buddhism in order that any man might be admitted.

After the martyrdom of Jesus, His promises yet rang in the ears of the disciples. Many returned to their former life, even as they may yet have aspired to earthly and heavenly wealth. According to the Book of Acts, the basic source material, ministeries of the disciple Peter, as he preached on the resurrection, were among the first. The prophecies of the Book of Daniel were met in Jesus' martyrdom. He was first to become the "Son of Man," a Jew, who would lead his people to glory. Only then could the Gentiles, becoming Jewish converts through marriage, be saved. Jesus would first appear to redeem Israel. This doctrine made up the theological nucleus of the first Christian communities.

It was chiefly to the fierce resentments of the poor that the communistic doctrine of the Essenic Christ appealed. Only a few of the wealthy were attracted to the cult. The latter must have truly believed in the earthly kingdom to come, and their sacrifice may have been considered as a kind of investment in the promised kingdoms.

The original doctrine was fivefold:
(1) Jesus was the Anointed One (Christ) of Yahweh.
(2) He was the Son of God.
(3) He was the soter, the all-time God-man, risen from the dead.
(4) He would return during the lifetime of the people of the sect to bring forth the Kingdom of the Jews. The Jews would inherit all earthly wealth from the wealthy and sinning non-believers.
(5) Any who would not accept Jesus would suffer everlasting hellfire.

Early Christian communities were organized under Peter in Jerusalem. An Essenic format was evident in the practice of baptism, the eucharist, and magical laying-on of hands to expulse demons. They practiced celibacy and communistic brotherhood. Wealthy converts at first provided major economic support of the order that numbered several thousand Jews. Later, membership among the wealthy fell off for, lacking the highly-ordered discipline of the Essenes proper, the wealthy members may soon have despaired in the unfair exchange.

Gentile converts were at first the Greeks living in Palestine and Syria from the time of the Alexandrian conquests. Jewish Christians discriminated against the Greek Christian converts, however, in such things as support of poor Grecian widows. A rising majority of the Hellenic population, converting to Christianity from Orphic-Pythagorean traditions, introduced the fundamental conflict that was eventually to give rise to the Gentile Christian Church.

Stephen, one of the treasurers of the Jerusalem church, first contended vehemently that Jesus changed the customs of Moses. Stephen became the second Christian Martyr, being lynched in Jerusalem by fanatical Jewish traditionalists.

The Pharisaic Saul, a Roman Jew living in Tarsus at the northeastern corner of the Mediterranean, had first undertaken to persecute and discourage the members of this most troublesome heretical sect in Jerusalem. Saul perhaps had instigated the lynching of Stephen and the punishment of many other Christians who went against the Law of Moses. It was through Saul, however, that Christian growth became greatly accelerated, for he himself was soon to convert to Christianity.

Chapter 21

Paul, The Christian Organizer

In the city of Tarsus in the Empire of Rome, an area that is now Turkey, there lived a Jew called Saul. He was one of many Jews living outside Palestine. The son of a rich merchant called Cissai the Benjamite, Saul was a Roman citizen also known as Paul.

As a boy, Paul watched great ships sailing along the Mediterranean. He may have indeed dreamed about going to sea but it could only have been a child's dream for his father planned for him to become a Rabbi. He was sent to study under Rabbi Gamaliel who was a descendant of Rabbi Hillel. The latter's teachings were preached throughout Palestine at the time of Jesus.

After Paul had finished his training he lived in Tarsus and taught the Mosaic Laws to his people. There he also worked at his father's trade. He may never have heard of the crucifixion of Jesus, nor of the death of John the Baptist. Even if he had, they were merely two religious radicals of the many who were punished for transgressing from the basic laws. Several decades after the death of Jesus, Paul received a message from the Rabbis (Pharisees) in Jerusalem: "If the Laws of Moses and the Mission of Israel are sacred to you, then come to Palestine and help destroy a group of insurgents called Nazarenes."

He left for Jerusalem immediately. A careful and competent organizer, Paul directed forces to seek out and arrest scattered numbers of Nazarenes. He systematically and bitterly persecuted these heretics in Jerusalem, Samaria, and other parts of Palestine. Then they began to spread to Damascus.

In journeying to Damascus Paul was stricken with fever. Weak and delirious, he no longer sought to persecute the Nazarenes but joined them. Then he traveled from city to city as a devout Nazarene. In each city he went to the synagogues to preach the

teachings of Jesus. His faith in Jesus as the savior God strengthened as he continued to teach. The Jews to whom he spoke
frequently could not accept the strange teachings of the sect.
Many Jews were outraged when Paul taught contrary to the
Law. The Romans could neither understand nor accept the
strange religions of the Jews. Paul traveled and preached in Syria, Cilicia, Macedonia, Crete, Sicily, and finally Rome. He
preached of Jesus, Christ, the Messiah, the Anointed, and organized groups to form a great brotherhood. The churches became
highly organized. Paul wrote letters to provincial church leaders, while he himself traveled spreading the gospel and explain-
ing the faith. Membership among the Nazarenes grew, but the
resentment and hostility of orthodox Jews also grew as the heretical doctrine was preached.

Paul was incarcerated in Palestine, charged with treason. He
was sent to Rome to appear before Emperor Nero, and was first
acquitted. Paul continued to preach in Rome but was again arrested and finally convicted. The third martyr died in the name
and cause of Christianity. His work in organizing the sect was
phenomenal. From written records, especially Paul's letters in
Greek, it is evident that if any single individual were responsible for the ultimate growth of Christianity, it was Paul. Paul
promoted Jesus as both divine and human. He drew parallels
between the Christian and other salvation cults. He established
Christianity as a distinct religion, breaking away from Judaism.
His methods were most effectively compromising. Pagan beliefs
were incorporated into Christian dogma. The Mithraic Sun-day,
rather than the Sabbath of Judaism, was adopted as the weekly
holy day, as well as other Mithraic holy days. The twelve days
from Christmas to Epiphany, celebrated as the sign of the Magi,
among early pagans were the days of prophecy for the coming
year, one day for each month. The birthday of Mithra, December 21st in the Julian calendar, was to become the birthdate of
Christ. The pagan celebration commemorating the Spring goddess, Astarte ("Easter"), and the pageantry of Attis, became
celebrated as the death and resurrection of Christ. In the passion
of Attis an effigy of the desexed god was affixed to a pine tree.
Desexed (castrated) initiates watched and fasted until dawn. At

the Christian Council of Nicaea in 325 A.D., the dates and tradition of "Easter" in the Christian Church were set precisely to be in keeping with the practices of the pagan celebrants. Christian sacramental ritual was taken from Mithraic practice rather than the Jewish sacrificial rites. Christ became the Son of God, conceived of the virgin Mary. Pictures of Mary and Jesus in Christian churches bore strong resemblance to the Egyptian hawk-headed god of day, Horus, and the god of the underworld and judge of the dead, Osiris. Christian mass was taken from Mithraic ritual. Architecture of columned Christian cathedrals resembled ancient worship grounds. The Christian Season of Lent, 40 days between December 25th and the Spring Equinox, also paralleled Mithraic elements. Both Mithra and Christ were described as, "The Way, the Truth, the Light, the Light of the World, and the Son of God." Mithraism was an abstract cult with no single titular head nor human image. Christianity provided a personification of such abstract characteristics in the man Jesus.

Perhaps, a distinction must be made between the gospel teachings, simple, straightforward, and sometimes impertinent, and the doctrines of the church. The church, whatever its claim, is an institution in time and place. Church growth is marked by a series of compromises with existing institutions, belief systems and social problems. Dogma of the Church, may, or may not, be traceable to authentic historical doctrine about Jesus. In this light only may the massive following and power of the church and its present condition be understood. From Paul to Constantine, from the first Roman Catholic Bishop, to Luther, Waldo, Calvin, and Billy Graham or Bishop Sheen, such developments in Christianity can be analyzed only with this in perspective. Religious developments frequently fail to change with the times and expediency necessary to meet current social needs. Paul provided the necessary compromises with existing institutions and adopted expediencies to meet the social needs of the Gentiles. When Paul converted to Christianity, the sect was still weak and promised only a small ultimate following. Certainly had he continued to persecute the Nazarenes as he started out to do, the Christian sect may never have acquired sufficient momentum even to carry it to Rome. When Paul was executed, Christianity not only had become extensively merged with the existing institutions, but its belief system was of sufficient potential breadth to become the major religion of the world.

Chapter 22

Proselytizing About the Mediterranean

The Christian movement first spread from Jerusalem to Samaria through the zealous efforts of the disciples Philip, Peter, and John. Saul (Paul) was converted after suffering a fever while on his mission to Damascus. He may have experienced extreme guilt in the merciless persecution of Nazarenes. In recompense he himself became entangled in the Judeo-Christian conflict. He incensed Jewish traditionalists so intensely in Damascus that they conspired to kill him. He became embroiled in controversy about Christian meanings among the Nazarenes themselves. In fact, just after his conversion Paul seemed to antagonize everyone. His friends encouraged him to return to Tarsus since he was still ill from the fever of sunstroke.

After Paul's conversion, the Jewish Christian sect gained momentum in Judea, Galilee and Samaria. Peter made concessions to the Romans of Caesarea. A Roman militarist, Cornelius, was first converted. A later disciple whose name was also Stephen preached in Phenice, Cyprus, and Antioch. Barnabas went to Antioch to convert Greeks. He later went to Tarsus to seek Paul's help. It was first in Antioch, where Barnabas and Paul preached, that the sect was called "Christians." (From the Greek word "Christos" meaning the Anointed One.)

Christian doctrine was heretical, and provoked hostility among those of orthodoxy as it did with Herod in Galilee. A disciple named James was slain. Peter was imprisoned, but other disciples arranged for his escape.

Peter selected John Mark from a Christian family to join Barnabas and Saul. They preached in Selencia, Cyprus, and Salamis. Saul preached vehemently in Cyprus and cursed those who refused to accept Jesus. In Antioch they told the Jews how

Jesus was descended from King Saul and David, the son of Jessie, and that Jesus was of the seed of Jessie. They spoke of how Jesus had been persecuted in Jerusalem, and was taken down from the tree (cf., Attis) and laid in a sepulcher to be raised by God. He offered forgiveness of sin contrary to Laws of Moses.

Paul spoke in frustration, angry that the covenant of Jesus was denied by the Jews. Jew and Gentile alike came to Antioch to hear Paul and Barnabas. The strong orthodox faction protested their heresy. The Jews, argued Paul, no longer listened to God. Gentiles would listen and hear and be ordained to eternal life. In Antioch, during this period, a book of the gospel was written, and the faith was opened to the Gentiles who neither then were required to become Jewish converts nor to marry into the line of Abraham.

The Apostles left Antioch in conflict and went to Iconium. There, too, Jews refuted the doctrine; but there were Jews, as well as Gentiles, who believed. The apostles fled Iconium in fear of their lives at the hands of angry Jews who denounced their heresy. They preached in Lystra, Derbe and Lycaonia. Many Lycaoneans believed Paul and Barnabas to be Jupiter and Mercury. In Lycaonia the resident Jews decried the Christian heresy. The disciples left in ill will and journeyed to Pamphylia and Attalia.

The appeal of Christianity among Jews and Gentiles alike was to the poor and discontent, a cry for more equitable distribution of privileges—an appeal that even today summons large numbers to Communism. This appeal gave Christianity its initial impetus. In departure from the status quo of the rigidly codified Mosaic Law, Paul began to sweep in the Gentiles, and win immediate converts among disgruntled Jews. The Gospel Jesus was simple, requiring only dutiful homage to Yahweh, while the strict discipline of the Essenes, and the compulsive conformity demanded by the Pharisees, often no more than promulgated the tribal caste system of the Iraelites. Many found no identity nor equality through the laws of the tribe. The promise of rewards and equality held great appeal in Jesus' preachment. Jesus taught that the Sabbath was made for man, not man for the Sabbath. He flaunted a rebellious spirit of disdain for the Judaistic priestly authority which ultimately had led to his execution. Paul capitalized on this central point of departure to admit the Gentiles. Any great numbers of Gentiles would hardly have accepted the Jewish form of Christianity. Paul held that even to practice the law was to justify it and to deny the covenant of Christ.* This became the fundamental basis for early growth of the Christian movement.

Jewish Christians at the Jerusalem church heard of the proselytizing heresy of Paul in freely admitting Gentiles. They ordered the immediate return of Barnabas and Paul to Jerusalem. In Jerusalem the Christians of Pharisaic background insisted that Christ adhered to the Jewish Laws. Only those circumcised and obedient to the Laws of Moses could be Christian. Peter defended Barnabas and Paul in their winning of Gentiles to the cause of Christ. A disciple named James proposed a compromise; that all converts abstain from offering meat, blood, and things strangled to idols.

Then, disciples named Judas and Silas joined Barnabas and Paul in returning to Antioch to continue proselytizing in the Gentile church. Paul advised Barnabas that they separate to be more effective in their work. They parted with some disagreement, for Barnabas proposed to take John Mark, and Paul contended that Mark was unreliable. Paul took Silas with him to seek converts in Syria and Cilicia. They journeyed to Phrygia, Galatia, and Macedonia. In Macedonia the disciples were imprisoned by the Romans for preaching the Jewish doctrine. After a day in jail they were released and made to leave the city. But in Macedonia the seeds of Christianity were already sown. They went thence to Thessalonica among the Jews and preached on Jesus Christ who suffered execution and arose from the dead. Both Jew and Gentile gathered to hear them. In Berea, Paul was threatened and left for Athens, and waited here for Silas and Timotheus who had remained in Berea. While in Athens Paul preached and was confronted by Epicureans and Stoic philosophers who listened with interest. Paul admonished the people for their ignorance; his God had overlooked their errors in

---

*It may be a moot question as to whether or not the Synoptics, describing Jesus' transgression of the Law, preceded Pauline transgression. The epistle content was composed prior to that of the Synoptics. This may suggest that Synoptic writers fictionalized stories of Jesus to conform with later Judeo-Christian conflicts.

the past but now demanded obedience for He had raised his Son, Jesus, from the dead.

Paul went to Corinth and found work tent-making. There he preached of Christ to the Jews; but he lost patience, for they disputed his word. He vowed he would leave them in their blindness and seek out Gentiles. But still he continued to preach to Jews in Corinthia, until they rose against him, and he fled. He returned to Syria, and then to Ephesus. In Caesarea he hailed the church community. Finally he returned to Antioch through Galatia and Phrygia.

Preaching in Ephesus he threatened the economy. The silversmiths there made shines and medals to the great goddess Diana, and to the god Jupiter. Those working in the lucrative silver crafts resented any heresy that might disrupt their trade. A mob formed and crowded angrily about Paul and his disciples. They decried the heresy and reiterated the greatness of Diana. The town clerk then spoke to Paul, admonishing him not to speak against Diana and Jupiter who were supreme in Ephesus.

Paul left for Greece and remained there for three months. He left there again in trouble with the Jews for his heresy. He preached in Asia with Sopater of Berea, Artistarchus of the Thessalonians, Secundus Timotheus, Gajus of Derbe, and Tychicus and Trophinius of Asia. Paul was indefatigable in his zealous proselytizing. In Troas he preached tediously and endlessly. A man named Eutychus fell asleep and toppled off a third loft. Then they went farther to Assos, Mitylene, Trogyllium and Miletus.

Paul desired to be in Jerusalem for the Pentecost. He lamented that he had been dutiful in serving the Lord, even while suffering the wrath of the Jews, wanting nothing for himself but repentance to God by both Greek and Jew. As he started out for Jerusalem, as Jesus had done several decades earlier, he knew he had antagonized the orthodox traditionalists. Nor did he know, like Jesus, what lay before him in Jerusalem. Paul, however, was clearly not ready to martyr himself. The Church elders of Ephesus accompanied Paul to Miletus and bade him farewell. He journeyed to Coos, Rhodes, Patara, Phenicia, Cyprus, Syria-Tyre, Ptolemais, and Caesarea. In Caesarea, his friends again warned him not to go to Jerusalem, but he refused to heed their warning.

When Paul arrived in Jerusalem, he told the elders of the Jerusalem church of the thousands of Gentiles he had converted. The elders severely admonished Paul. He had also converted thousands of Jews who had openly turned from the Law of Moses. This could not be tolerated. Jews must follow the Law.

When Paul went to the Temple for purification, Asian Jews pounced upon him. He was a Gentile baiter denying the Laws of Moses and bringing the heathen Greeks into the Holy Temple. Paul was dragged outside the Temple to be beaten into submission when Roman soldiers arrived. "What has this man done?" demanded the soldiers.

"I am a Roman citizen and demand to be heard," cried Paul, mounting a staircase above the crowd. Then He spoke in Hebrew: "Hear me! I was brought up in Tarsus and studied under the great Rabbi, Gamaliel. I was most devout of all Jews, and persecuted others, as you do me, for their transgressions. As I proceeded to Damascus on a mission to rid us of Christians, I saw the spirit of the Lord Jesus. He bade me not to persecute Him, and I was blinded by the light. When I could see again, I knew it was the word of God I should preach. I was baptized to be cleansed for I alone was blameful for imprisoning and beating Christians, even the martyr Stephen. The Lord sent me to the Gentiles . . . "

"Gentiles, indeed!" cried the Jews.

The Roman soldiers threatened to scourge Paul for inciting the people. Paul again protested, and claimed his rights as a Roman citizen to be heard fairly.

The following day Paul was brought before the Chief Priests for a hearing. "I have lived a clean and good life," said Paul, standing before them.

Attendants of the priests slapped Paul's face. "You are an affront to God!" shouted Paul in anger. Then he noticed that Sudducees were among those present with the Pharisees, and contrived for dissension. "Merely because I have preached in good faith on the hope and resurrection of the dead I must answer before you."

Sadducees denied resurrection while Pharisees believed in life after death. "He speaks the truth," exclaimed a Pharisee.

"You all speak nonsense," retorted a Sadducee. Wild argument ensued.

The Roman soldiers rushed Paul away to the castle before he was injured in the turmoil. "It will be the same from here to Rome," thought Paul.

Jews in Jerusalem swore to see Paul dead and vowed to slay him when he appeared before the priests the next day. But Paul's nephew told the Roman captain of the plot which was conspired by more than forty Jews. The chief captain, Claudius Lysias, ordered two centurions to alert 200 soldiers in order to escort Paul to Caesarea, to be delivered to Felix Antonius, the Governor of Caesarea. A letter was prepared relating how Paul was being set upon by the Jews. "As a Roman citizen he must be protected, since the charge is merely a question of their tribal laws. While nothing is clearcut, he is in danger here, so therefore I send him to you . . . "

Paul, under guard, left by night, and was finally delivered to Caesarea. Felix received Paul. He would be heard, and kept in the Judgment Hall. After five days, priests came with the prosecutor, Tertullus. Tertullus praised Felix, accusing Paul of sedition as a ringleader of the Nazarene sect and profaning the Holy Temple. Paul defended himself. He had been in Jerusalem only 12 days: " . . . I was not disputing in the Temple, nor inciting the people in the synagogues anywhere in the city; nor is there proof of what I am accused. I believe all things written of the Law and the Prophets, and in the resurrection of the Just. And I am neither guilty of offense to God nor man . . . "

Felix waited for Lysias, the Chief Captain, to give his version. Felix heard Paul tell of his faith in Christ, and righteousness in temperance, and judgment. Felix was impressed, but Paul had neither money nor gifts to give Felix. Felix, wishing to please his Jewish friends, kept Paul captive.

The Jewish priests conspired to have Paul returned to Jerusalem where he could be assassinated. Jews from Jerusalem appeared before Felix in the Judgment Seat to accuse Paul. Paul reiterated that neither against the Temple, Caesar, nor the Law had he given offense, and refused to return to Jerusalem for judgment. " . . . I appeal to Ceasar . . . " Felix agreed that, as a Roman citizen, he should be sent to Rome for Ceasar's judgment.

When King Agrippa and Bernice visited Felix, he told them of Paul and the charges against him. As a Roman, his accusers were required to face him. This they did and their accusations were unfounded. Only their superstitions confronted Paul. Felix told then of Paul's belief in a man named Jesus, who was dead, but whom Paul believed to be alive. Agrippa and Bernice pompously agreed to hear Paul speak. Paul repeated his position of first being a most devout Pharisee who was condemned for his hope in the promise of God and prophecy. He, too, had been committed to punishing the heresy found in the words of Jesus. He had pursued the followers of Jesus and ruthlessly imprisoned or put to death these good people, working in the authority of the priests. This he did in many distant cities.

" . . . On the way to Damascus," he related, "I saw, at midday, a light, greater than the brightness of the sun, and heard a voice call, 'Saul, why do you persecute me? It is hard to kick against the thorns . . . ' I answered the call of Jesus to become a minister to the Gentiles and turn them from darkness to light, from the power of Satan to the goodness of God. I could not be disobedient to the heavenly vision, but preached to Jews and Gentiles in Damascus, Jerusalem, and throughout Judea, to repent, and turn to God. For this the Jews would have me die. The prophets themselves have told of how Jesus would be the first to rise from the dead and bring light to Jew and Gentile alike."

Festus Porcius broke in, crying that Paul was insane. Paul quietly denied the accusation. Agrippa mused that Paul spoke so convincingly that he himself was almost persuaded to become a Christian. After Paul left, it was agreed that he surely had done nothing wrong. Indeed, he could have been set free had he not already appealed to Caesar.

Under the custody of Julius, a centurion of Augustus, Paul was taken to Rome together with a shipload of other prisoners. They sailed along the coast of Asia to Aristarchus in Macedonia and Sidon, thence bypassing Cypress due to contrary winds, to Myra of Lycia, transferring to a ship from Alexandria.

Sailing south of Crete to the city of Lasea, the tempestuous Mediterranean slowly seethed into a sea of violence. Paul, knowing the sea, warned the Centurion of the imminent danger; but Julius was determined to reach Phenice before the winter. The wind whipped the ship violently about the cascading foam of the sea. Steerage was lost and holds were flooded. In desperate fear of sinking they lightened the ship of cargo and supplies. Paul prayed and assured the others that God would watch over them. The ship tossed and creaked, cast high on the waves for many days. Finally, it was pounded to pieces on a reef near the Island of Melita. The people of Melita assisted the crew and the prisoners ashore and cared for them.

On shore they built fires to warm and dry themselves. Paul lifted a bundle of sticks from which there crawled a viper. The poisonous snake curled about Paul's hand. He would be bitten and punished for his crime, gasped people of Melita, for he was deserving of such punishment as a prisoner. Paul merely flipped the snake into the fire. Truly he must be a god, murmured the Melitians. A mortal would surely have been bitten and died. During the three months on the island, Paul moved among the Melitians, who believed him a god, performing miracles, curing the sick and infirmed.

In the Spring the crew and prisoners were put aboard another ship for Syracuse. They sailed first to Rhegium, and Puteoli. In Puteoli, Christian brethren of Paul had journeyed from as far as Appiiforum to greet him.

Finally the prisoners were delivered to Rome. On first arriving, Paul summoned leaders from the Jewish communities of Rome and appealed to their sense of justice:

" . . . I have followed the law and done nothing against those in Jerusalem, but here, as you see, they have delivered me as a prisoner. I am bound with the stigma of the hope of Israel . . . "

The Jews in Rome had previously heard nothing concerning the charges against Paul, but were aware of the Christian sect and its heresy against orthodox tradition. Paul explained the teachings of Jesus, how His words had originated in the Laws of Moses. He spoke of prophecy fulfilled and promises of the

Kingdom of God. Paul met denial, protest and hostility among these Jews as he had among thousands on other occasions. "Your hearts are waxed closed. Your ears are dull to hearing and you are blind. The salvation can only be for the Gentiles who will listen and know the truth," lamented Paul.

The Jews he had summoned left Paul in ill will. He remained captive within a private dwelling for two years. He received whomever would come to hear the gospel. He told of the Lord Jesus and the Kingdom of God. He preached with the fire of conviction, and thousands listened. His work was consolidated with that of Peter's. The Roman church grew to be the largest of all the many churches in communities about the Mediterranean. In the final two years of Paul's ministeries, he may have remained in Rome preaching and converting. Legend, however, has him traveling throughout the continent as far west as Spain. In any case, he was finally tried and executed under Nero in 62 A.D.

Thirteen letters are recorded to Christian Mediterranean churches, though traditionally Gentile Christians deny validity of the Epistle to the Hebrews. Proselytizing and church building about the Mediterranean may very well have been the least significant of Paul's work when weighed against the influence and unrecorded myriad conversions he accomplished in Rome.

Chapter 23

Theological Developments After Paul

From Syria, Greece, Italy and throughout the Mediterranean World, Christian congregations sprouted. The seeds were sown by Paul, Peter, Barnabas, and scores of other proselytizers from the original Jewish church. The fertile ground of cults, such as those of Dionysus, Mithra and the prototype Osiris, nurtured the unprecedented growth of the Christian religion.

Other epistles than Paul's, upon which church doctrine is based, include:

(1) Epistle of Barnabas (70 A.D.). Christ is considered to be the Savior, the Son of God, who was manifest in human flesh.

(2) First Epistle of Clement (97 A.D.). No mention is yet made of the virgin birth.

(3) Epistles of Ignatius (117 A.D.). Jesus is described to be conceived of the Holy Ghost in the womb of Mary. At this date, it was supposed that the Virgin birth had been kept secret from Satan. The faith is found in the symbol of the Cross, the Passion Story, and the Resurrection. Much of this epistle was later exposed as Christian forgery, however.

(4) Justin Martyr and Tatian in Rome (145 A.D.) emphatically claim the virgin birth of Christ. Tatian's "Diatessaron" (170 A.D.) combined two versions into Church dogma, viz., the pre-existent Christ, the Virgin Birth, and the Trinity of the Father, Son, and Holy Ghost. Jesus Christ is clearly a God man.

These early documents are still those cited today. They evidence the fundamental Gentile-Hebrew conflict, viz., a gospel kingdom for all men versus a Jewish chiliastic kingdom with a

1,000-year reign of Christ and Jews supreme over all the world. Conflict of theologies originating in pagan tradition versus those of Judaism appears again and again in the writings of early church fathers. First-century fathers such as Jerome, Justin Martyr, and Irenaeus, all expected the millenarian kingdom, as did the second-century castrated priest, Montanus. The Holy Ghost spoke to Montanus and his prophetesses instructing them to renew the Apostolic hope for the millenarian. Organized resistance developed against Montanism, when it seemed to threaten the newly-organized secular church. Bishop Serapion of Antioch first refuted Montanists. In 230 A.D., Montanist baptism was not recognized. At the time of Constantine, edicts were issued against Montanists in Phrygia. In 550 A.D., all Montanists were finally and completely exhumed under Bishop John of Ephesus. The Tertulian, written at the turn of the third century, described the divinely-built city of God where the saints would be received upon their resurrection, their last judgment and investiture with celestial bodies. In Egypt, Greece, and Lactantius, this Christian millenarianism was engrafted on the pagan doctrine of the Golden Age. Others promoting eschatological doctrine were Anthanasius, Cyril of Jerusalem, Sulpitius Severus, and St. Martin. Then Augustine (around 430 A.D.) wrote that world history would encompass 6,000 years, after which would come the sabbath of the saints. In 1,000 years would be the year 6,000. The church on earth would be both the Kingdom of Christ and the Kingdom of Heaven. Christ would reign with all His saints for 1,000 years. In this official doctrine, the world was to come under control of the saints and the Catholic Church until the world's end and universal judgment. This provided a place for the Church through eternity, while only a vestige of the millenarian doctrine was integrated into the superstructure. Pope Gregory (circa 600 A.D.) saw the havoc in the events of his time that was supposed to precede the millenarian. This he interpreted from the ravaging of the land by Arian Lombards, the dissensions of the Manichaeans. Hestorians, Donatists, and Montanists. He saw in the East the precursor of the prophesied Anti-Christ in the figure of Bishop John who attempted to set himself up as the universal hero of the Catholic Church.

DEVELOPMENTS AFTER PAUL

In the Virgin Birth and Millenarian disputes, it can be seen that the Christian sect at first diverged into essentially two conflicting theological factions, viz., Jew and Gentile. This division also occurred throughout the Pauline ministeries in conflict with Mosaic law. New theological disputes arose with each generation. Jewish theology saw Jesus in Hebrew lineage born of Mary and Joseph. In the Jewish version, He was anointed with the Holy Spirit at baptism. In Hellenic-gnostic versions of the Gentiles, as seen in the Book of John, the Trinitarian dogma emerged. Then a third version, the Orthodox, appeared in which the Greek soter, half mortal and half divine, gave His life in sacrifice for repentant sinners. One hundred and fifty years later, the virgin doctrine was adopted to become church dogma interpolated in the gospels. Further sects emerged. By the year 200 A.D., there were almost forty sects, and late in the 4th century Epiphanius described eighty sects. As the church became increasingly dogmatic, however, sectarianism became a capital offense.

The thinking of these early Christian fathers has been sampled in their letters and is presented in Appendix A. Ignatius called for growing unity early in the first century. In the letter of Ignatius, however, is evident redaction, by a later church proponent, to herald the primacy of the Catholic Church, viz., it was not until the fourth century that such extensive church power, about which Ignatius writes, was clearly in perspective. Other writers evidence the power struggle and the essential lack of structure in the early church. Clement cites the strife that prevailed in acknowledging the bishop's office. Tertullian seemingly gives directive for the lineage of the Apostolic churches. In the writings of Athanasius, whose creed, per se, was purportedly adopted three centuries later in 600 A.D., may be seen a more elaborate theology taking form. Others, such as Jerome, insistently point to the seat of Rome as final authority.

Augustine's writings presage the beginings of a heresy that was to crystallize in Protestantism a thousand years later. The works of Thomas Aquinas are still in authority among modern Catholic intellectuals. Aquinas used the apocryphal work of II Maccabees, which was Zoroastrian in character and written about

60 B.C., to formulate much of what was to become Catholic dogma. In II Maccabee, Judas had offered sacrifices for those who had fallen in battle. Through this, the period of eschatological purification could be shortened by the burning of candles, saying of prayers and masses, and the offering of sums of money. Such practices could reduce the period of purgatorial confinement for the deceased. This doctrine was employed extensively during the crusades in the practice of Indulgences. Thomas' scholasticism was otherwise patterned after that of the 3rd-century B.C. Aristotle. Aquinas formulations are given a most prominent role in modern Catholic theology to cover any matters dealing with individual nature and society.

Other sources of doctrinology dealt with basic theological formulations which serve to instill fear for the gathering of constituents. The Apocalypse of Peter, for example, written about 125 A.D., postulated that "Hell" was full of harlots, adulterers, murderers, perjurers, scoffers, blasphemers, and the persecuters of saints. This was a Brahamic hell which was to become part of the Christian theology. Hippolytus, at the turn of the fourth century, described Hades as a place beneath the earth serving as a guardhouse for souls, where temporary punishment was administered according to the magnitude of the sinner's transgressions. The unjust were sentenced to dwell in a lake of unquenchable fire and endless punishment. Augustine saw purgatory as a place where even the most saintly underwent further purification. Pope Gregory made this version Catholic dogma in 604 A.D.

Through an administrative structure, first developed by the Roman Empire, the Church grew into fantastic proportions. Its claims to supernatural ordination, in an adaptive theology, were built out of age-old pagan god-men and Zoroastrian hell fire. As the secular empire declined, a supernatural one developed. Finally, in the year 1870, the Pope became veritably deified as an infallible Vicar of Christ as pronounced by a Vatican Council. This also followed a pattern established in Rome by ancient Roman senators, who often declared the emperors to be gods.

Chapter 24

Administrative and Ideological Models

At the beginning of the Christian era, the Roman Empire encompassed all the civilized world. The governing system was one of central control from Rome. Provinces throughout the empire reported to Rome. These were subdivided into dioceses and counties, and subsequently into parishes, the units of local government.

Ecclesiastical models of the church were selected from the Brahmanistic hierarchical system, from which the designation of "father" was derived for individual priests.

The Church of the Middle Ages modeled its organization after that of the empire of the Ceasars. In the all-embracing spiritual domain of the Church, Europe was divided into the essential erstwhile imperial organization of the Empire. The provinces originally laid out by Rome, and subdivided into dioceses and parishes, were assumed in the ecclesiastical hierarchy, e.g., an archbishop held jurisdiction over the bishops of the dioceses. In some instances, ecclesiastical boundaries remain the very same as orginally laid out for Roman administration.

Ideologically, Christianity has been founded as much on conflict and militarism as on love and brotherhood. Early Christians bitterly denounced each other when they differed on theological points and practices. New sects developed that taught different beliefs about Jesus. Some insisted that He was God, others that He was only a teacher. The claims of Church leaders and bishops to final authority on the word of Christ and God became the basis for endless conflict, culminating in the Thirty-Year War. Hatred among Christians or the sectarians became the rule. Each group sought converts as even today.

An issue of Life Magazine late in the year 1960, carried a picture of Jewish survivors in a Nazi Concentration Camp. It illustrated the implementation of Eichmann's assignment in the German Reich to annihilate European Jews. Eichmann was proud of his record and outstanding achievement for the Fatherland, in most efficiently exterminating six million of these enemies of the German Reich. His was part of a massive intrigue that resulted in mass murder of one-third of the entire Jewish population. It was the modern Jewish Exodus without the benefit of Yahweh's intervention. This, rather, was the story of lamp shades made of human flesh, of tens of thousands of Jews marching daily to their death, aligning themselves along ditches to be machine-gunned into open mass graves. Here were warehouses filled with rag dolls, shoes, and eye glasses, and the gold fillings knocked from mouths of myriad yawning corpses. These were deals made for the acquiesence of hundreds of thousands of Jews to save a few of the more ruthless of their own. The picture of survivors showed a group of women in slovenly camp uniforms. They were forlorn looking as a group; but a woman at the center of the picture stood barefoot with pained expression. On her face seemed writ the horror and tragedy, and misery and suffering that has indelibly marked the centuries of man's inhumanity to man.

In the busy hurry and scurry of modern life, men still have but little patience for the small annoyances. Slippery roads, the slow moving driver, and the misunderstood mischief of the adolescent easily provoke us to anger. Ideals of brotherhood are not implicity cherished. Occasionally even common courtesy and civility, so necessary for peace among ourselves, are neglected. Rather, we revert to ancient demonology, seeing in others, from lack of personal insight, demons of distrust, suspicion, deliberate vengeance, and acts of malice, albeit there are none except as we may induce these. The greatest meaning for humanity still lies in such simple ideals, whether under titular Christianity or in the name of human dignity. The simple peace and profound satisfaction in deeply human relationships can still penetrate the stuff out of which malice comes. Perhaps, too, if we merely sought a wholesome understanding and equitable relationship with one another, the highest of all religious ideals would be achieved. Yet, Christianity, or the Church, throughout its history seems not to have lighted that eternal spark that could truly set fire to an ideal of universal botherhood. Rather, these historical institutions seem largely to transfer only in title without spawning functional ideals.

The early Christian sect was small. Its locus was the Middle East. Emperor Constantine Augustus adopted it as his personal religion early in the fourth century, This became, perhaps, the singularly most notable event promoting the Church and accelerating its growth throughout the world.

Since the matrix of Rome is of such importance, both organizationally and ideologically, in the history of Christianity, some discussion of the ancient empire may also help to delineate the milieu in which world-wide Christianity was incubated. Some seven or eight hundred years before Christ, several communities were settled about the plains of Latium in Central Italy. The communities were later united under Etruscan rule to form early metropolitan Rome. Rulers in the early days of Rome were severe, tyranically governing the provinces.

Roman history, as religious history, is obscured by mixing of fact and fable. Legend describes Romulus as founding Rome in the year 753 B.C. Pompilius succeeded Romulus. His wife was a nymph named Egeria who traditionally brought god worship to Rome. Hostilius followed Pompilius. Under his rule, Alba Longa, a troublesome Latin city was conquered. Martinus, the next king, brought other neighboring cities under Roman rule. Rome then became a large seaport on the Tiber. The city prospered and grew. Work projects were completed. Beautiful temples and roads were built. Sewage systems were constructed such as the famous Cloaca Maxima sewage system, the ruins of which can still be seen in Rome today.

Rome became a republic in the year 510 B.C. The Brutus Rebellion overthrew King Tarquinius Superbus. It was then a city state with a population of about 150,000. The wealthy "Patricians," politically and economically dominated the "plebians." The plebs slowly gained civil rights, though they were grievously oppressed by wealthy patricians. In 494 B.C., the plebs left Rome as a body threatening to set up a new city. Patricians conceded to the plebs' demand for better representation at the "tribunes."

Economic conflict, however, continued. Land owners strived to maintain ascendence over, and legal control of, the small proprietors. The latter were indebted to the status of slaves. Reforms were slow. Large segments of the population remained impoverished and subservient throughout the whole of Roman history.

Roman wars continued to increase the expanse of the empire. Powerful Etruscia to the north was weakened by battles with Syracuse and the Gauls. Rome moved in and took Etruscia around 200 B.C. In increasing strength, Rome won in battle Latin states and Greek cities throughout Italy. During this period Roman genius had built a unified empire by granting full privileges of citizenship, save voting, to all conquered people. Rome was a militaristic state, a nation of soldiers. She won over Phoenicia of Carthage in a war that lasted nearly 100 years. The character and mettle of sternly devoted Romans brought Rome to victory. At the end of the first century, B.C., Rome ruled most of the civilized world—all of Italy and as far west as Spain and Britain, south to the borders of the Sahara Desert and Egypt at the Red Sea, east to Athens, Greece, Crete, Cyprus, Armenia, Mesopotamia, the land of Israel, and to the borders of Arabia. (See Figure 4).

The republic, once thriving when it conferred citizenship upon the conquered, became increasingly totalitarian. Conquered lands were later administered by governors. Inordinate taxes were wrung from the people. Wealth poured into Rome. A wide class breach developed. Civil war, inspired by individual interests in a struggle for power, marked the final years of the Republic. Then there developed a period of emperor worship beginning with Julius and Augustus Caesar. For a period the empire was again consolidated. Literature and art flourished. Paved roads were built throughout the Mediterranean World from Italy to France, Germany and Britain. During this time, Christianity also began to grow with little interruption, until under Constantine it became the official faith of the Roman Empire.

The luxurious splendor and its softening effect on the Roman character is to what some historians attribute the eventual decay and decline of the empire. Reverence for family, state, and the gods waned. Corruption increased. Patricians gave feasts of unparalleled splendor and surfeit, where vomitoriums were provided with attendants to assist guests in throwing up so they might continue eating. Middle-class backbone of the society disappeared. Only the very idle and extravagant pleasure-seeking rich contrasted with a disemboweled peasantry reduced to serfdom and begging. Rule was absolute with a highly efficient bureaucratic organization. Individualism promoted by the republic that marked the earlier period, was gone, as was the incentive for growth and national survival. A malarial epidemic, and the continuing Christian thrust, were the final episodes leading to the disintegration of the secular empire. Varying degrees of dictatorship were found in the administration of each succeeding emperor: Tiberius, 37 A.D.; Caligula, 41; Claudius, 54; Nero, 68; Vespasian, 79; Domitian, 96; Nerva, 98; Trajan, 117; Pius, 161; and Aurelius, the philosopher king who reigned to 180 A.D. A period of militaristic vying was followed by Emperor Diocletian ascending to the throne in 305 A.D. During the Diocletian period, Rome lost its central importance in the empire. The government was split into east and west, with Augustus ruling to the west. Constantine later transferred the total seat of government to Byzantium in Greece and named it Constantinople. The Byzantine empire in the east continued for several centuries. The western empire at Rome lost both political and military power, falling prey to invading hordes of barbarians. New kingdoms grew out of Roman provinces once making up the empire. France, Italy, and Spain developed autonomy in government. Languages evolved from the old Latin of the Romans. The laws were Roman, and the religion was Christianity, all of which came from Rome. The dominion of Rome became that of religion. Christianity spread throughout the lands that pagan Roman power had first brought together. Rome had earlier aspired to extend the power of the Empire to encompass the civil affairs of the civilized world. The ideal of the church then became to extend Christianity to govern spiritual affairs. Constantine's official act in the Fourth Century, adopting Christianity as the state religion, brought together

Church and State. The once secular empire later became known as the Holy Roman Empire.

Remnants of ancient Rome are both exposed and hidden beneath buildings and houses in Rome today. The famous Colosseum was constructed in 80 A.D., with twenty tiers of seats accommodating 50,000. Here, amid the luxurious dazzle of 3,000 statues, tiers of marble, glass, gilded wood, and precious stones, the emperor and crowds in a Roman holiday watched gladiators and criminals in combat with each other, or with hungry animals. Vast building shells and columns, harking back to days of the Roman bath fad, still stand. Side by side, above or below modern buildings stand the ruins of ancient Rome. These reveal both its advanced culture and the erstwhile extravagances of its emperors. There, too, can be seen the vastly glorifying monuments of the Christian Church of the Vatican, with magnificient structures laid over more than thirteen acres of land, with a thousand halls, chapels and apartments. On one ceiling alone, Michelangelo, during the Renaissance, worked for four years, and Raphael labored in his art for twelve. Visitors see paintings and sculpture that were for centuries exclusively devoted to edifying the Church. On the walls are such images as Augustus, the Emperor who in tradition ordered the census that brought Joseph and Mary to Bethlehem. There is the traditional "Last Supper." The Vatican also houses six separate museums bulging with Christian relics. From this Christian Mecca, the center of ancient Roman power, religious affairs of over one-half billion people have now come to be regulated.

Final years of the Empire were marked by power struggles, widespread, unbridled, primitive sadism, and increasing numbers of untutored, unproductive citizenry. In its last face turned to history, Rome was an efficiently administered bureaucracy, gutted of an effective middle-class. No note-worthy ideological patterns were to emerge among Romans for centuries after Christ. Nor was Christian theology advanced in Rome. Traditionally, as perhaps epitomized by the Curia Romana, Rome has clung to the status quo, doing only what she has been best prepared to do—to administer, and this was the model on which Christianity was based.

IDEOLOGICAL MODELS

Ideological models for Christianity were those of the Greeks. The theology, indeed, was derived from that of Greek soters. Even as late as the 13th century, most venerated of Church philosophers, the Italian Thomas Aquinas, formulated his rational scholasticism based on Grecian ideological postulates. Thomistic philosophy is based wholly on third century B.C. Aristotelian formulations.

In summary, the administrative system of the Roman Catholic Church was inherited by-and-large, from the ancient Romans. The Romans, however, contributed but little ideologically or theologically to Christianity. This doctrinal content was derived largely from the Greeks. Roman tradition has been one of organization. In its declining years, the populace, over which the Church assumed control, was, in the majority, subservient and unlettered. The resultant, a perfunctory Christianity, may yet leave a moral-ethical vacuum where the world still needs to know a religion espousing progressive ideals in human relations.

Chapter 25

Rome and the Roman Church

By the end of the second century A.D., Christians boasted a following larger than any single cult of the period. Christians were frequently militantly proselytizing and politically offensive. The Roman imperial policy was normally one of indulgence toward religion, i.e., any reasonable, untreasonable belief was permitted. Faith was treated largely as a private matter. Christians, however, held to many treasonable elements, openly declaring that the Empire would fall when the savior returned. They would neither worship nor make sacrifices to Roman emperors who had been deified by proclamation. Christians also refused to acknowledge Roman holidays and festivals. Many refused to serve in military service. Some were even considered immoral for breaking up families, (a long-venerated institution in Rome), to serve Christ in the primitive format of the Essenes.

Yet, historically, there is no evidence of extensive discrimination against the Christians. Even Emperor Nero was interested more in finding convenient scapegoats among the unpopular Christian fanatics than in eliminating the cult. Early retaliations against Christians could not be considered persecution, per se, but rather, punitive action taken for acts of vandalism or when the rights of competing cults were violated. The only extensive persecution occurred when Christians employed under Emperor Diocletian were fearful of his successor, Galerius. In a crude attempt to bring Galerius into disfavor with Diocletian, Christians set fire within the palace contriving to fix blame on Galerius. The plot was discovered. Diocletian saw in this clumsy maneuver a vast Christian conspiracy. For a period, from 303 to 305 A.D., it was considered treasonable to be a Christian. (Refer to Eusebeius).

A successor of Diocletian, Constantine, earlier favored the Christian cult as his personal religion. Politically he also saw a major threat to be posed by the Christian movement. The only alternative to complete annihilation of Christians, was integration of the religion into the empire. Concomitant with Constantine's rise was a power struggle with frequent episodes of intrique, in the expedient execution of close relatives including his wife. Christian bishops promised Constantine purification through baptism when becoming Christian. Constantine thenceforth was always accompanied by a priest who was ready to administer baptism should he die. Constantine was thus given impunity in the unscrupulous conduct of his office until his death. His first act as emperor was to issue the Edict of Toleration in 313 A.D., which was rescinded in 325 to make Christianity the imperial religion. In the west it was tax exempt. Legacies, private and public funds were committed to construction and operation of Christian buildings and churches.

Thenceforth, Christian tradition was embellished to provide dramatic emotional appeal. Severus, for example, described "ten persecutions" under emperors from Nero through Diocletian, including such noble and liberal emperors as Marcus Aurelius under whom no record of such persecutions has been found. The conversion of Constantine is also dramatized for such effect. As Constantine went into battle, a fiery cross appeared in the heavens inscribed with the words, "Hoc Signo Vinces." (By this sign shall ye conquer.) Under the cross he conquered for Rome and Christianity. Christians practiced underground burial, in the tradition of Osirians and Mithraists, leaving the body intact to permit the soul free departure. Subterranean Pagan chambers, catacombs, were used to interr Christians in burial vaults. Catacombs later became identified as places of refuge for persecuted Christians.

In the year 305 A.D., Galerius, the man Christians sought to discredit in the eyes of Diocletian, became Emperor. He jointly ruled Rome with Constantine Chlorus. Galerius took the eastern half. When the elder Constantius died in Britain, the troops in Britain and Gaul transferred their allegiance to his son, Constantine, with Galerius retaining control of the east. Constantine's rise gave impetus to the church in the west, when his celebrated son converted to Christianity. This cleavage in control between west and east was the precursor of the major church division to come. A later eastern emperor, Theodosius, withdrew government support of pagan temples. In close ties with a priest of the Eastern Church, Ambrose, he made Christianity the sole and official religion in the east. Christianity, after three centuries, gained major impetus in both eastern and western empires. Through this extensive political favoritism, and the fanaticism of zealous Christian martyrs, Christianity was saved from the obscurity that proved to be the fate of myriad other salvation cults in Rome. Now there can be no doubt that the vast military power and secular organization of Rome predated Christianity, and implemented its world-wide import.

Ancient Romans have been described as creators of the home. Centuries before Christ, the stout fabric of the patriarchal Roman family instilled manliness and self-control in male children. This strength of character produced dutiful citizens who revered the home and nation with a firmness of discipline that molded the stolid character of Rome. Perhaps it was to reinforce the family and nation that women of Rome intuitively turned to Christianity, to an ostensibly family-bound religion of the Jews.

What had once been a great Roman republic of sturdy hardworking farmers and plebians became an empire where hoards of unemployed and soldiers returning from Roman wars petitioned the government for food and entertainment. Slave labor and military contracts spawned vast numbers of profiteers and fortune hunters. By the first century A.D., the great Roman Republic had already lost its greatness. Emperor Julius Caesar instituted despotism in full dictatorial authority. Some in the senate, such as Brutus, aspiring to maintain the republic, plotted the death of Caesar. The assassination of Julius did nothing more than perpetuate Caesarian rule, with Octavian through Tiberius, Claudius, Caligula, and Nero. The monarchy continued through the Flavian imperial line to the Antonines, becoming firmly entrenched by the time of the beneficent philosopher-king, Marcus Aurelius. After the assassination of Aurelius around 200 A.D., the empire became rent by internal strife and barbarian wars. A brief period of restoration seemed evident under Diocletian and Constantine, but eventual decadence was inevitable. Absence of a fixed imperial lineage, loss of a strong central authority, and the lack of leadership and discipline in the armies under attack by barbarian hordes, brought quick demise to the secular empire. State militias were mobilized and independent territorial governors assumed rule, as in Britain and Spain. Disintegration of the secular empire is attributable to multiple causal conditions. Economically, only a small few possessed the wealth in large estates, maintaining slave labor and subservient tenants. Vast numbers of unemployed demanded government support. Coinage values became erratic. Industry was stilted. Commerce declined. The provinces lent inequitable support in taxes and received little or nothing from the central government. An unnatural caste system was imposed by Constantine, who decreed that all tradesmen should be bound to their trade as should their children and childrens' children who were to wed and breed only among those of the caste.

Decay of the empire cannot be ascribed to singularly causative responsible events as is sometimes implied. Was it the graft of an entrenched bureaucracy, unscrupulous political vying, breakdown of productive and patriotic strivings of a healthy middle class, or limited dissemination of educational benefits to an elite few? Was it massive ignorance in over-populated urban areas that yielded a helpless hopeless mass of common men? Was it that half the population was forced into slavery status? Was it bureaucratic absolutism and literally frozen social statuses, and the loss of individual liberty? Was it interbreeding with the barbarians? Did decline occur, as Christians hold, through the corruption of morals and widespread licentiousness? Was poor morale and mass psychological depression responsible? Was it just that things came too easily, that wealth and culture were imported, and the typical Roman became self-indulgent, indolent, and self-satisfied? The historian Arnold Toynbee suggests that Rome lacked challenge, purpose, and the freedom of self-criticism fundamental to the growth and development of a citizen or nation. The zeitgeist of decaying Rome was a kind of sophisticated sadism. All citizens, from Emperor to unemployed plebian, relished the free entertainment provided in the great ampitheaters and arenas. The sports were brutal and inhumane.

Chariot racing was most subdued, but during a single day twenty to thirty gruelling races were held. A wild, unruly crowd of 50,000 filled stadia, such as the Circus Maximus, gambling on each race. Most popular were gladiatorial contests. Large numbers of assorted beasts—lions, tigers, or panthers—would be set loose into the colosseum. Gladiators would enter to slay them or be slain. Dead gladiators and animal carcasses were dragged out, and in would drive chariots with death duels of the drivers. Blood was spewed throughout the day. The contest of retiarii and thracians were lightly clad, nimble netters with a three-pronged lance, versus heavily armored warriors armed with huge swords. The netters danced and cast their nets about the helmeted heads of the Thracians. Crowds wagered on the victory of the agile netter or a death blow of the lumbering Thracian. They fought for hours on end and blood was spewed throughout the day. Scores of gladiators died in each day of dueling, and crowds of men and women shouted in animal-like hysteria, "Occide! Occide!" ("Kill! Kill!") A scarred gladiator, skilled and trained in a school of gladiatorial art, may have enjoyed moments of idol worship by the women of Rome, but his ultimate destiny was death in the arena. All Roman citizens eagerly attended these contests of bloodletting and massacre, so vividly dramatizing the unpretentious cruelty of the Roman character of this period. A public spectacle was also made of a criminal's death in such arenas. He would be confronted by a huge lion with only a small sword to defend himself. As criminals, frequently, Christians were so punished.

Within a climate of failing nationalism, dwindling prestige of the secular empire and a degutted citizenry indulged in unbridled sadism, Christianity made its thrust. The disciple Paul preached in scores of urban centers throughout the empire from Jerusalem to Antioch, from Thessalonica, Athens, and Corinth to Rome. He strengthened the churches by frequent letters to the converts. They, in turn, became as zealous as he. Through the aggressive proselytizing of these converts, an extensive church organization was formed. The Christian Churches became zealously militant, absolute and unwavering. The competitive cults were fiercely denounced, while the abject massochistic martyrism of many of the Christians also led the Romans to be more tolerant. Galerius issued the Eastern Edict of Toleration in 311A.D. In 313, the Edict of Milan was issued, which under Constantine, became the Edict of Legalization of Christianity in the West. Emperor Theodosis, in the Eastern Empire, also made it the state religion. By the middle of the fourth century, the Empire was forcefully swept clean of pagan alters.

Politically-minded clergy espoused the doctrine of the "Second Coming" to prepare a hierarchy for the long wait. Church Elders were first appointed. Later church "bishops" were designated, based on a title coming from high office in Roman municipal government. Elders (or presbyters), stewards and recorders of the Church were all subservient to bishops. Within a century a bishop headed every Church region. Large urban areas appointed "Archbishops" to regulate Church affairs in dogma. The administrative divisions of the Roman Empire were then assumed, i.e., provinces and dioceses.

Christian proselytizing in Greece resulted in fusion with Greek philosophies. Christian theology became systematized. The New Testament was written. The "Apostolic Church" creed was formulated from the "rock" or "cave" precepts of Mithraism. Petrine (meaning rock) became "Peter," the favorite apostle of Jesus, who nominally became the chief bishop of Rome. Eventually this became tradition, in the designation of a papal lineage originating with Peter. By the end of the seventh century the Roman bishopric was recognized as the Western "Christian Emperor." A creed was formalized at the Council of Nicene, when such controversies as the trinitarian were resolved. When Emperor Constantine first called for a Council of Bishops in 325 A.D., differences in dogma were extensive. In the conference, a dogma was drafted which was to become that of the Church, as even today:

" . . . I believe in one Lord Jesus Christ, the only begotten Son of God, begotten of the Father before all Worlds, God of God, Maker of Heaven and Earth, and all things visible and invisible, Light of Light, very God of very God, begotten, not made, being of one substance with the Father by whom all things were made, who, for us men, and for our salvation, came down from heaven, and was incarnate by the Holy Ghost of the Virgin Mary, and was made man, crucified for us under

Pontius Pilate; He suffered and was buried; on the Third Day, He arose again, according to the scriptures, and ascended into Heaven and sitteth on the Right Hand of God; and He shall come again, with glory, to judge the quick and the dead, whose Kingdom shall have no end . . . "

In the last two centuries of the Roman Empire the government had become bureaucratic and distant. Traditional religions, such as the Dionysian, Apolloian, Epicurean, and Stoic, with their theologies and ceremonies, failed to satisfy the great masses. Religious feeling degenerated. A new emotionally congenial and universal belief system was essential to solidarity. Romans had turned more and more to the Middle Eastern cults of Cybele, Isis, Osiris, Sol and Mithra. Roman worship was highly formalized, controlled, impersonal and prosaic. The new cults brought in personal elements, centered about the individual, his salvation, and a blessed after life. It was from these elements that Christianity evolved.

Elements of the Christian creed had been almost universal in the tradition of Middle Eastern pagan cults. Minor politico-theological controversies were evident, but the creed was essentially that of the pagans. Some preferred Christ to be God, while others thought of Him as the Son of God. The Greeks, whose basic theological material was adopted in Christianity, were steeped in mythological traditions. Their country was at the center of the world. At the apex was Mount Olympus where the gods lived. Far off from the land of Greece was the Isle of the Blest where good people were taken at death for eternal life. This they achieved by being patrons of the gods: Jupiter, king of the gods; Juno, Queen of Heaven; Apollo, god of sun, medicine, music and poetry; Venus, goddess of beauty, laughter and marriage; Neptune, god of the waters; Pluto, god of hell. The gods fell in love, hated, suffered pain and anger, sought pleasure and became jealous as did human beings. Half-gods like Hercules, and ordinary human beings, were also worshipped as gods. Many things had become sacred to the Greeks, including words. Words, they reasoned, were unchanging. The meanings of words had substance. Such words as "courage", "love," "loyalty," and "faith" seemed to stand for a pure abstract state that had a complete and independent existence apart from communication. Such a tradition of word usage continues today. We hear such word usages as, "God is Love . . . Faith, Hope and Charity, and the greatest of these is Charity . . . " All of these nouns, in tradition, stand for unchanging, abstract entities that exist for all time.

Bishop Athanasius saw such absolutism in the formulations of the Nicene doctrine to which, he insisted, Christians must rigidly adhere, lest other cults distort Christianity and change it to conform with their own beliefs. Christ was the one life in which God completely revealed Himself. He was the goodness of God in the form of a servant appearing in the likeness of man.

The Church dogma was chiefly developed from the 3rd to 5th centuries by such Greeks as Origen, Athanasius and Basil. Ambrose and Jerome dominated Roman theology. Jerome translated the New Testament books from Greek into Latin. This Roman version, the "Vulgate," continues as the official version for the Roman Catholic Church. The Bishop Augustine, an African of Latin stock, also crystallized many theological precepts in his work, *The City of God.*

The Rituals developed were taken from the basic pagan cults. The Last Supper was made a liturgical rite suffused with pagan symbolism. Mass and baptism were purification rites. Veneration of saints, penance and confession were gradually introduced developing out of the old religions. The Church became the intermediary, indispensable for patronizing God, and the only means by which Christian and pagan alike could gain passage to the "Isle of the Blest."

Early Christian converts came from all ranks of Roman life. The Christianity to which the Romans subscribed, however, was extensively modified from that of Christian Jews. Hebrew tribal laws were severe and demanding. Their God was jealous and provincial. Bound as they were in the rigid tradition of Yahweh, no quarter was given to heretics, who were stoned or driven over cliffs. The death of Jesus was contrived for his heresy. Stephen was stoned when attempting to disrupt the code. Paul lived in constant danger, saved only by being a Roman citizen as well as Jew. The Gospel Jesus originated in, or bore marked resemblence to, Essenic doctrine. The Essenes were a persecuted minority who taught forebearance. Modern psychologists describe such behavior as a "reaction formation." And today the earth still inherits the meek. Among the Essenes and in the Gospel Jesus there was unity through a communistic code. This was not the nucleus of Christian idealism that eventually spread to Rome, thence throughout the Occident. The Church in Rome compromised with paganism. After Constantine's victory over the Eastern Empire, with the seat of secular power set up in the East, the power of the clergy in Rome was then unimpeded. The Church hierarchy was provincially subordinate not even to the emperor. Scores of bishops served in the hierarchy. At the top were five Church Fathers known as "Popes" (Latin, father).

The secular empire continued to hold sway in the East. There the Patriarch Chrysostom, who officially set the date for Christmas based on Mithraic tradition, preached on primitive Christianity, the blessing of being poor, and the folly of wealth. Such a position against the secular values in the East became the eventual cause for the banishment of Chrysostom. Even in the Eastern Empire, however, secular authorities feared the Church. They believed, as in the West, that the Church mediated with God. Emperor Theodosius, in blind fury, had ordered an indiscriminate killing of thousands of people in the amphitheater of Thessalonica. A protesting crowd had killed the arresting officer of a favorite chariot driver. The races went on, but Theodosius had sent soldiers in angry retribution. They plunged swords indiscriminately into everyone they came upon in the amphitheater. Later Emperor Theodosius attempted to attend church in Milan. His friend, the Patriarch Ambrose, stood at the door of the Cathedral. "Your hands are smeared with blood, and you come to the House of the Lord. Go and clean yourself!" Theodosius repented.

Emperors in the East were reverent. They were not subservient. In the West the ascendency of the Church grew over the secular empire. There later appeared the forged document, "Donation of Constantine," in which it was claimed that, at the baptism of Constantine by Pope Sylvester in 326, control and rule of the empire was awarded to the vicar of Christ, the Roman Catholic Pope, to rule supreme over all the earth.

Suggested Further Reading

1. Althein, F. *A History of Roman Religion* 1938
2. Atwater, D. *The Christian Churches of the East* 1949
3. Asch, S. *The Apostle* 1943
4. Barrow, R. *The Romans* 1949
5. Burnet, J. *Greek Philosophy* 1960
6. Carcopino, J. *Daily Life in Ancient Rome* 1940
7. Cary, M. *History of Rome* 1935
8. Cullmann, O. *Peter: Disciple, Apostle, Martyr* 1953
9. Deane, H. *The Political and Social Ideas of St. Augustine* 1963
10. Diehl, C. *Byzantium: Greatness and Decline*
11. Enslin, M. *The Prophet from Nazareth* 1961
12. Eusebius *Life of Constantine*
13. Frazer, J. *The New Golden Bough* 1961
14. Hamilton, E. *The Greek Way to Western Civilization* 1942
15. Hamilton, E. *Mythology* 1940
16. Jones, H. *Studies in Roman Government and Law* 1960
17. Latourette, K. *History of the Expansion of Christianity* 1945
18. Lavender, L. *A Thousand Ages* 1962
19. Lebreton, J. and Zeiller, J. *The History of the Primitive Church* 1949
20. Lucas, H. *A Short History of Civilization* 1953
21. McSorley, J. *Outline History of the Church by Centuries* 1943
22. Muller, M. *Sacred Books of the East*
23. Pieper, J. *Guide to Thomas Acquinas* 1962
24. Robinson, C. *Selections From the Greek and Roman Historians*
25. Rose, H. *Ancient Roman Religion* 1949
26. Rose, H. *Ancient Greek Religion* 1946
27. Severus *Sacred History*
28. White, E. *Why Rome Fell* 1927

VI

The Tri Christian World

After decay of the secular Roman Empire in the west, the Church grew more insistent, claiming power and authority to control the very lives and thinking of men. Theology tightened and solidified, and priests labeled even skepticism as heresy punishable by death. Thus, the most extensive theocracy in history, compared even to that of Islam or Brahmanism, enveloped virtually all the Occident.

The secular stronghold of the Eastern Empire continued until the seventh century, when Islam swept through the east and challenged all that was sacred in Christendom. In the east, Christians traditionally differed from those of the west in claims of authority, on fine points of theology, and in rites and practices; most of all, they contested supremacy of the western pope. Then others, emerging from the side of western Christianity itself, began to dispute papal claims. Dissidence, conflict, cruelty, and mass murder reigned in Christ's name for centuries. Today this traditional conflict is still with us; we are deeply religious people divided three ways.

These developments are briefly reviewed here.

Chapter 26

Christian Political Dissension

During the 20th century Catholic Ecumenical Council in Rome (1965), final chapters of schema were drafted on Christian unity. Several compromises were made purporting to achieve good Catholic relations with Orthodox, Anglican, and Protestant churches. One such, for example, was that Catholics were henceforth allowed to receive certain sacraments in the Eastern Churches, but not in the Anglican nor Protestant.

These latter Roman Catholic views are perhaps classical, for some recognition has always been given the Eastern Church; but it was in bitterness, and veritable bloodshed, that Protestants and Anglicans broke away from Roman Catholicism. The falling away from the Roman Papacy, and, at times, the vehement condemnation of the heresy by Rome, and of Roman bigotry by protesting Christians, became the titular cause for armed conflict, and of vicious personal attacks and retaliation. This has been built into our Christian-pagan tradition, but has perhaps become obscured by shame and guilt. Yet, the traces of these hostile relations are still evident.

The Roman and Orthodox Churches were first to find major differences in their political and theological expediency. After Constantine, the breach between east and west widened. The western Church grew in strength and influence, while, at the same time the control of the secular emperor there weakened. The picture was thus one of a strong church in the west, and an imperial empire weakened in waning nationalism.

The church in the east, on the other hand, was much less influential. The Roman Empire there retained its political-nationalistic spirit for many centuries. This comparative situation is evident today, where the Roman Catholic population, obedient

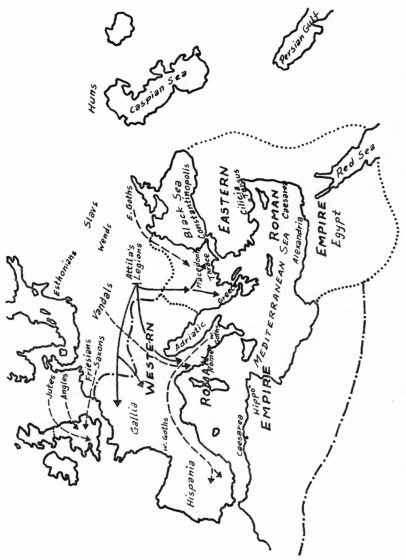

Fig. 7. Divisions of the Roman Empire and Barbarian Intermingling (5th Century A.D.)

to the pope, outnumbers that of the Eastern Church, under several separate patriarchs, by a ratio of more than four to one.

The 11th century brought a final break between the Roman Church and the Church of Constantinople. The churches then became independently identified as the Roman Church of the West, and the Orthodox Church of the East.

Translations of the new testament from Greek into Latin, for Romans, changed word meanings. Eventually, practices also began to differ. East and west church leaders antagonized each other with theological bickering; popes of Rome and patriarchs of Constantinople vied in claims for the highest authority.

From the time of the early Hebrews, idol worship had been discouraged. Christians, however, began anew to make and worship statues and paintings of their martyrs and saints, and of the apostles, and Mary and Jesus. The faithful knelt and prayed before these.

"They worship mute stone idols," observed Jews and Mohammedans, "yet theirs is a superior religion—this Christianity."

Bishops of both the Eastern and Western Churches were against idol-worshipping practices, and attempted to discourage them. The Constantinople Patriarch could bring little influence to bear against the power of the emperor, and the whims of wives of rich citizens who desired these images in the church. For a time, prior to the period of Pope Gregory, the Church in the west checked such practices in its political superiority.

European hordes of Goths, Huns, Gauls, Danes, Franks, etc., later to establish the Kingdoms of England, Spain, France and Germany, were converted to Christianity under the influence of the Western Church. (See Figure 7) Power of the Western Church continued to grow and dwarf that of the Church in the east.

In the 6th century the Prophet Mohammed inspired massive numbers in the east. Not unlike the Christians, the Mohammedans zealously sought converts. The "Flaming Sword of the Desert" cut its way to the west and conquered the sacred city of the Christians, Jerusalem. Jerusalem was where Jesus the Nazarene preached and died. The Mohammedans desecrated His sacred land and His very name. Itinerant preachers, such as Peter the Hermit, rallied the French to form an army to retake Jerusalem.

The sins of all would be forgiven. In the Eleventh, Twelfth and Thirteenth centuries, throughout the Christian world, thousands joined the armies of the Crusaders, recruited from among those believing themselves to be sinners, or those believing that the Mohammedans sinned against God and must be destroyed, or some who sought the freedom and adventure of armed conflict, or still others seeking secular power; and even non-Christian pagans joined the crusading armies for the sheer thrill of battle.

Several Crusade armies, under papal sanction, departed to battle for Jerusalem in the Twelfth and Thirteenth centuries. The city was repeatedly won and lost over this period. Those who perhaps suffered most, however, were the Christians of the east in the Orthodox Church. Crusaders, marching to Jerusalem, demanded and requisitioned food and housing from those whose lands they passed through. During their sojourn in these lands it was claimed that they also attempted to negate the Church of Constantinople and usurp its authority with that of the Church of Rome. The Greek Orthodox Church leaders accused many leaders of the Crusades with plots against the Orthodox Church, under the guise of marching for the cause of Jerusalem.

The Crusades failed, both in vanquishing the Mohammedans, and in uniting East with West; but gross evils arose in the practice of Indulgences. Sins and past sins, even of the dead, were forgiven those who joined the Crusades. Centuries following the Crusades, these became lucrative and highly commercialized practices, and served as a major source of income for the Church. (Even today, for example, such vestiges remain as the sale of mass cards for the deceased.)

The Church of Rome had thus grown and spread its influence throughout Europe. Missionaries were constantly being sent out from Rome to convert pagans. As the Pope's authority became supreme, he decreed laws, and wrote encyclicals of instruction. Popes were elected by a College of Cardinals in the hierarchy. Once elected, a pope had absolute power to write or re-write the laws of the land. He often decreed that given portions of everyone's earnings be paid to the church. In pre-Reformation Germany, approximately only one out of every six in the population worked and produced. The remainder belonged to religious orders, of the contemplative variety, who did little but sing and pray. The heavy financial burden fell upon the working peasants, who were a very small minority,

The very lives and thinking of Christians were controlled and regulated. Communicants were told what they could or could not read, what absolutely they must believe, under coersion and threat of severe punishment here and in the hereafter. Many objected to making payments to the Church; some chose to read what the Church forbade, or not to observe the proclaimed holidays. These were declared to be crimes against God and the State, and the offenders were arrested, tried, and punished; but the numbers of dissenters grew, as had the number of Christians increased under earlier secular Roman rule against the dictates of the emperor. With an ever increasing number of rebellious Christians, the Church began a series of intense and severe conversion programs. During the 13th century, conversion by force began, and dissenters were officially punished. This became known as the "Inquisition." The methods of the Inquisition were severe and inhumane, as were those of the earlier Romans almost a thousand years before. Those who refused to accept the ways and reasons of the Church were burned alive, or crushed to death with heavy weights, or torn apart by specially designed instruments. Many were non-Christians, but Christians too suffered the same punishment when refusing to accept mandates of the Church, or when speaking against the pope. Resentment increased, and the rebellious grew in number until in the 15th century a new and systematic affront to the Roman Church began, and spread within its own hierarchy.

Chapter 27

Early Christian Forms and Conflict

Authoritative literature on the Gospel Jesus began to appear around 200 A.D., including the *Second Clement, Justin Martyr,* and the Synoptics. The Church based its authority on faith in the Old Testament and in the prophecy of Christ. Followers of the apostles of Jesus became deacons, presbyters and bishops of the Church, inheriting the alleged power given the apostles, "to bind and loose on earth and in heaven."

Before the third century, the Church possessed a complete canon consisting of diverse documents. Hebrew, Latin, Egyptian, Ethiopic, Armenian, and other bible versions of the canon all differed. The enigma of such contradictions prompted Justin Martyr to pronounce the basic Christian dogma that no scripture is to be understood to contradict another.

Records existing prior to the development of printing were hand-written. The earliest Saxon version was written in the seventh century. In the 14th century the bible was translated into German. Later it appeared in the various languages of Europe including Danish, Swedish and French. The bible was first printed in England in the year 1538. Later, in 1560, it was divided into verses. It was later revised under Henry VIII, again under Queen Elizabeth, and finally under King James. The latter version was published in 1611 and is the most widely used bible among English-speaking Protestants.

The diverse versions of Christian history reflect the breaches in interpretation that led to later disputes and conflicts, and eventual development of sectarianism. The early church doctrine had developed as an eclectic expediency. *The Church fathers conceded to every important group those compromises necessary to insure allegiance of the converts where such compro-*

mises would not alienate other equally powerful and important groups. This became the early mark and measure in the success and growth of the Church. The process was reinforced by demanding obedience and severely punishing heresy from whatever theological or philosophical sources it originated. Epistles of Ignatius declared that all members of the Church are subject to their bishops as they are to the commands of God. Tertullian wrote that heretics must be opposed by refusing them any discussion of scriptures. "Truth," according to Tertullian, was only that which agreed with the Apostolic Church, that was received from the Apostles, the Apostles from Christ, and Christ from God. Cyprian declared that heresy arose from disobedience to God's priests. The early concessions made in development, together with demands for strict obedience, laid dormant the potential conflict that later erupted into sectarianism.

Christianity inherited from eastern cultures, particularly Judaism and Brahmanism, an intense drive for absolute and statelike control. (cf., theocratic insistence evident in the Old Testament and in the Manichaean practices inherited from the east) In the early church the cardinal sin was one of ignoring authority of the Church. Dissenters were severely dealt with. Earlier divergencies condemned as heretical were the Jews—the Ebonites, the Simonians and Cerinthians. The major Jewish heresy was, of course, in emphasis upon the Jewish heritage of Jesus with lineage traceable to David, Moses and Adam. The Gnostic heresy in the second century was Greek. The Greeks Cerdo and Marcion taught that Christ was the "word" that the Supreme God sent to Judea, i.e., an apparition in the form of Christ. This was an attempt by Platonically oriented Greeks to develop a consistent theology, to expunge the Jewish fleshy heritage. The Gnostic heresy, too, was vigorously denounced by the Church after 325.

Countless heresies arose, so defined because they failed to meet the practical exigencies of the Church and its developing dogma —the Valentinians rejected the Jewish God; the Pythagorians espoused sacredness of numbers; the Manichaeans held to a Zoroastrian dualism. From the latter heretical sect, however, Christians adopted several practices and disciplines, such as the unmarried priesthood and prevenient grace. In the heresy of the Arians, the divinity of Christ was denied. The Macedonians, or Pneumato-machi, declared the Holy Spirit as simply divine energy diffused throughout the universe, and not a person. The Marcellians held that the existence of the Son began with His human birth. Then, the other extreme, the Apollonarians, denied the human character of Jesus. The Nestorians refuted the divinity of Mary as mother of God. The Monothelites taught that Jesus was but one will, one energy and an exclusive spirit. In the midst of such conflicting dogma, Tertullian, a third century priest, coined the word "Monarchian" seeking to establish Christianity as an uncompromising monotheism. There was but one God, but at the same time the divinity of Christ was maintained. Christianity claimed a supreme God whose unity could not be questioned. Too, Jesus Christ could be nothing less than God or His atonement could not be sufficient for salvation. The enigma, (logically unresolved to this day) was this: How could Christ and the Father both be God without breaking His unity. The resolution of this enigma in the seventh-century Athanasian Creed became the substance of the Christian faith, a dogma in final resolve that was built on compromise over the bodies of tens of thousands of heretics flushed from the core of the creed. Over the centuries such heretics have been condemned, excommunicated, anathematized and assassinated for taking exception to the main stream of a developing creed that has since been zealously defended by the traditionally conservative elements of the Catholic Church. Following are listed several councils recorded over the Centuries that have acted on heresies in defense of the dogma:

1. (325) The Nicean Council condemned the Arian heresy.
2. (381) The First Constantinople Council defended Catholic doctrine against the troublesome Arian heresy and refuted Apollonarianism. The Nicene Creed was also completed.
3. (431) The Council of Ephesus decreed the Virgin Mary to be Mother of God.
4. (451) The Council of Chalcedon declared papal supremacy, and defined the nature of the soter.
5. (553) The Second Council of Constantinople condemned the Nestorian heresy.

6. (690-91) The Third Council of Constantinople condemned Pope Honorius I for his failure to reject the monothelite heresy.

7. (787) The Second Nicean Council condemned iconoclasm which opposed the use of images in the church.

8. (869) The Fourth Council of Constantinople affirmed the Catholic religion to lie in communion with the Holy See.

9. (1123) The First Lateran Council approved the Condordat of Worms and banned marriages of churchmen.

10. (1139) The Second Lateran Council condemned and banished Arnold of Brescia for inciting the people against the bishopric.

11. (1179) The Third Lateran Council condemned Albigensians who taught the evil of flesh and the goodness of the spirit, and the Waldensians who preached against Church property. Rules for bishops were also established requiring them to be at least 30 years old, of legitimate birth.

12. (1215) The Fourth Lateran Council established the dogma of incarnation and the presence of Christ in the Eucharist, banned new religious orders and required a minimum of one yearly confession and communion of all communicants.

13. (1245) The Council of Lyons excommunicated Frederick II Barbarossa.

14. (1274) The Second Council of Lyons alledgedly reunited the East and West Churches. This was later repudiated.

15. (1311-12) The Council of Vienne, France, censured the order of Knights Templars, and reformed the clergy.

16. (1414-18) The Council of Constance condemned the heresies of John Wycliff who claimed scriptures alone to be sufficient, denying the power of the Holy See; John Huss was outlawed for proposing to abolish the liturgy, and adopting communistic and promiscuous sexual practices among his followers.

17. (1431-43) The Council of Basle, Ferra, Florence and Rome, compromised with Hussites. Reunion with Greek Orthodox, Armenian and Coptic Churches, was decreed. This was later repudiated.

18. (1512-17) The Fifth Lateran Council outlined papal jurisdiction over Councils. Church jurisdiction over pawnshops was decreed.

19. (1545-65) The Council of Trent declared war on Protestantism. The hierarchy of the church was reorganized and new dogmas were established covering original sin, purgatory, veneration of saints, indulgences, Church discipline, morals and canon law.

20. (1869-70) The First Vatican Council pronounced papal infallibility.

21. (1962-65) The Second Vatican Council attempted to resolve points of the dogma and practices most unacceptable within and outside the Church.

It is perhaps now difficult to imagine the intensity of conflict coming from the early theological controversies. Thousands of wild-eyed fanatics could be incited at any moment to attack violently the adherence to a different formulary. The meaning of the vague differences were understood by none, but all were convinced that temporal and eternal wellbeing depended upon precise terms of respective dogma. Mobs in Alexandria, Antioch, and Constantinople were incited by monks and priests to assault the opposing religious faction, looting, destroying and killing. The rage enveloped priests and laymen alike (cf., Arian vs Orthodox factions in the massacres of fourth-century Antioch). As the Roman Church grew in power such theological conflict became more in the nature of persecution. The Edict of Toleration, issued under Emperor Constantine in 313, at first proclaimed the right of any to worship their gods as they chose. In 325 this edict was rescinded. Christianity was adopted as the imperial religion. Christian clergy became exempt from taxes and military service. The Church became heir to unclaimed properties of the deceased. Other cults were forthwith outlawed, with their temples and places of worship converted to Christian temples. In 383, Bishop Gregory Nazianzen decreed that allowing pagan worshipers to practice their faith was tantamount to conceding to the truth of their views. During this period, tenets of philosophies were crushed. It was decreed that all follies of earthly wisdom be dispelled. The "most blessed Peter" was appointed citadel of the Roman Empire, to assume the power of the throne of the Caesars. In the power of the papacy, it was pronounced that the devil was busily engaged in contaminating Christian minds for which he employed legions of heretics. The task of all good Christians became to identify and destroy all heretics who practiced in the company of the devil.

The Roman world had enfolded a major portion of the Occident into a single political entity. It was through this comprehensive administrative control, too, that the state religion of Christianity was able to exact its control over all the Occident. Otherwise each sovereignty would surely have developed its own national religion, with a Roman Christian international priesthood becoming impossible. There were, for example, Arians in Antioch and Alexandria who exiled the Christian priest Athanasius and burned the Christian baptistry. In 390, the Christian Bishop Theophilus ordered the razing of the Temple of Serapeum in Alexandria. This enraged the pagans who defended the shrine with every bit of the fanaticism of the Christians. The Christian campaign against Manichaeans continued for decades. In 443, Pope Leo finally decreed that throughout Italy, the Manichees (as well as free-thinkers) be deprived of all rights and privileges, and suffer the death penalty if they refused to convert.

A brief period of toleration was introduced during the reign of Emperor Julian during the mid 4th century in the empire to the east. Jews and pagans enjoyed a measure of freedom, but this too was short-lived. Theodosius acceded to the throne of the Eastern Empire. During his reign, suppression and terror was the lot of non-Christians. Violent punishment and massacre befell all those who opposed Christian theology. Christians drove the Jews from Alexandria early in the 5th century. In the year 443, Pope Leo issued a circular to Italian bishops instituting the banishment of Manichaeans. Heretics were hunted out, their properties confiscated and, if adamantly refusing conversion, the death penalty was dealt. Pope Gelasius published the first index of forbidden books in 496. This served subsequently to destroy all remnants of Greek culture and of the healthy skepticism that had given Greece its golden age. It became a kind of institutionalization of ignorance that is with us even today, in Mariolatry, the uncritically encysting of pagan superstition into Christian culture, the belief in the magic of sacred medallions and scapula, of the Manichaean-Zoroastrian doctrine of purgatory, and of the celibate priesthood.

Generous support of the Church was first instituted by Constantine giving special privileges and grants to the clergy. This also established the prestige and the Brahmanistic-priestlike status still enjoyed by the Christian clergy. The Church became increasingly involved in a kind of power politics, and, with this, the increasing acquisition of wealth. In fact, it became so extensively involved in secular affairs that the behavior of the opulent clergy glaringly belied the Gospel of Jesus. The Gospel in the Books of the New Testament, until recently, has been at the top of the proscribed list to prevent such inconsistencies from becoming evident. It was indeed punishable by death to read or possess a copy of the Bible, lest the enormity of the Gospel incongruity become evident.

a. Pre-cursors of the Reformations

Augustine

Before the turn of the 5th century, one of the giants of the Catholic Church was born. He was an African, a Latin, at first a pagan, and a man of rare genius who in another time and place may well have contributed truly monumental work to the progress of mankind.

Augustine had been a Manichee for almost ten years before converting to Roman Christianity. Later appointed bishop of Hippo, Augustine sought to solidify Christian theology through the scriptures. He rejected such practices as in the use of amulets, relics, or charms, or the indulgences. He cited no creed, nor did he revere the Roman See, or ecumenical authority. For Augustine, the scriptures remained the ultimate authority, with reason determining their meaning. He met with strong logical opposition (though much personal misgiving), the Pelagian heresy, which held that human nature was basically good. Being once himself a rogue and sexually licentious, Augustine embraced the total doctrine of Pauline sexual wickedness. The Donatist heresy or schism he declared invalid, holding that purity was unnecessary to administer the sacraments. This came only from the Grace of God. He persuaded the western Emperor Honorius to take military action against the Donatists after the Council of Carthage in which headstrong Donatist and Catholic Bishops could agree on nothing. Ostensibly a champion of the Catholic Church, Augustine laid the theological foundation for the Protestant revolution. On baptism he held that the ministrant need not be a man of the Church, for the act cleanses in its own right. In his determination to ascribe this and the other sacraments to Christ, he inadvertently took them from the Catholic Church, thus laying the theological basis for Protestantism.

Early in the 5th century, a mild British monk named Pelagius had arrived in Rome to attract but little attention. He was both a Christian monk and an analytical thinker who could not easily accept the doctrine of human depravity as being consistent with the theory of free will. Pelagius had formulated an independent theology in which he held that Adam was the source only of our bodies. Each soul he considered as a new creation without sin. Heaven was thus attainable without baptism. As a creature of God, man was basically good and could achieve atonement through the gospel ethics as well as faith.

Pelagius was a timid man. When called to answer for his heresy, he evaded and denied the charges. But his formulations had already influenced the churchly protagonist Augustine who, in correspondence with Jerome, wrote, "When we come to the penal sufferings of infants, I am embarrassed, believe me, by great difficulties, and am wholly at a loss to find an answer by which they are resolved."

From these earlier theological enigmas, from the heresies of the Arians, the Pelagians, and the Marcellians, and the inadvertent undercurrents of rebellion in Augustinian theology, the substance of 16th century Protestantism had begun to take shape. At the Council of Orange in 539, superficial aspects of Augustinianism were adopted as Church dogma. The underlying theses of Augustine, in the blind age of the Church, would not be examined scrupulously, nor exploited in new theologies, for nearly a thousand years. During the interim period, a kind of stagnancy settled over the theological world, with a reawakening coming only with Protestant enlightenment.

CHRISTIAN CONFLICT

b. A Thousand Years of Trivia

The period of the "dark ages," which lasted nominally for a thousand years, is seen as an era of an almost complete stall in scientific and technological progress. It can, in fact, be considered to have been a serious withdrawal of humanity from the pursuit of happiness. We can look to no one, for example, in the 8th century, for an item of astronomy, an advancement in medicine, an innovation in physics, or anything but triteness in philosophy. With the rise and ascendence of Christian dogma, a proportional decline of this-worldly pursuits and ideals began.

Buddhistic elements of renunciation gained in popularity, as did celibacy in the western Church. As late as the 3rd century a celibate priesthood had been condemned in both Eastern and Western Churches. Under Augustinian influence, from the 5th to the 7th centuries, celibacy became mandatory. It was decreed at the Council of Chalcedon in 451, and then again at the Council of Trullo in 692.

Civil law became replaced with church canon, and the secular penal system with penance. Homicide, for example, was punished by exclusion from the sacrament for 20 years with the penitant required to weep for four years, to pray among the kneelers for seven and stand among the faithful for eleven. An adulterer was committed to such penance for 15 years, a thief for two. One who was actively incestuous was also required to do penance for 20 years. Those who denied Christ and repented, were condemned to weep throughout their lives, to receive the sacrament only on their deathbed.

The Christian priesthood had largely derived from Manichaean influence, which was in turn, modeled after Indian Brahminism. The conflicting rebellious elements of Buddhism, incorporated into Christianity, had also come from Indian culture as a reaction to the Brahmanistic caste system. Today we still have, as then, the luxuriating, opulent priesthood on the one hand, and the austere self-abnegating orders of monks and cloistered nuns on the other. A conflict that had begun as a reaction to the caste system of India, in the theocracy of Hinduism, again flared up in Christianity. The potential wealth and power in the profession of the clergy attracted men of avarice and demagoguery, who resorted to subterfuge, deception, intrigue and violence in climbing the hierarchy of power. (In the Simonical heresy church offices were sold to the highest bidder.)

Heroes developed during this period of history from among those renouncing the wealth and luxury of the priesthood. Many became the saints to whom we yet pay homage. These models of men, that developed as a reaction to the exploiting clergy, were frequently masochistic, often tragic, and always morbid:

Jerome - " . . . Tears and groans were every day my portion, and my bare bones, which hardly held together, clashed against the ground. Now, although in my fear of hell I had consigned myself to this prison, I often found myself amid bevies of girls. My face was pale and my frame chilled with fasting. Yet my mind was burning with desire and the fires of lust kept bubbling up before me when my flesh was as good as dead . . . and so miserable was I that I could fast only that I might afterwards read Cicero . . . Suddenly I was caught up in the judgment seat. . . 'Thou art a follower of Cicero. . . .' Accordingly, I made oath and called upon His name saying, 'Lord, if ever again I possess worldly books. . . I have denied Thee . . .' Taking this oath I returned to the upper world. I opened eyes so drenched with tears that my distress served to convince even the incredulous . . . "
(Letter to Eustochium)

In the Life of Saint Antony, demonology and superstition of this period of Catholic Europe were epitomized. Antony gave his land to the villagers, and his money to the poor so that no clog of sin might burden his soul. In the desert he was tempted by the devil in the form of a beautiful, seductive woman; but in fear of hell he spurned the adversary, and passed through the temptation unscathed. He fasted constantly and dressed in a hair shirt. He neither washed his body nor feet to free himself from filth, and he reeked with the odor of sanctity. His nights were filled with dreadful visions of Satan who swallowed up souls of those who had served him on earth.

St. Martin lived as an Anchorite in a cell at the top of a precipitous rock in the company of some eighty brethren. Holy idleness was the rule since no art was practice. The devil was always at hand. St. Martin saw him in a thousand shapes and disguises.

Pope Leo the Great was the first of the Roman popes to assume prominence in secular affairs. At the Council of Chalcedon in 451, Leo was declared chief of the 520 bishops present. The east and west sees then became equal in status. With the fall of the western division of the secular empire in 474, the patriarchs of Constantinople made a bid for political supremacy. The secular strength of the Church in the east may have indeed outstripped that of Rome but for the victory of Islam in the east. As early as 787, none of the African, and but little of the oriental Greek Christianity remained in the east after the onslaught of the Mohammedans. The primacy of the priesthood in Rome was officially claimed by Constantine VI in the year 787. By the turn of the 9th century, the east and west had already become the separate communions of the Latin Roman Church and of the Eastern Orthodox. A Holy Roman Empire was set up in the west. Frankish kings were in charge of the armies. Roman popes were at the head of the ecclesiastical polity.

Decay set in directly as solitary Roman Catholic power grew. Pope Gregory, at the close of the 6th century, admonished monks for illiteracy, though he himself, by many literary standards, was poorly educated. He knew nothing of philosophy and but little of Christian theology. Gregory was an intensely superstitious man who gave parishioners amulets to wear about the neck that would protect them from harm. Illiteracy became more universal among the clergy. The Church was forced to rely more and more upon the plastic and pictorial arts to implement its faith. This increasing use of images was, of course, in conflict with the second Mosaic commandment. Gregory maintained, however, that so long as pictures and statues were not adored, they were harmless. Moreover, he held, they were necessary to serve the ignorant.

When the armies of Mohammed surged through the eastern Christian world of the 7th century, Islam won easy converts among Eastern Christians. Eastern Christians yielded to the Moslem faith perhaps because they had grown weary and skeptical of the developing demagogic priesthood and its inconsistencies.

Islam presented a distinct contrast to Christianity. It espoused diametrically opposed doctrines. Islam was militant, poylgamous, and openly secular, purporting to establish a great temporal kingdom by force and violence with intolerance to all opposed. It promised a secular paradise of physical luxury and sensual pleasure, with the winning of glory through deeds. It had no soter but Mohammed, the prophet. During the early period of Islam in the east, a brief resurgence of skepticism and individualism produced a culture prolific in the arts and classics, but this again was short lived. There again developed, as in the west, a priest state, that, by nature, seemed always to lay the culture in waste, generating poverty, ignorance, repression, and cultural retardation as a theocratic by-product. Christendom had early suffered a severe setback in its conflict with militant Islam. Christian and Moslem factions established a truce during the Crusades, though they were indeed not to live in friendship. Even today they compete in the winning of converts.

Over the Christian world there seemed to settle a universal lethargy. Intellectual activity was wasted in bitter disputes over meaningless speculative doctrines, in a kind of neurosis of theological obsessions. Ruin and decay were at every hand until invading barbarians injected new life. The Aryans, then the Teutons, came, reawakening in Rome elements of the ancient culture of Greece. After rumblings in England and Hungary, a movement began in Germany that was to wrench much of barbarian Europe from the grasp of the hierarchy of the Church. These successive rebellions laid the foundation for modern civilization and our present secular republics.

Chapter **28**

The Period of Protest
and
The Reformations

The time between the decline of the Roman Empire in the fourth century, and the reformations of the fifteenth century, is classically known as the "Dark Ages." This was the period of increasing church domination. Suppression and enforced obedience were the rule of order, to be climaxed in the twelfth century with the Inquisitions. Ignorance and fear abided. Art was lost. Studies in Greek, Hebrew, philosophy, and classical mythology were sternly suppressed.

At the turn of the fifteenth century, leaders throughout Europe, particularly in the universities, revived the classics, philosophy and literature of the ancients. The study of Greek history brought renewed interest in the Bible, and stimulated interest in art. The talent of such men of science as Leonardo da Vinci, Copernicus and Galileo was nurtured. The artistry of Michelangelo flowered in frescos, sculpture and architecture. World borders expanded. Diaz, Vasco da Gama, and Columbus set sail across unchartered waters of the Altantic in search of new routes to India, but to find instead a land where the edge of earth was believed to be. A Polish astronomer, looking up at the stars with magnifying lenses, completely changed man's regard of the universe; for at the turn of the sixteenth century, Copernicus published his theory of the solar system, holding that the sun was at the center of life about which the earth and other planets revolved. The Coperican theory was iconoclastic, eventually to change the view of man and God. The earth became a tiny, insignificant speck in a timeless universe of infinite space. This realization more and more broke men loose from their theological shackles and induced them to think. Dante wrote his Divine Comedy. On a trip through Purgatory, Hell and Heaven, his main character was neither angel, apostle, nor saint, but the poet Virgil, a heathen. This became the first of heretical writings daring to challenge the authority and omniscience of the Church, even under threat of death. Ancient Greek mythologies were studied, Greek philosophies were again pondered, and Greek literature esteemed. Men began anew to scrutinize the world about them. Humanism was advanced through such men as Valla and Erasmus. The tyrannical dictates of the Church were challenged. The yoke of Christianity loosened. Reformation of the faith had begun.

In periods of enlightenment a truly expansive outlook emerges. The faith changes, and is reshaped as men see the universe and God in new perspective. The Renaissance, the classical period in history when a new era of understanding emerged, may have come about as a result of something in man, an eternal curiosity and malcontent that does not lend itself to easy explanations; or it may have simply been an angry reaction of such men as Luther to the unreasonable, inequitable demands of the theocratic papacy, the overpowering resentments building up as a reaction to the avarice, unpretentious sensualism and demagoguery of men in the fifteenth century church. In any event, in Germany, England, Switzerland, Sweden, France, Spain and throughout Europe, rebellion mounted, and new leaders in heresy emerged.

a. Germany

Near the end of the fifteenth century, a son, called Martin, was born to poor peasants named Luther in the city of Eisleben, Germany. The family was large and their income at first meager, but Martin managed to obtain a good education. Martin Luther was always a poor student. Like others of his day, as a college student, he begged meals and literally sang for his supper. He attended law school, but was later to enter a monastery. An inquisitive man of high intelligence, Luther soon became a professor at Wittenburg. He preached and taught about the Church, and its organization. A conscientious and devout Catholic, his scrutiny of the Church eventually led to disillusionment: "No one can compel a man's belief by force. It must come from his heart," affirmed Luther.

On a visit to Rome, he was appalled by the shamefully un-Christ-like conduct of men of the Church. Pope Julius II, Luther's great religious leader, languished in the splendor of a king. Julius prostituted the holy office by bestowing divine favors on whomever paid him well. This was seen by Luther as blasphemous hypocracy, even though vowed and dutiful to his Pope, the vicar of Christ on earth.

After Julius II died, Leo X was elected Pope. Leo was an intensly ambitious man. During his reign the magnificent St. Peter's Cathedral was built, a project that demanded funding greater than any that had been yet undertaken by the papacy. Pope Leo resorted to practices begun during the Crusades when complete forgiveness of sin was granted those ready to sacrifice their lives. Under Leo, whoever paid money to the treasury would be forgiven, or they could pay for the forgiveness of the sins of relatives and friends, alive or dead. "Indulgences" were marketed in a thoroughly business-like manner. Not only clergy, but lay agents were commissioned to receive one-third of the proceeds. This was, in Luther's eyes, merchandizing of the "Forgiveness of the Lord." Long disillusioned by what he had seen in Rome, he was now incensed. A man could kill or commit any unsavory act. Yet, for a sum, all blame could be purged and the wicked would be judged innocent. Under the autocratic authority of the Pope, and with the cruelty of the Inquistion still upon them, many German priests remained fearful and obedient. Luther appealed to his fellow priests through letters to protest the selling of Indulgences. A Pope's representative appeared shortly thereafter in Germany to begin the sale. Outraged, Luther nailed to the door of the church in Wittenburg a long inscription in wood. Swarms of people in Wittenburg read his denouncement of the Indulgences. Soon his dissention became known throughout Europe. Pope Leo himself heard of the affront and contemptuously derided Luther as a drunken German. The sale of Indulgences, however, fell off, and Leo became alarmed. Luther was excommunicated. He was thoroughly incited and no longer even nominally obediant to Rome. He lectured and wrote in acid criticism: "The Holy Church of Rome has become a law-less den of thieves, a most unholy place of sin."

Once freed of Rome, Luther expounded his own theology. He translated the bible into German. He preached and organized churches, later to become known in his name as "Lutheran." Lutheran Churches spread throughout Germany, Norway, Sweden and Denmark.

The spirit of rebellion in both laymen and Churchmen against Rome had become increasingly intense after the period of the Crusades; political, religious and intellectual dissentient factions abounded. Only strong leadership was needed. This was nominally provided by such men as Luther.

Luther lived in the first half of the sixteenth century. The earth was known to be round, but only a spotty knowledge of geography was available to the scholar. Superstition and fear still dominated. Peasants were filled with ideas of monsters and evil spirits. Servitude and absolute authoritarianism prevailed with strict obedience demanded of the subservient masses by an endowed royalty. Printing was just becoming an industry. The practices of a corrupt clergy were being made known through writing with many stories passed along by word of mouth on the fornication and graft among monks and nuns.

Luther had the background of a peasant. His father, at first a farmer, had turned to mining, eventually to work in a foundry. In the latter industry he was to become a wealthy man. Luther's mother always remained a simple peasant woman, superstitious and devout. Encouraged by his father, Luther earned the B.A. and M.A. degrees at Erfurt University. He studied the classics and the physics of Aristotle and hoped eventually to obtain a professional law degree. While still a student, however, he was struck by lightning during a thunder storm. Having an intense religious backround, particularly under the influence of his mother, he vowed, in gratitude for his life, to enter a monastery. His father vigorously opposed his forsaking a most promising career in law for the deprivation of the clergy, but Luther doggedly carried out his vow. He then went on to earn his Augustinian Doctor of Theology degree.

As a man of sound intellect who had once been intent on a secular pursuit, Luther became a disquieted theologian. On the one hand he denounced knowing God through philosophical reasoning. God could be known only by revelation, maintained Luther. Yet, having his doctorate, he once commented, "Although I am a doctor, I have to do just as a child and say word for word every morning and whenever I have the time, the Lord's Prayer and the Ten Commandments, the Creed and the Psalms."

On another occasion, he remarked that he would gladly surrender his doctor's hat to anyone who could reconcile the writings of James in the New Testament with those of Paul. In a pilgrimage to the Eternal City of Rome, representing the Erfurt monastery, he did not, as most, delight in the antiquities of Christendom, nor in the Renaissance splendor of the city. He, rather, became disgruntled and disturbed by the ignorance, immorality and frivolity of the Italian priests he met. In Rome, these churchmen, said Luther, went mechanically and irreverently through mass. While in Rome, Luther climbed the Stairs of Pilate on hands and knees, kissing each step as he went, symbolically to help someone be delivered from Purgatory. This was the practice of devout believers. When he reached the top, Luther raised his head in doubt, "Who knows if it is so!" Throughout his career as a Roman Catholic priest, Luther did, in fact, seem always critical and rejecting of both dogma and practice.

Luther became increasingly militant in his opposition to the papacy. His letter to the newly elected German Emperor, Charles V, early in the 16th century, is perhaps typical of Luther's rhetorical struggle against Rome. It can be seen that the appeal was largely to the nationalistic feeling of the Germans:

"... It is not out of mere arrogance and perversity that I, an individual, poor and insignificant, have taken it upon me to address your lordships. The distress and misery which oppress all ranks of Christendom, especially in Germany, have moved not me alone, but everybody, to cry aloud for help; this is that which compels me to cry out and call upon God to send down his Spirit upon someone who shall reach out a hand to this wretched people ... I now intend, God helping me, to expose, so that, being known, they may cease to effect such scandal and injury. God has given us a young and noble sovereign for our leader, thereby stirring up fresh hope in our hearts; our duty is to do our best to help him, and to avail ourselves to the full of this opportunity and his gracious favor.

The Romanists have, with great adroitness, drawn three walls around themselves, with which they have hitherto protected themselves, so that no one could reform them, whereby all Christendom has suffered terribly.

First . . . they have affirmed . . . that spiritual power is above temporal.

Secondly . . . no one may interpret the Scriptures but the Pope.

Thirdly, if they are threatened with council, they invented the notion that no one may call a council but the Pope.

. . . As for the unction by a pope or a bishop, tonsure, ordination, consecration, and clothes differing from those of laymen —this may make a hypocrite of an anointed puppet, but never a Christian or a spiritual man . . . If a little company of pious Christian laymen . . . had not among them a priest consecrated by a bishop, and were there to agree to elect one of them . . . and were to order him to baptize, to celebrate the mass, to absolve and to preach, this man would as truly be a priest as if all the bishops and all the popes had consecrated him. That is why, in cases of necessity, every man can baptize and absolve, which would not be possible if we were not all priests. This grace and virtue of baptism, and of the Christian estate, they have annulled and made us forget by their ecclesiastical law . . . a priest should be nothing in Christendom but a functionary; as long as he holds his office, he has precedence; if he is deprived of it, he is a peasant or a citizen like the rest . . . temporal power has been ordained by God for the punishment of the bad and the protection of the good, we must let it do its duty throughout the whole Christian body, without respect of persons whether it strikes popes, bishops, priests, monks, nuns, or whoever it may be . . . whatever the ecclesiastical law has said in opposition to this is merely the invention of the Romanist arrogance.

The second wall is even more tottering and weak: namely their claim to be considered masters of the Scriptures. If the article of our faith is right, 'I believe in the holy Christian

Church,' the Pope cannot alone be right; else we must say, 'I believe in the Pope of Rome,' and reduce the Christian Church to one man, which is devilish and damnable heresy.

The third wall falls of itself, as soon as the first two have fallen; for if the Pope acts contrary to the Scriptures, we are bound to stand by the Scriptures to punish and to constrain him, according to Christ's commandment . . . I must collect the Church together . . . Italy is almost a desert now . . . towns are decayed, and the country and the people ruined because there is no more any worship of God or preaching . . . Because the cardinals have all the wealth . . . Now that Italy is sucked dry, they come to Germany. They begin in a quiet way, but we shall soon see Germany brought into the same state as Italy. We have a few cardinals already. What the Romanists really mean to do, the 'drunken Germans' are not to see until they have lost everything . . . If we rightly hang thieves and behead robbers, why do we leave the greed of Rome unpunished? For Rome is the greatest thief and robber that has ever appeared on earth . . . Poor Germans that we are - we have been deceived! We were born to be masters, and we have been compelled to bow the head beneath the yoke of our tyrants, and to become slaves. Name, title, outward signs of royalty, we possess all of these; force, power, right, liberty, all these have gone over to the popes, who have robbed us of them . . . It is time the glorious Teutonic people should cease to be the puppet of the Roman pontiff. Because the pope crowns the emperor, it does not follow that the pope is superior to the emperor . . . "

Lutheranism soon spread north to Sweden, Denmark, Norway, and Finland. A 16th century Swede, Olaus Petri, a literary man who had been trained at Leipzig University, adapted Lutheranism to a nationalistic movement that was to make Swedish royal power independent of the papacy. His younger brother, Olavus Petri, became the first Lutheran Archbishop in Sweden. Lutheranism had become so firmly established in Norway that Nielsen Hauge, an 18th century independent lay preacher, was imprisoned for heresy by the State Lutheran Church. The American Norwegian Lutheran Synod was later named "Haugean" in his honor. King Christian II, in 16th-century Denmark, also sought to weaken the power of the Roman Church in Denmark by instaling Martin Reinhart as a Lutheran minister. Though King Christian was later overthrown for his treachery in the famous "blood baths," Lutheranism had also become firmly implanted in Denmark.

b. England

In the sixth century, the pope of Rome sent the missionary Augustine to the distant land of Britany to convert the heathen Saxons. Augustine established a branch of the Roman Church in England. It remained, for many centuries, a replica of the church in Rome.

Rulers in the remote land of Britany, from the first, resented Church interference with civil affairs. In 1534, leaders of the Church in England elected to recognize the Roman Pope only as equivalent to any other bishop in a foreign country. This marked the decline of the pope's political power in England and the rise of the Church of England (later to become known on the American continent as the Protestant Episcopal Church). The Church of England retained the essential beliefs, rituals, and ministry of the Church of Rome.

Other more radical Protestant sects, however, also evolved in England. In the 14th century, an Oxford University professor named John Wyclif criticized practices of the Roman Church, and its insistence upon having the final authority. Wyclif objected to the Latin being used, which was a language that the English did not understand. Wyclif organized a group of priests who would preach to the English in their own language. He and others translated the Bible into English. Though Wyclif was considered by many to be a crank, his influence reached across the channel to reformers in Germany and Bohemia. His propositions were later denounced by a Council of British bishops, particularly those holding that grace could be derived directly from God without intermediaries. The Bible he considered to be sole source of faith, independent of historicity. Several of Wyclif's propositions included that:

.... if a bishop or priest be in mortal sin he does not ordain, consecrate or baptize.

. . . it is not laid down in Scripture that Christ ordained the Mass.

. . . if a man be duly penitent . . . outward confession is . . . useless.

. . . it is contrary to . . . Scripture that ecclesiastics should have possessions.

. . . any deacon or priest may preach . . . apart from the authority of the Apostollic See or a Catholic bishop.

. . . temporal lords can . . . take away temporal goods from the Church, when those who hold them are sinful.

. . . excommunication by the Pope . . . is not to be feared because it is the censure of anti-Christ.

. . . the Roman Church is the synagogue of Satan.

. . . the Pope is not the next and immediate vicar of Christ and the Apostles.

The followers of Wyclif, called "Lollards," were also extreme in their criticism of the Church. Their position is often seen to have been more in the nature of political revolutionaries than of reformers:

" . . . our unusual priesthood, which began in Rome, pretended to be of power more lofty than the angels, is not that priesthood which Christ ordained for His apostles . . . the priesthood is bestowed with signs, rites, and pontifical blessings of small virtue, nowhere exemplified in Holy Scripture . . . it is a grievous play . . . to see bishops trifle with the Holy Spirit in the bestowal of orders . . . this is the unrestrained introduction of anti Christ into the Church.

. . . the law of continence enjoined on priests . . . brings sodomy into all the Holy Church . . .

. . . the pretended miracle of the sacrament of bread drives all men, but a few, to idolatry, because they think that the Body of Christ which is never away from heaven, could by power of the priest's word be enclosed essentially in a little bread which they show the people.

. . . exorcisms and blessings performed over wine, bread, water and oil, salt, wax, and incense, the stones of the altar, and church walls, over clothing, miter, cross, and pilgrims' staves, are genuine performance of necromancy rather than sacred theology.

. . . holy water (should) be the best for all kinds of illnesses —sores, for instance; whereas we experience the contrary day by day. . . "

The Lollards (meaning "prayer mumblers") were eradicated at the turn of the 15th century by the statute, De Heretico Comburendo, at a time when the full force of the reformations was not to develop for several decades.

The impudence of the Lollards, and Wyclif in particular, was anathematized. Wyclif had preached and translated the Bible into the vulger English. He had harrassed the Church up until the time of his death. He did, however, remain a Catholic even at death. In bitter renouncement, years after his interment, his remains were dug up and burned in papal ceremony.

In England, resentment had been growing against the papacy in its rigorous demands on a poor peasantry. The Church was seen to be wealthy, while still mendicant friars went about demanding gifts and donations. Rebellion mounted.

During this early period of bitter conflict, the famous Tower of London was built. Here may still be seen the axes, head blocks, stretching racks and various and sundry skin puncturing and limb stretching devices and instruments of cruelty used literally to wring conformity from dissenters—a monument with its artifacts that still dramatizes the major paradox in Christianity. Thomas Hawkes, in 16th century England, refused to have his son baptized. He was subsequently imprisoned and tortured. Continuing to defy Church authority, he was burned alive. Hugh Latimer, a Cambridge educated bishop, refused to sign a document pledging loyalty to Roman-worship practices. He preached for reformation of the Roman format. He, too, without trial, was impounded and tortured in the Tower of London, later released under Edward the Sixth and recommitted under Mary Tudor. At the same time, a former chaplain to Henry the Eighth, Nicholas Ridley, was also committed. Both Latimer and Ridley refused to recant, were accused of heresy, and together were burned alive at Oxford. A former reformation leader under Henry the Eighth, Thomas Cranmer, who wrote the "Book of Common Prayer," was also burned to death.

The fifteenth century was alive with religious revival and academic adventures. This was the background in which the English reformation began. Printing was becoming commonplace. The first printed Bibles and the classics appeared early in the 15th century. The clergy were increasingly being educated in colleges rather than monasteries. The time was right for change and progress.

Henry the Eighth appealed for papal sanction in his divorce from Katherine of Aragon. Failing to receive the Pope's blessing and suffering excommunication, he broke off relations with Rome and instituted himself as head of the Church and State of England. Monasteries were abolished. Tax payments to the Papacy were withdrawn. Bibles were distributed to every parish throughout England. Henry's successor, the boy King Edward VI, permitted reformers to gain further control.

During the devout-Catholic Mary Tudor's rule, the papacy was reunited with England. Latin mass was reinstated. Leading Protestants were excuted. Under Elizabeth, the situation was yet in flux. Many English remained Catholic in sentiment, yet resented papal absolutism. The Catholic King Philip of Spain also stood ready to enforce the Catholic persuasion, and threatened England with attack. Elizabeth compromised, retaining much of the traditional rule of Church bishops (episcopacy), while yet permitting public Bible reading. Unlike Henry, she did not place herself at the head of the Church. Within the laws of the Roman Church, she made attendance mandatory to be subject to payment of fines for failure to attend. Her religious dictates were severe:

" . . . if any persons above the age of sixteen . . . go about or move or persuade any of her majesty's subjects, or any other within her highness's realms or dominions, to deny, withstand, and impugn her majesty's power and authority in causes ecclesiastical, united, and annexed to the imperial crown of this realm; or to that end or purpose, shall advisedly and maliciously move or persuade any other person whatsoever to forbear or abstain from coming to church to hear divine service, or to receive the communion according to her majesty's laws and statutes aforesaid, or to come to or be present at any unlawful assemblies, conventicles, or meetings under color or pretense of any exercises of religion contrary to her majesty's said laws and statues; or if any person or persons which shall obstinately refuse to repair to some church, chapel, or usual place of common prayer, and shall forbear by the space of a month to hear divine service as is aforesaid, shall . . . be committed to prison, there to remain without bail or mainprize, until they shall conform and yield themselves to come to some church, chapel, or usual place of common prayer, and hear divine service, according to her majesty's laws and statutes aforesaid, and to make such open submission and declaration of their said conformity . . . "

Pope Pius V found the Elizabethan compromise unsatisfactory. He called upon France and Spain to enforce a Bull against Queen Elizabeth:

" . . . He . . . to whom has been given all power in heaven and earth, entrusted the government of the one Holy Catholic and Apostolic Church (outside of which there is no salvation) to one man alone on the earth . . . the Roman pontiff . . . chief over all nations and kingdoms . . . declare Elizabeth . . . a heretic and an abettor of heretics, and those that cleave to her in the aforesaid matters to have incurred the sentence of anathema, and to be cut off from the unity of Christ's body . . . we declare her to be deprived of her pretended right to the aforesaid realm, and from all dominion, dignity and privileges whatsoever . . . all who disobey our command we involve in the same sentence of anathema . . . "

Elizabeth retaliated:

" . . . For reformation whereof be it ordained, established, and enacted by the queen's most excellent majesty, and the Lord's spiritual and temporal, and the Commons, in this present Parliament, that all and every Jesuits, seminary priests, and other priests whatsoever made or ordained out of the realm of England or other of her highness's dominions, or within any of her majesty's realms or dominions, by any authority, power, or jurisdiction derived, challenged, or pretended from the see of Rome, since the feast of the Nativity of St. John the Baptist in the first year of her highnesses's reign, shall, within forty days next after the end of this present session of Parliament, depart out of this realm of England, and out of all other of her highness's realms and dominions, if the wind, weather, and passage shall serve for the same, or else so soon after the end of the said forty days as the wind, weather, and passage shall so serve . . . after that he shall hereafter come into this realm, or any other of her highness's dominions, submit himself to some archbishop or bishop of this realm, or to some justice of the peace within the country where he shall arrive or land, and do thereupon truly and sincerely, before the same archbishop, bishop, or such justice of peace, take the said oath set forth in anno primo, and by writing under his hand, confess and acknowledge, and from thenceforth continue, his due obedience unto her highness's laws, statutes and ordinances . . . "

Elizabeth had retained much of the Roman form of worship in what was to become the Anglican Church, or Church of England. Many British reform factions wished to purge the Church of all Roman elements. The Separatists, Purists or "Puritans," as they were called, began a struggle within England against the Anglican Church. The Calvinist Puritan, Oliver Cromwell, made England the Protestant stronghold of Europe, allying with France to stop the onslaught of Roman Catholic Spain. The Scottish King James I, under Puritanical pressure, appointed a committee of learned men to re-write the Bishop's Bible, first written in 1568. This King James Bible became one of the most monumental literary document in the English language, and still serves as a model for the speech in the preachment of English speaking clergy.

King James, contrary to the Puritans, had issued a "Book of Sports," to encourage sports on the Sabbath. James' successor, Charles I, re-issued this in the "Declaration of Sports." The latter book the Puritans later burned in public ceremony. During the Cromwellian period, the Archbishop of Canterbury, William Laud, was executed by Puritans as a proponent of Charles I and the Anglican Church. Charles had sought to establish the divine right of kings, which antagonized the Puritans. He later lost public support and was publicly beheaded in 1649. After Cromwell died, Charles II became king, reinstating the Anglican Church. During the reign of King Charles II, the Puritans became subject to censure and prosecution. Such men as John

Bunyan, famous for his "Pilgrims Progress," and William Tyndale, who had completed a racy English translation of the Bible from the original Greek, were severely harassed. Tyndale was eventually strangled and burned for heresy. Other important Puritans of the 17th century were Richard Baxter and Milton of *Paradise Lost* fame.

The outstanding character of the Puritans was the zealous dissemination of Christian doctrine through Scriptures. They distributed inexpensive books on catechism, Christian behavior, Bibles, and "The Book of Common Prayer."

Another major sect developing in Britain was Presbyterianism. The name was derived from its organization of "presbuteros" or elders. A group of churches and clergy form presbyteries, which make up a synod. Synods form the assemblies. Presbyterian doctrine stems from the reformed wing of Protestantism, which was focalized in Scotland under John Knox. It originated with Puritan groups which were active during the reign of Elizabeth, and many of whom were partial to a Presbyterian polity. Other Separatists, or Pilgrims, were congregational in form. John Knox had been earlier influenced by the Swiss Zwingli, and the French Calvin. He had also befriended George Wishart, a reformer strangled at the stake. Knox was persecuted for his association with Wishart by being condemned to slavery. He escaped to England at a time when the anti-Protestant Mary Tudor was Queen. He was again threatened with persecution, and took refuge in Geneva, Switzerland. There he met the French John Calvin and Swiss Ulrich Zwingli. When the Protestant Elizabeth came to power in England, Knox returned eventually to settle in Scotland. There the Catholic Mary of Scots was on the throne. The Knox variety of Presbyterianism, patterned after Calvinistic doctrine, was again in conflict. After much political and civil strife, Presbyterianism finally became established as the chief religion of Scotland. The Presbyterian doctrine in Ireland resulted in severe conflict. In the Massacre of 1641, 40,000 Protestants were maimed and burned to death. Soldiers were finally brought in from Scotland to control the rioting Catholics.

Protestant developments in England also included Methodism, which gained impetus in the 18th century. The founder, John

Wesley, was not concerned with implementing a new creed, nor forming a new sect, but, rather, bringing about spiritual revival in the Church of England. John, his younger brother, Charles and George Whitefield were chiefly responsible for the early developments in Methodism. Their fraternity, which they dedicated as a holy society, became a somewhat ridiculed group in the eyes of the general public. John had been influenced by the Moravians, particularly Peter Bohler. He was also completely sympathetic with the Anglican Church doctrine. However, these sects lacked the essential ingredient of "holiness" that was so important to the Wesleys and Whitefields. Whitefield preached to the people in the streets, out of which practice grew the famous Wesleyan revivals. He traveled throughout England, Scotland and Ireland, crying out for righteousness and salvation. Some eight thousand societies were formed in England and Wales. The Methodist Episcopal Church in America (Philadelphia) also grew out of this movement. Charles Wesley, who was also a major leader of the fraternity, is credited with hymnal lyrics sung today throughout the Protestant Christian World, including, "Hark the Herald Angels Sing," "Love Divine," "All Loves Excelling," "Jesus, Lover of My Soul," and "Come Thou Almighty King."

Late in the 17th century a final attempt was made to restore the throne of England to an absolute monarchy, and to reinstall Roman Catholicism. This failed due to the widespread Protestant-Puritan elements in England. The Toleration Act finally brought lasting freedom of religion in England.

c. Switzerland

John Calvin was perhaps the most important leader in the Protestant movement of Switzerland. Born in France in 1509, he entered the University of Paris in 1523. Paris was then a center of new learning and religious excitement. Here Calvin studied religion, law, Hebrew, Greek and the classics. He was undecided about his career until he wrote a paper on Protestantism for a friend who was to present it before an assembly. Protestants in France, during this period, were outlawed, but in 1536, Calvin issued his "Christianae Religionio Institutio." He fled from France to Geneva, Switzerland, joining Farel in the work of the reformation movement. Calvin was a thoroughgoing fundamentalist, and abhored the libertine Severtus whose speculations on the trinity were heretical. Calvin contrived the death of Servertus for these theological excursions. In fact, John Calvin was so much a fundamentalist that his theology is frequently characterized as the grass roots of Protestant Fundamentalism. "Christianea Religionio Institutio" was his only major theological work. He was more involved with extensive organizing work than theology, which perhaps accounts for the fundamentalism. Following are excerpts from the Calvinist theology:

" . . . original sin is seen to be an hereditary depravity and corruption of our nature, and diffuses into all parts of the soul . . . wherefore those who have defined original sin as the lack of the original righteousness with which we should have been endowed, no doubt include, by implication, the whole fact of the matter . . .

. . . but they have not fully expressed the positive energy of this sin. For our nature is not merely bereft of good, but is so productive of every kind of evil that it cannot be inactive. Those who have called it concupiscence have used a word by no means wide of the mark, if it were added that whatever is in man, from intellect to will, from the soul to the flesh, is all defiled and crammed with concupiscence; or, to sum it up briefly, that the whole man is in himself nothing but concupiscence . . .

. . . when His Light is removed, nothing remains but darkness and blindness; when His Spirit is taken away, our hearts harden into stone; when His guidance ceases, we are turned from the straight path . . .

. . . (when) we attribute foreknowledge to God we mean all things have ever been, and eternally remain, before His eyes; so that to His knowledge nothing is future or past, but all things are present; and present not in the sense that they are reproduced in imagination . . . but present in the sense that He really sees and observes them placed, as it were, before His eyes . . . and this foreknowledge extends over the whole universe and over every creature . . . A testimony of God's grace to us confirmed by an external sign, with our answering witness of piety towards him . . .

Calvin's view of man was one of an intellect vitiated, and morals depraved. Divine Truth, as he saw it, could be attained only by revelation. God was absolute and elected only whom He willed to salvation; all mens' destinies were determined by God. This was so first with the Jews. Then the newly elected Christians became God's chosen. Election could be had only through proper faith, and participation in the sacraments.

Calvin condemned dancing, gambling, drunkenness, obscenity, card playing, and theater going. When he died, he was buried, as requested, without a grave marker. A Calvinistic community was set up in Geneva, active in community affairs and militantly intolerant. At the Council of Geneva, the Catholic custom of naming children after saints was prohibited. The Calvinists decreed that names from the Old Testament should be used instead.

Switzerland traditionally has been a land of freedom, perhaps due to its isolation in the Alps. In many ways it may have been similar to the early periods of settlement in the United States, a land that provided refuge from political and religious persecutions. Switzerland was a geographic haven, sheltering such men as Calvin, Knox, and Zwingli. It was for this reason, perhaps, that Calvin spent most of his professional life in Geneva, free to develop his own tyranny of dogma. From Geneva the Calvinistic doctrine spread throughout the continent, saturating the Presbyterianism of Knox and the Puritan doctrine that arose in England. The Calvinistic doctrine, holding man to be fundamentally depraved, later became dominant among early American Puritans. It was both theocratic and intolerant, condemning religious liberty as a most diabolical license that permitted man to go to hell in his own way.

Switzerland's native son, Ulrich Zwingli, was a Swiss Army chaplain. He later became a pastor in the city of Zurich. A contemporary of Luther, Zwingli lived in a land of democratic liberties that were not permitted in Luther's Germany. Zwingli married in opposition to the mandates of the priesthood. He attacked the practice of statue or image worship, and was influential in having all pictures, statues, crucifixes and other liturgical accruements removed from the churches in Zurich. He militated against the celebration of Mass. He and Luther clashed in debate, Zwingli being the most radical in his opposition to Romanism. Luther dissented bitterly.

Zwingli aspired to organizing Protestant churches all over Europe. He attempted to enlist support of the heads of government in order to separate church influence from state affairs. Like Wyclif in England, Zwingli failed to achieve widespread political liberty. His influence, however, did give additional major impetus to Protestantism.

d. France

The twelfth-century Peter Waldo was a wealthy and deeply religious man. He undertook translation of the New Testament into French, as Luther was to do several centuries later into his native German. Waldo had pondered the meaning of the Bible. He was convinced that Jesus was being denied by the luxuriating popes. Peter Waldo was wealthy. It was not, as Waldo saw it, that Christ intended for His disciples to have worldly possessions. So he worked and preached the word of Christ, giving up his fortune.

After Waldo's death, his followers continued reformation of the faith. Many were sought out by the pope's soldiers and executed, but the movement spread throughout France and England. The Waldenses preached, as did the early Christian sect, on the rule of poverty. Itinerant preachers admonished the people throughout France against worship of images, wearing of clerical vestments and subscribing to Crusade Indulgences. Waldenses were condemned by the clergy for their liberal interpretation of Scripture. They managed to survive the purges of the pope's soldiers by hiding in caves high in the rugged Alps. Their heresy, as that of tens of thousands of others, was in the reading and peddling of Scriptures.

The Albigenses, of 11th, 12th and 13th centuries in Southern France, also severely criticized the materialism of the Catholic priesthood. "Evil is matter and light is good," was the motto. They denied the pope and his Church. It was then that Pope Innocent III iterated the universal dominion of the pope as Vicar of Christ.

e. *Spain*

The tradition of Spain has been strongly pro-Catholic. Its history is one of intolerance and even today non-Catholic sects are subtly or overtly suppressed.

Spanish history has always been strongly anti-reform. Juliano, while visiting Germany, was influenced by the reformation movement there. Returning to Seville, Spain, with a number of bibles, he was immediately arrested and eventually burned for heresy. All with Bibles in their possession were publicly whipped and enslaved or imprisoned. The "Auto-da-fe," or "Act of Faith" became an elaborate public ceremony for the treatment of heretics. They were first condemned, then given a sermon. A reconciliation, or rejection was pronounced. If the heretics continued to reject the faith, the ceremony continued with the somber march and the execution.

The medieval Inquistion had begun under Pope Gregory IX. The latter had commissioned priests of the Dominican order to investigate heresy among the Albigenses. Inquistitors at first pardoned those who recanted, but brought to trial all who had not abjured. The trials, conducted secretly by bishops, usually resulted in a verdict of guilty. Burning at the stake was punishment for unrecanted heresy, as the Romans had done centuries earlier for treason. Property of the guilty was confiscated by civil authorities. Later the Inquistion became used as a weapon of state, with or without appreciable evidence of heresy. The Inquistion was conducted largely in France, Italy, Germany, and the Papal states. It continued in mild form until the 19th century, with the Inquisition Office later becoming the Congregation of the Holy Office guarding the faith. (The latter office later came to publish the index of forbidden books.) Thirty thousand Albigenses had been executed during this early Inquisition period in Bezieres.

The Spanish Inquisition was instituted under Ferdinand V and Isabella. It continued from the 15th to 19th centuries, and was more severe than the original Inquisition of the papacy. In Spain it was originally intended to extricate heretical Jews and Moslems. It later became so widespread that no Spaniard felt safe from the Inquisitions. The papacy objected to the Spanish kings usurping the Church's prerogative in defining heresy, which had become arbitrary and frequently political within Spain.

On the continent and in England, heresy grew from year to year over the centuries. Dante Alighiere, 14th century Italian poet, author of the "Divine Comedy," was exiled. He brilliantly caught the folklore, mood and symbolism of his day, but was blasphemous in neglect of saints and clergy. In the 16th century, the Swiss priest Conrad Grebel protested vehemently against the Church interfering in state affairs. Grebel, a follower of Zwingli, preached the doctrine of absolute love and opposition to militarism. His congregation became the Anabaptists. A Catholic priest in the 16th century, Menno Simons, united his group with the followers of Obbe Philips, Obbenites. The joint communities were later called Mennists or Mennonites. In the 18th century this reform movement was formalized in the General Conference of the Mennonite Church Confession documented by Cornelis Ris in Holland. The Mennonites today publish a periodical, "Martyrs' Mirror," which is martyrology illustrating in gory detail, the burning to bone of martyrs such as Levina, the drowning of Felix Manz in Zurich, and the beheading and maiming at the block of scores of other Mennonites. The Hutterite order of Mennonites, as well as Amish, survives today in the United States and Canada. In the 15th century, a Czech, John Hus, working with Wyclif, denounced the pope and cried out against war, political power, human law, and affluence of the clergy. He, too, was executed for heresy. There was Jerome of Prague, and another named Jerome in Florence, whose Bohemian sect, the Moravians, survived.

As early as the 16th century it was clear that no small isolated movements in heresy were involved. The life of the Catholic Church was threatened. It must, for survival, mobilize physically and rhetorically lest the very Church of Peter be washed away in a flood of protest.

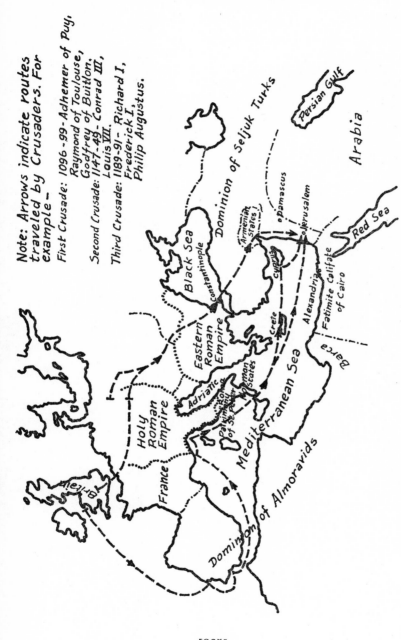

Note: Arrows indicate routes traveled by Crusaders. For example –

First Crusade: 1096-99 - Adhemer of Puy, Raymond of Toulouse, Godfrey of Buillon.

Second Crusade: 1147-49 - Conrad III, Louis VII.

Third Crusade: 1189-91 - Richard I, Frederick I, Philip Augustus.

Fig. 8. Europe and the Mediterranean in the 11th and 12th Centuries during the Crusades.

Chapter 29

The Roman Fortress
and
The Counter-Reformation

Leading up to the time that the Imperial Holy Roman Empire was instituted, the Church continued to acquire large tracts of land. The territories were governed by the clergy, even as today is Vatican City. In the year 756, the large land donations presumably given by Pepin-the-Short made the pope a powerful lay prince as well as the vicar of Christ. His role then became a semi-spiritual, semi-secular king over rulers, whose lands were known as Papal States. Pope Leo III crowned Charlemagne emperor in the year 800. Two centuries later, under Otto I, the center of Catholic Europe became the Imperial Holy Roman Empire.

The years of the Holy Roman Empire were marked by a vicious vying for power among the crowned heads of Europe. For many years even the papacy became a pawn to be bought and sold. Whereas, prior to the Imperial Holy Roman Empire the political scene had been dominated from Rome, after Otto I secular power became increasingly assumed by non-ecclesiastics. In Germany there developed claims to the ancient Roman Empire, denying those of Byzantine in the East.

For several centuries political bickering occupied the main interests of popes, imperial Emperors, and kings of France, Naples, Spain and England. The pope's political strength determined the extent of his spiritual domain and secular influence. For half a century, after 1309, the seat of the Church was uprooted from Rome and carried to Avignon, France. The secular power of the French king dominated the papacy during this period, called the "Babylonian Captivity." The holy office was administered from France, with those of the Papal States yet obedient, viz., Germany, Austria, Bohemia, Moravia, Belgium, Switzerland and the Netherlands.

It was during the crusades that major impetus had been given secular powers. At first the Christians of Europe had answered the call of Pope Urban to mobilize and retrieve the holy city of Jerusalem from the Moslems. After two centuries of prayer, political intrigue, and plunder of their own Christian cities enroute to Jerusalem, the secular powers of Europe had usurped the essential militancy, the political drive and secular authority of the pope. Then, in the 17th century, the nucleus of what had once been the seat of papal power, the Imperial Holy Roman Empire, declared war on growing Protestant forces. Motives, for what became a thirty-year war, were both religious and political. Alliances shifted as the balance of the power changed, but Catholic armies always moved under the banner of the Church with the blessings of Rome.

A century earlier, the growing number of Protestants had alarmed the papacy. It had then begun an internal purge on its own, and acted to reverse the tide of the reformation. At the Council of Trent in Bologna (1545-47, 1551-52, and 1562-63) internal reforms were implemented. New proselyting orders were formed. Foreign missions were established, and such sternly devout orders as the Society of Jesus (Jesuits) came into being. These were to become the armies of theological technicians that adamantly defend the faith to this very day.

The Papal States, in later years, continued to develop independent political power, acting in the name of the Church of Rome, yet setting up its own clergy when expedient. The Papacy, in order to maintain its political position, was forced to negotiate concordats, or agreements, with these states; though even this practice did not bring about complete accord, as was the case of the Spanish Inquisition*

---

*A modern counterpart of the Holy Roman Empire may be found in the Third Reich of Adolph Hitler who promised to build a third empire, a successor to the Holy Roman and the Hohenzollern empires. He capitalized on Christian theological tradition, holding that it would reign for 1,000 years (cf., the tradition of Christian Chilism which has Christ and His saints reigning for a thousand years.) A concordat was signed with the Vatican to guard the faith. This resulted in persecution of such non-Roman Catholic sects as Jehovah's Witnesses, and, notably, non-Christian Jews.

COUNTER-REFORMATION

During and following the Crusades, the Holy Roman Empire became only a shell of what it had once been. It became so thoroughly secularized that it was finally renounced by the pope in the 19th century. The Papacy reverted to a spiritual appeal in renouncing secularism (anticlericism). Today they continue to be pitted against secularism, and find deadly enemies in the hideous religions of atheism and communism. On the other hand, perhaps with its widespread discipline and lay support, and ever-increasing monetary wealth, the Papacy may again emerge as a secular power.

a. The Crusades

The tradition of armed conflict, inspired by the Papacy, is largely traceable to the Crusades from the 11th to 13th centuries. Several earlier appeals had been made by Byzantine emperors for military aid from the west in the face of advancing Turks. It was not, however, until the Roman Pope Urban II at Clermont, using his appeal as a play against the political harrassment of the German king, exhorted Christians to take up the cross against the heathen to retrieve magnificent Christian relics, e.g., the Sepulcher and splinters of the Cross, and to free Jerusalem from under the heel of the blaspheming Turks. "Deus volt" (God wills it) was the battle cry, eventually to be taken up by hundreds of thousands of crusaders.

Count Raymond of Toulouse was among the first military leaders to take up the cross. The itinerent preacher, Peter the Hermit, carried the pope's appeal throughout Europe and gathered a motley mass of followers for his expedition. Practical implications were found in territorial gains for the secular lords, and more freedom for those of the lower classes. The Normans seemed as much interested in taking the Byzantine Empire for the West as in defeating the Turks. Cities enroute were frequently pillaged and subject to the demands of military requisitions. They were often sacked and left in ruins, particularly when resisting the demands of the marching Crusaders. (See Figure 8)

For nearly two centuries the Crusades ebbed and flowed. Early assaults were put down. The Crusaders were defeated in the Battle of Asia Minor. Then, Raymond IV of Toulouse, Bohemond I Tancred, Robert of Normandy, and Robert II of Flanders, took Nicaea, Antioch, and Jerusalem in 1099, massacring the Moslems. A Latin Kingdom was set up in the city of Jerusalem. Subsequent Crusaders embarked to secure the military position in Jerusalem and outlying areas. The holy city, when lost in new attacks by the Turks, was subsequently the supreme prize through a period of centuries.

Second Crusade. (1147) Louis VII of France, and Conrad III sought to conquer neighboring cities about Jerusalem, such as Damascus. The crusade failed.

Third Crusade. (1189) Pope Gregory VIII made a plea for further military action after the Turks, under Saladin, had retaken Jerusalem. Richard I of England, Philip II of France, and the then emperor of the Holy Roman Empire, Frederick I, mustered forces again to lay siege to the holy city. Political dissention, with changing alliances and suspicion, resulted in only moderate success of the military operations. An uneasy treaty was finally negotiated with the Turks to permit Christians to have access to the Holy Sepulcher.

Fourth Crusade. (1202) Pope Innocent III again summoned Christians to come forth against the Turks in Jerusalem. This time only the French and the Flemish answered the call. The contingent was never to get beyond the Eastern Empire. It, rather, laid seige to the city of Constantinople. This Crusade was almost a complete failure. It was also during this period that the famous Children's Crusade was launched by the French boy fanatic, Stephen of Cloyes. Thousands of children tragically starved to death or were sold into slavery.

Fifth Crusade. (1217) Pope Innocent III once again appealed to Christendom. King Andrew II of Hungary, Leopold VI of Austria, and John of Brienne, struck at the seat of Moslem power in Egypt only to be defeated.

Sixth Crusade. Emperor Frederick II led his armies to Jerusalem in 1244 on a kind of peace mission. He secured a truce with the Moslems which permitted Christians to have access to the holy city. The treaty, however, was shortly broken, with the Moslems again closing off the city.

Seventh and Eighth Crusades. (1248-70) Louis IX of France moved against Egypt. He was captured at Cairo, later released, regrouped his forces and was finally defeated.

Ninth Crusade. (1271) Edward I of England concluded the long series of Crusades. He successfully negotiated a truce with the Moslems. The latter again broke the treaty and took Tripoli. This became the final Crusade to the Holy Land.

Several additional attempts were made to rally Christians to move against the Moslems, but none were effective. The word "Crusade" then came to mean any action taken against political dissenters, heathens and heretics, as sanctioned by the pope, e.g., against the ambitious Emperor Frederick II in 1228, and against the Albigenses and Hussites.

The Roman pope continued to lose his political strength. During the Crusades, secular leaders came to power and usurped authority that had previously been that of the pope. The massacre of the French in the "Sicilian Vespers" is also frequently cited as a case of waning papal power. Even later religious wars were more political and nationalistic than religious or in bearing papal sanction. The Hussite wars were crusades led by the Catholic Emperor Sigismund against followers of John Huss. Czech Hussites defeated the Catholics, but the war became largely a struggle between the nations of the Czechs and Germans. The Hussites, per se, returned to the Roman Church.

b. The Thirty Year War

The Reformations in Europe had developed to an alarming magnitude by the mid-sixteenth century. Minor politico-religious wars broke out all over the continent. The Peace of Ausburg, in 1555, had been only an interim truce. Settlement was not to endure until after the exhausting conflict of the Thirty Year War. Meanwhile, the Scandinavian countries of Sweden, under Gustavus I, and Denmark and Norway, under Frederick I, had become firmly Protestant.

The Thirty Year War (1618-48) may be characterized as one of mixed political-religious interests. It was primarily a conflict between the Protestants of Germany, France, Sweden, Denmark, and England, and the Catholic Holy Roman Empire (See Figure 9). It began when Bohemian Protestants ousted King

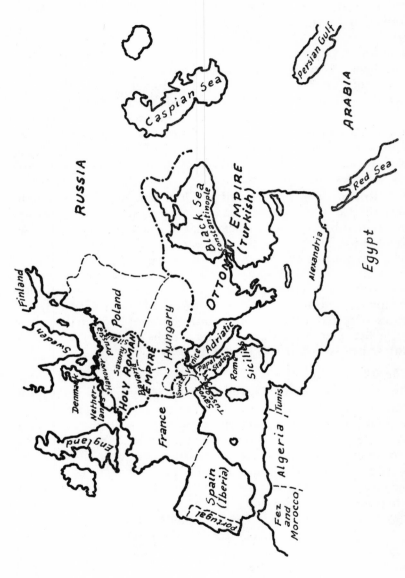

Fig. 9. Europe and the Mediterranean of the 17th and 18th Centuries.

Ferdinand from Prague in 1618. The newly-elected Protestant Bohemian king, Frederick V, was first defeated at Mt. White, Wimpfen, and Hochst by the Catholic League under the Generals Tilly and Wallenstein. In the 1620's the war was expanded to include Denmark, while England entered token forces. Catholic armies swept through Germany defeating the Danes. The Danish withdrew from the war in 1629. The Edict of Restitution followed, which attempted to enforce ecclesiastical mandates on Protestants. Their lands and property were seized, and it was demanded that they return to the Church. Provoked by the harsh terms of the treaty, the Swedes entered the war in 1630. They marched into Germany, meeting and defeating the Catholic armies of Tilly, and later Wallenstein. The Peace of Prague in 1635 resulted in the Edict of Restitution being revised, thereby laying the ground work for more equitable terms in reconciling Catholics and Protestants.

The French declared war in 1635. English and French troops engaged the Spanish. Until this time, the battlefields had been primarily in Germany. Now battles were fought in Italy, France and throughout the Iberian Peninsula.

In the north, the once allies Denmark and Sweden went to war against each other. The Swedish General Banar was again victorious in Germany. The Catholic armies of the Empire were repeatedly routed and their strength depleted. Spain conceded in 1643. The French and Swedes were moving successfully on all fronts when the Treaty of Westphalia was signed in 1648.

Under terms of the treaty, the sovereignty of the German States was recognized. France was given several bishoprics and land titles, as was Sweden. Religion, it was agreed, would be determined by territorial rulers, though subjects would continue to worship as they were accustomed. Calvinism was recognized. Religious questions were no longer to be decided by a majority of imperial states. Disputes were to be compromised. Toleration became a function of each individual ruler's discretion.

The Thirty Year War had been contrived and perpetuated by individual rulers with political and territorial, as well as religious, interests. The Holy Roman Empire was reduced to a shambles. The papacy had lost major political power, and became progressively less important as a secular force in policy determination. For example, after the Peace of Prague, hostilities continued while the pope attempted to intercede and mediate. He was unheeded. Protestantism, through nationalism, became firmly established as a result of the Thirty Year War bringing an end to religious passion and intolerance.

c. Counter Reformations

To the extent that fundamental and central religious issues were involved in the Catholic-Protestant wars of the 17th century, motives were plain. Catholics wished to damp out heresy and arrest growth of Protestantism. The Protestants, as an essentially persecuted minority group, sought to win religious liberty and shake loose the shackles of the papacy. Roman Catholicism reeked of a power-oriented, surfeiting, corrupt clergy who plainly sought personal political strength under the guise of religion, and in the name and glory of God. Clements VII, who founded such religious orders as the Capuchines to evangelize the common people, and other Catholic leaders became increasingly aware of the degradation, indolence and lethargy within the Church. They increasingly recognized that this was largely responsible for the loss of constituents. With this realization there began a renewal of vigilance and proselytizing within the Church which was popularly to become known as the "Counter Reformations."

Reformation began within the Church, when such men as Paul III were elected to the papacy. The Council of Trent became oriented to the reconstruction of the Church, to review and institute new effective definitions and regulations. Foreign missions began with new proselytizing orders. The Vatican took on the quasi-monastic character we find today. Worship was standardized. The law of the Church was reorganized. Educational requirements were established for parish priests. Discipline in the lives and conduct of priests was redefined, and the orders reformed. Catholicism took an offensive stance with the Jesuits and Capuchins. Austria, Poland, and the southern Netherlands, parts of Germany, Hungary, and Bohemia were won back. Jesuit foreign missions sprung up in America. Carmelite reforms were instituted in Spain by Theresa and John of the Cross. Catholic reforms in France began under Francis of Sales and Vincent de-Paul. In England, Catholicism was saved from extinction by Jesuit missions.

The Order of the Society of Jesus, the Jesuits, is the largest and most rigorously disciplined of all Catholic orders. The Spaniard Ignatius of Loyola took the original oath sworn to papal loyalty. The discipline developed into an extreme devotion. They daily recite the divine office as do other clergy, but wear no distinct habit. Thus they can accept no ecclesiastical office nor honors, taking vows of chastity, poverty and obedience. The training is prolonged and tedious. Religious indoctrination is required for two years, with study and teaching for thirteen. The Jesuit is then ordained as coadjutor, taking final vows to the pope. Foreign Catholic missions are largely Jesuit, including those in Japan (now defunct), China, India, and, most extensively, in Latin America.

Early in the Counter Reformations, the Jesuit mission was to reclaim Protestant Europe for the Church, and to excite religious fervor in Southern Germany, France, Hungary, and Poland. They were suppressed in the middle 18th century, but again commissioned in 1814. The Jesuit tradition has since grown in strength, with the Jesuits becoming a determined, unrelenting body of Catholics. Their doctrine, dating back to the period of the Counter Reformations, dramatizes the rigid code and militant stance under which the order operates:

1. Always ready to obey with mind and heart, setting aside all judgment of one's own, the true spouse of Jesus Christ, our holy mother, our infallible and orthodox mistress, the Catholic Church, whose authority is exercised over us by the hierarchy.

2. To commend the confession of sins to a priest as it is practiced in the Church; the reception of the Holy Eucharist once a year, or, better still, every week, or at least every month, with the necessary preparation.

3. To commend to the faithful frequent and devout assistance at the holy sacrifice of the Mass, the ecclesiastical hymns, the divine office, and, in general, the prayers and devotions practiced at stated times, whether in public in the churches, or in private.

4. . . . esteem . . . religious orders . . . and give the preference to celibacy or virginity over the married state.

5. Never engage by vow to take a state that would be an impediment to one more perfect . . .

6. . . . praise relics, the veneration and invocation of Saints . . .

7. To praise the use of abstinence and fasts as those of Lent, of Ember Days, of Vigils, of Friday, of Saturday and . . . pure devotion.

8. To commend, moreover, the construction of Churches and ornaments; also images, to be venerated with the fullest right . . .

9. To uphold . . . the precepts of the Church . . . to defend them promptly, with reasons drawn from all sources against those who criticize them.

10. . . . never attack superiors before inferiors . . .

11. To value the sacred teachings.

12. . . . blamed and avoided to compare men who are still living on the earth with the Saints . . .

13. . . . the Church . . . if she shall have defined anything to be black which to our eyes appears to be white we ought in like manner to pronounce it to be black. For we . . . the Spirit of Christ and of the Orthodox Church is the same . . .

14. . . . speak with circumspection concerning (predestination) . . . lest perchance, stressing it too much . . . we may seem to shut out the force of free will and the merits of good works . . .

15. . . . not speak on the subject of predestination too often . . . whence many are wont to neglect good works and the means of salvation . . .

16. . . . praise of faith without distinction and explanation added, the people seize a pretext for being lazy with regard to any good works, which precede faith, or follow it when it has been formed by the bond of charity.

17. . . . nor . . . must we push the . . . inculcating of the grace of God, as that there . . . might raise doubts as to liberty and efficacy of good works.

18. . . . the fear of God . . . is not only useful . . . often necessary to raise man from sin . . .

Jurisdiction was founded upon the principle of subjection of the whole life of the individual to a visible authority. The extreme consequence of this is the institutionalizing and subversion of all morality. Perhaps in such mandatory and uncritical obedience lies the secret of Jesuit success, as well as that of modern Catholicism.

The Jesuits are considered by those within the Church hierarchy, as well as the laity, to be the "best educated" of all Catholics. A political scientist, Max Lerner, once pointed out the difference between training and education as evidenced in the USSR. Education is dangerous to dogma in the sense that a free spirit of criticism is imparted. Jesuits, in this sense, are, then, not educated. Rather, they may be considered to be "trained" Catholic technicians, perhaps even as a kind of army ant, solely dedicated to perpetuation of the faith.

Clergy at the Council of Trent patterned their precepts in keeping with mediaeval scholasticism. The binding power of the church was reiterated, as were the dogmas of original sin, the seven sacraments, the transubstantiation, penance, extreme unction, the Host, the consecration of priests and the hierarchy, the sacrament of holy matrimony, purgatory, the worship of saints and relics, and of monastic vows. These became binding as Church creedal document and law. The axiom of Church authority, in deciding about the truth of dogma and to act autonomously in all theological matters, was reiterated, viz., all Catholics must believe in the holiness and infallibility of the Roman Catholic Church, and that alone which the church teaches is Catholic. The Church alone has the right to command the conscience and faith of the individual. Many theretofore abuses originating in the Church were modified, such as the perversion of indulgences as a source of gain, and devotion of the clergy to the mere personal administration of their office. Foremost among internal reforms was in abolishing the secular Papacy.

Protestant or heretical precepts anathematized and condemned by the Council were prepared in the Canon on Justification. The following were so denied:

1. . . . man can be justified . . . by his own works.
2. . . . this grace is given . . . so that man may more easily live justly and earn eternal life . . .

3. . . . man can believe, hope and love . . . repent . . . (and) the grace of justification can be conferred.
4. . . . the free will of man . . . does not cooperate at the call of God, . . . nor can it refuse . . . it does nothing at all, like some inanimate thing, and is completely passive.
5. . . . man's free will was completely lost and destroyed after Adam's sin.
6. . . . evil works, as well as good, are wrought by God . . . the betrayal of Judas is no less his works than the calling of Paul.
7. . . . the more strongly a man strives to dispose himself to receive Grace, the more grievously he sins.
8. . . . a man reborn and justified . . . is assuredly in the number of the predestinate.
9. . . . he that falls into sin was never truly justified . . .

Anathematized propositions in the Canon on Penance were:
1. . . . that penance is not truly a sacrament.
2. . . . baptism itself is . . . penance.
3. . . . that the words of our Lord . . . "Whosoever sins ye remit, they are remitted unto them; and whosoever sins ye retain, they are retained" . . . are not . . . understood as the power of remitting . . . in the sacrament of penance . . . (and) refer to the authority to preach the Gospel.
4. . . . for . . . remission . . . three acts are not required . . . contrition, confession and satisfaction.
5. . . . sacramental confession was neither instituted by divine authority . . . nor . . . private confession to the priest alone . . . is alien from the institution and command of Christ . . . a human invention.

The Holy Sacrifice of the mass was revivified; Christ, proclaimed the Council, once offered himself with the shedding of his blood. God was propitiated by the offering, through the ministry of the priesthood of a holy bloodless Mass. Through it, the Council maintained, we attain mercy, and find grace and help in time of need.

Purgatory was again avowedly proclaimed as real, and that the souls residing there are helped by intercessions of the faithful and acceptable sacrifice of the altar. The power of conferring indulgences, it was insisted, had been granted to the Church by Christ, and had always been used by, and was salutary for, Christian people. This would be retained by the Church. Honor due saints in the Catholic Church was re-emphasized: . . . it was the concensus of the Holy Fathers, and the decrees of the Sacred Councils, that the intercession, the invocation of saints, was true and valid. Honor is due relics and the lawful use of images. The Saints, who reign with Christ, offer prayers in supplication in obtaining benefits from God through his Son, Jesus Christ.

During the Council, the profession of faith was revivified:

" . . . I recognize the Holy Catholic and Apostolic Roman Church as the mother and mistress of all churches, and I vow and swear true obedience to the Roman Pontiff, the successor of blessed Peter, the chief of the Apostles and the representative of Jesus Christ.

I accept and profess, without doubting, the traditions, definitions and declarations of the sacred Canons and Oecumenical Councils, and especially those of the holy Council of Trent, and, at the same time, I condemn, reject and anathematize all things contrary thereto, and all heresies condemned, rejected and anathematized by the Church. This true Catholic Faith without which no one can be in a state of salvation, which at this time I, of my own will, profess and truly hold, I vow and swear, God helping me, to my life's last breath, and that I will endeavor, as far as in me shall lie, that it be held, taught and preached by my subordinates or by those who shall be placed under my care: so help me God and these Holy Gospels of God . . . "

Erroneous thinking and premises at large devaluating the Church were identified and denied:

" . . . That there exists no Divine Power, Supreme Being, Wisdom and Providence, distinct from the Universe . . . That the prophecies and miracles narrated in Holy Scriptures are fictions of poets . . . that the decrees of the Apostolic See and the Roman Congregations fetter the free progress of science. That the method and principles, by which the old scholastic Doctors cultivated theology, are no longer suitable to the de-

[279]

mands of the age . . . that every man is free to embrace and profess the religion he shall believe to be true, guided by his reason . . . that Protestantism is nothing more than another form of the . . . Christian religion . . . in which it is possible to please God equally as in the Catholic Church . . . That the Church ought to be separated from the State, and the State from the Church . . . that, in countries nominally Catholic . . . persons coming to reside therein shall enjoy the free exercise of their own worship . . . that the Roman Pontiff can, and ought to, reconcile himself to, and agree with, progress, liberalism, and modern civilization . . . "

The counter-reformations swept through Bavaria, Trier, Wurzburg, Bamberg and Salzburg. Protestant ministers were soon replaced by students of the Jesuits. The original reform doctrine was dying. Lutheran ministers were driven from Styria, Carinthia, and Carniola. Jesuit guidance of the Counter-Reformation in England forged new conflict under the Catholic Queen Mary. In the sixteenth century, the Massacre of St. Bartholomew in France was engineered under Jesuit influence. Mutual intolerance between Catholic and Protestant increased under the force of the Counter-Reformation movement and culminated in the Thirty Year War.

Neo-Catholicism, as Counter-Reformation doctrine was called, was formulated at the Council of Trent, though "new" is perhaps a misnomer. Actually the doctrine was but a revivification and restatement of earlier doctrine. The chief innovation, rather, was the renewed unrelenting insistence upon absolute loyalty to the Church, the Pope and his hierarchy. Most desperate and urgent measures were taken during a period of waning church power. The Counter Reformation brought about much of modern Roman Catholicism, in a singular fanatical doctrine, with a resiliency of purpose not unlike that of the early Christian sect.

The Catholic hierarchy now seems often to look in retrospect upon the romance-ladened Protestant tradition, and such men as Luther. Modern Catholics are not completely forgiving, but, Pope Leo notwithstanding, they concede that Luther may have had some justification. He, and others like him, were, after all, the catalytic agents that brought about badly needed reform within the Church. Now, in twentieth-century Roman Catholic perspective, Luther is seen as a zealous man of God, first a Roman Catholic seeking worthy reforms. It is indeed not incomprehensible that Luther's hymn, "A Mighty Fortress Is Our God," should be published in the Catholic publication, "The People's Mass Book" in Cincinnati, Ohio, September of 1964. God is yet the Roman fortress. Though Catholics may detest, anathematize, reconcile and deny divergencies of view, attacks on this fortress have not ended. Perhaps in the face of such dogma, when it infringes on human liberty, we cannot expect them to end.

Chapter **30**

The Modern Christian World

Since the 17th century, Christendom has been essentially tripartisan in character. There were first Eastern Orthodox and Roman Catholic Christians; then came the Protestants. Protestants are divided into multiple sects, but generally include the Anglican, and generic categories of Protestantism originating on the mainland of Europe.

a. Eastern Orthodox

The terms "Catholic" and "Orthodox" are not technical, for both groups refer to themselves by either designation. Eastern Christians who have returned to communion with the Pope are called Uniates. Repudiation of the Bishop of Rome (the Pope) otherwise is the principal dividing point.

The Eastern Church differs on several points of faith and celebration. Liturgy is not celebrated daily, and it is always sung. Raised bread is used in the sacrifice, and the communion is given with a spoon. Infants receive communion as well as confirmation, with the confirmation being conferred by priests. Unction is given to the sick as well as the dying. Also, the practice of confession is less frequent than it is in the Roman Church. Orthodox parish priests may marry, with only monks and bishops abstaining. Orthodox Churches are governed by a holy synod, a board of bishops and laymen, frequently appointed by the government. The patriarch is only the synod moderator.

The Patriarch of Constantinople, after the Eastern Empire was established, enjoyed the highest respect. He ruled the churches of Asia Minor and the Balkan Peninsula. He was, however, subordinate to the emperor in the east. The Turks later gave the Patriarch greater freedom; his quarter in Constantinople, the Phanar, became the Greek center of the Ottoman Empire, but the Patriarch never was to achieve the absolute jurisdiction that the Western Pope enjoyed.

Separate Orthodox churches were set up in Russia, Greece, the Balkans and Bulgaria. Independence of such Orthodox patriarchates has now become typical, including the Coptic Church in Alexandria and the Jacobite in Antioch. There are also separate Orthodox Churches in Palestine, at Mt. Sinai, and Cyprus.

The Russian Orthodox Church is the largest in the Eastern communion, established first in Kiev under the Constantinople Patriarch; the Moscow Patriarch was first set up in 1589 under the Tzar. In the year 1712, Peter the Great established a synod under his control. In 1917, following the Bolshevik Revolution, all churches in Russia were closed, their priests executed or exiled. They were reopened during the Second World War, with the new Russian Patriarch since being loyal to the Communist Regime.

Other separate Orthodox Churches include Greek (a State Church), Yugoslavian, Rumanian, Albanian, Finnish, Polish, and Japanese (founded by a Russian mission in 1860).

In the United States, there are separate hierarchies consisting of Greek and Russian Orthodox Churches. In 1950, the American Orthodox Church merged with the Protestant groups to form the National Council of Churches of Christ in the U.S.

The Orthodox Church actually differs only in matters of discipline and worship with the Roman Catholic, not in beliefs. However, Orthodox Christians in America, and perhaps as minority groups in other lands, stand as strange, misunderstood sects. This may be attributed to their scattered numerical strength (as compared with that of Roman Catholics), to the poverty of Orthodox Church members who were later immigrants to the United States, and to the cold indifference of Roman Catholics in recognizing Orthodoxy. Still, the Orthodox Church claims collectively to be the second largest Christian body in the world.

Orthodox clergy proudly hold that its theology is unchanged since earliest times. Roman Catholics, they contend, must believe things to attain salvation that would be strange to their ancestors. The 1854 dogma of the Immaculate Conception, as well as the 1950 dogma on the Assumption of the Blessed Virgin, is unacceptable, nor is, traditionally, papal infallibility as officially declared in 1870, acceptable to the Orthodox.

Orthodoxy seems more to assume kinship with Protestantism in America. While Catholics elaborate and expand teachings, Protestantism tends to simplify. Orthodoxy, like Protestantism, does not require legal exactness in such mysteries as Holy Communion. Unlike Protestants, however, the Orthodox feel that a priest is necessary to interpret scripture; and they, like Roman Catholics, without hesitancy, profess to have a unique status: The Orthodox Church is the one Holy Catholic Apostolic Church of Christ; it is the cosmic constant, the standard by which other churches are to be judged. Orthodoxy, it is claimed, has never found earthly kingdoms necessary, whereas Roman Catholicism has always sought wealth. The Church itself, they maintain, is eternal because it is spiritual. Temporal sovereignty is the state's charge. They characterize Roman Catholicism as a centralized form of religion, and Protestantism as centrifugal, the latter overemphasizing individual judgment. Orthodoxy achieves unity, but welcomes diversity in non-essentials. Like Protestantism, they would emphasize a church that Jesus founded, and strive for betterment in life here and now. Saints, in this regard, are to be marveled at and not imitated.

The Orthodox Church goal primarily, however, is sanctification through holiness to save one's immortal soul. Thus even infants are given holy communion. Essentials of such doctrines as birth control are also held fast in the Orthodox creed.

b. Roman Catholicism

The chief distinguishing characteristic of the discipline and belief in this group, numbering one-sixth of the world's population, is the communion with the Pope who holds supreme authority as the Vicar of Christ. Other designations are "Holy Catholic" and "Apostolic Church." "Roman Catholic" was a term of the 19th century British coinage to distinguish it from other forms of Catholicism. "Roman church" properly means only the Archdiocese of Rome.

Roman Catholics vary somewhat in belief, but all generally hold according to Roman Catholic catechism that: (1) Theirs is the one True Church. (2) God objectively exists and has interest in individual men who can contact Him through prayer. (3) Each individual has a soul. (4) He is accountable at death for his actions in life. (5) He will accordingly be sent to Heaven or Hell. (6) The Gospels are historically authentic. (7) The Church is divinely commissioned, as are the pope and bishops. (8) The dead are never forgotten, nor the Virgin Mary and the Saints, nor those in Purgatory. (9) God conveys His grace directly through the sacraments. (10) Penance is required once a year. (11) The Eucharist is required at least every Easter. (12) Private prayer is essential. (13) Contemplation is ideal. (14) Self renunciation is a necessary part of prayer, as it is in fasting and Lent. (15) Every act is an offering to God. Thus, the main object of ethical behavior is in loving God. (16) Every act lies in the intent. (17) What God has created is never bad, but bad use can be made of His creations, e.g., drinking to excess, fornication, etc.

The keystone of Roman Catholicism is the Doctrine of Apostolic Succession, i.e., that the Pope and his appointed representatives have, in varying degrees, the spiritual authority Christ assigned to His apostles. Theoretically, any adult male Catholic is eligible to become pope, but practice limits candidates to Cardinals. Popes were first elected by the clergy and laity of the diocese. This was discontinued in 769. Then Nicholas II limited election to Cardinals in 1059. Gregory X set up the present form of conclave in 1274. This is now a College of Cardinals who meet secretly for not less than 15 nor more than 18 days after the death of a Pontiff. Two-thirds plus one vote, in secret balloting, is required for election, which, per se, confers on the new Pope full jurisdiction.

The Roman Catholic doctrine concerning non-Catholics is that all will be saved (in the Church) if they persevere. Only those are damned who persist in denying the Church when they *know* that she is right (The principle or tactic of hypnotic certainty.)

In Roman Catholicism, there is no distinction between the religious and non-religious life, e.g., stealing and failing to attend church are both wrong. Likewise, "truth" is equally valid if derived through science, reason, or church pronouncement (cf., "seamless robe," in the Greek Book of John, 19,23-24)

Ceremonial practices have been designed to reinforce the tradition in aesthetic ritual, in the use of Latin, the intonation of liturgy, the softening of light by colored glass, the burning of incense, the copius use of statues and images; also insistent belief elements, such as the doctrine of miracles, serve to reinforce the faith.

The new English mass now reveals clearly the liturgical content previously obscured by the Latin. An entrance hymn greets the priest mass-celebrant. A Latin prayer is spoken with altar boy response. The priest then chants the mass introit, ending with "Glory be to the Father, Son, and Holy Ghost." A commentator then calls upon the Lord for mercy and praises Him for His goodness. The priest takes up the chant: "Lord have mercy, Christ have mercy," followed by the reiteration of the congregation. Except during Advent, the Gloria follows:

"Glory to God . . . we praise, bless, worship, glorify, give thanks for your great glory, God the Father Almighty. Lord Jesus Christ, the only begotten Son, Lord God, Lamb of God, Son of the Father. You take away the sins of the world, receive our prayer. You, who sits at the right hand of the Father, have mercy on us. For you alone are holy. You alone are Lord, You alone, O Jesus Christ, are most high. With the Holy Spirit in the Glory of God the Father. Amen."

A prayer is again chanted, the priest washes his hands, to begin the Sacrifice of the Mass. He recites the preface, still in Latin, with response from the congregation, with communicants again affirming their faith in the Christ. The Canon is recited in Latin. Then the commentator states, "We have offered the Father our gift, Christ. He has received it. Now He invites us to feast on this same gift, Christ. To prepare for this saving banquet we will say together the Lord's Prayer."

The Lord's Prayer is recited, led by the priest. They then recite, "Lamb of God, who takes away the sins of the world, have mercy on us." repeated several times. Distributing of the wafer is accompanied by a series of similar chants, followed by a hymn of Thanksgiving for the Eucharist. Thus at last is revealed the mystery of Osiris to the English speaking communicants.

Except for foreign missions, all organization is by diocese, under a bishop's jurisdiction. Archbishops are given sees, and supervise bishops. Dioceses are divided into parishes with churches and priests who are supervised by bishops. The pope controls bishops through general legislation. The pope's government is run by cardinals, including such matters as missions and secular state relations. Several Roman Catholic groups of the Eastern rites, e.g., Uniates, Chaldean (Syrian), and Armenian, also have their organization under the pope.

The monastics cut across territorial lines, running missions, hospitals, schools and colleges. The latter generally receive subsistence allowance only, while parish priests receive fixed salaries. Training is usually in seminaries maintained by the Orders, the Bishops or the Vatican.

There is no Church-wide census, but the Church claims that their communion numbers one-half the world's Christians, or the largest single world religion.

Traditionally, Roman Catholic countries abound with signatures of the religion, such as road-side crosses and national observance of saints' days. In other countries, such as the United States, it is merely part of the Christian complex.

The church has undertaken characteristic reforms in its cycle of ascendancy following decline, always emphasizing goals of "spiritual revival." At first, reformation began in monasteries. Then popes, such as Gregory VII and Urban II in the 11th century, attempted to exclude civil rulers from making Church appointments. The vying for power in the Church by Catholic princes, however, continued for centuries. Following a quarrel between the Pope and Philip IV of France, the papacy was brought to Avignon in 1309, becoming cluttered with French politics. By the 15th century, the Popes were so shorn of power that they could do but little to halt the revolt of such men as Wyclif, Luther and Calvin. Protestants sought to restore primitive Christianity based on the Gospel Jesus. Great Britain, Northern Europe, parts of Central Europe and Switzerland then largely broke away from the Church. As a consequence in the

17th century there came the most extensive Roman Catholic church reform, with the militant Jesuits developing in Spain, and the cult of the Sacred Heart in France. State control, however, increased during the 17th century. In the 18th century, the Bourbons attempted to do away with the papacy, suppressing the Jesuits. In 1878 Pope Pius IX did much to re-institute church unity in issuing the Doctrine of Papal Infallibility. Leo XIII later urged Catholics to take part in modern life. In some countries Catholic political parties were again formed. Marxism, however, grew as an anti-papal influence. Increasing antagonism in Italy, France and Portugal, suppressed religious orders. This was later followed by active hostility toward the church in the USSR, Mexico, Spain, the Baltic States, Yugoslavia, Hungary, Czechoslovakia and China. Roman Catholic religious revival has since continued, however. Religious orders have expanded, and foreign missions revivified. Indoctrinated Catholics claimed to have apparitions of the Virgin Mary. Catholic emancipation and the Oxford movement revived Roman Catholicism in England. A series of encyclicals, e.g., Rerum Novarum (Leo XIII, 1891), Quadrigesimo Anno (Pius XII, 1931) and Mater et Magistra (John XXIII, 1961) have stressed fundamental adjustment to, or confrontation of, modern life. The Liturgical movement in France, Germany, Britain, and the United States, has recently emphasized non-political internationalism of the Church, culminating, perhaps, in the Second Vatican Council.

In the United States, Roman Catholicism originated independently with the Spanish Franciscan missions in Florida, New Mexico, and California, with the French in New Orleans, and, in Maryland, with the English. Northern colonists otherwise largely suppressed it. In 1790, John Carroll in Baltimore was made Bishop of the United States. By 1840, with increasing Catholic immigration, there were 16 dioceses. In the 1840's, the Irish came, followed by Germans, Italians and Poles. Thousands of churches and schools were built. The heavy Irish Catholic population concentrated in urban areas, which accounts for traditional urban Catholicism in America. Several anti-Catholic spokesmen in the United States, such as Beecher and Morse in the 1830's, and organizations such as those in the Know-Nothing movement of the 1850's, the American Protective Association in the 1890's, and the Ku Klux Klan in the 1920's, have perpetuated the traditional Protestant-Catholic antagonism. The Catholic movement in America has further increased in scope from the early period, to include the liturgical movement, the Catholic Youth Organization, Catholic social work, and Catholic trade unions. Catholic parochial schools and universities in the United States now number in the thousands.

c. Protestantism

Protestants, the third group of Christian partisans, make up from $1/4$ to $1/3$ of the Christian body. These include the Anglican Communion of 30 to 40 million constituents who are ritualistically close to Roman Catholicism and Orthodoxy, and who also claim precedence in the Creed of Apostolic Succession. They are, however, traditionally Protestant in the sense of having historically broken with the Roman Church.

1.) Anglicanism (Church of England)

This Christian body, composed of regional churches, provinces and separate dioceses bound together in agreement found in the Lambeth Conference in communion with the Church of England, is referred to as "Anglican." National member churches included the Episcopal Church of America, the Scottish Episcopal Church, the Church of Wales and the Church of Ireland. Here, as in the Eastern Orthodox and Roman Catholic Churches, is the doctrine of Apostolic Succession, or the unbroken tradition as handed down through the Holy Ghost, with apostolic power to administer grace through sacraments. Other Protestant divisions reject the Doctrine of Apostolic Succession, and substitute the authority of scriptures alone, maintaining that the true Church is invisibly present in all Christian denominations.

The Church of England had its origin in the Synod of Whitby in 663 combining the Romano British Church, the Celtic Church and the mission of St. Augustine of Canterbury. Henry VIII later broke allegiance with Rome, assuming church headship. The Act of Supremacy (1543 and 1552) established the king as the only supreme head of the Church of England. This was provoked, as well as by Henry's personal cleavage with the Roman Church, through resentment of the populace of required monies to be paid to Rome. Henry authorized the revised Tyndale-Coverdale bible translations. Cranmer's Book of Common Prayer was adopted in 1552.

Queen Mary briefly reunited with the Church of Rome, but later Elizabeth again broke off, establishing a middle course between Roman Catholicism and Calvinism. The Hampton Court Conference in 1604 decided in favor of traditional Catholic practices, against the protests of the Puritans. The conference also brought about the King James English Bible (1611). The civil war of 1652 resulted largely from Archbishop Laud's insistence upon maintaining discipline of the Roman Church against the Calvinists. Under Cromwell, Independent, rather than Calvin Presbyterian, doctrines were established. The Episcopacy, however, was re-instated by the Restoration Act of 1660, when the prayer book was revised toward Catholicism in the Act of Uniformity. In defiance of this act, many nonconforming clergymen resigned to form their own chapels.

Before the turn of the 18th century, James II again attempted to style the English Church more after that of Rome, requiring that his declaration of toleration be read in all churches. Midway in the 19th century the Catholic and Apostolic Creeds were strongly reaffirmed in the Oxford Movement led by Kible, Pusey and Newman (before the latter entered the Roman clergy). This movement re-emphasized ritual, and the Doctrine of Apostolic Succession.

The Church of England thus crystallized during the 19th century into essentially about what it is today, though since World War II, canon law and the prayer book have undergone further revisions.

The clergy of the Church of England are based on ancient order: deacons, priests, and bishops, with the bishops ordaining and confirming the membership and consecrating the churches. The Archbishop of Canterbury is the Chief Primate, with the Archbishop of York being the primate of England. The Church is established by the state, but clergy are paid by the congregation. Creeds are the Apostles, the Nicene, and the Athanasian. Doctrinal standards are found in the revised Book of Common Prayer and the Thirty Nine Articles of 1552, the Catechism, and 16th century books of homilies.

The enigma of three separate communions, viz., Eastern Orthodox, Roman Catholic, and Anglican, each claiming Apostolic Succession, remains one of the major points of contention among these churches. The Petrine claim of the Roman Catholic Church, viz., that the apostle Peter was first in Rome, is disputable by asking, what was Rome? If it were the empire, intended to be encysted in control by all apostolic descendants, then this was Constantinople, later becoming seated in Germany of the 11th century. In an Anglican's persuasion might also be asked, by whose admission does a Roman pope succeed, other than through a political Kremlin-like power struggle in the Vatican? The claims stand, each disputing the other in the bid for primacy; all, that is, but for the Generic Protestants who seek salvation through scriptures alone.

2) Generic Protestantism

The term "Protestant" is derived from the Latin word, "Protestatio," referring to a defiant protest of Lutheran princes at the Diet of Speyer in 1529, when the emperor's ruling against heretics was ordered to be enforced. Earlier a storm of protest had erupted in the theological formulations of Hus, Wyclif, Luther, Zwingli, Knox and Calvin. Within Protestantism itself there was a conflict of Lutheranism with Calvinism and the radical Calvinistic emotional Evangelic religions (Calvinist Churches were identified as "Reformed" on the continent, and "Presbyterian" in Britain). Such Protestant divisions from the beginning were sharp, with only a modicum of union ever achieved between the Lutheran and Evangelical doctrines.

Religious reformation in England assumed more of the character of church-state conflict than evidenced on the continent, though currents of Calvinist and Evangelical doctrine were also strong in England. Fierce hatreds arose within Protestantism, e.g., the burning of Servetus. These divisions within the Reformation Churches also served to further the work of the Counter-Reformation, during which the the Catholic Church won back Poland, Hungary, Bohemia, and parts of Germany.

The Reformation movement gave emphasis to personal responsibility and individual freedom. It fostered adamant refusal to accept any authority blindly, and served to break the centuries-old grip of the Church on the life of the individual.

The word "Protestant" was first adopted by the Protestant Episcopal Church in the United States (1783), an Anglican communion. It has since been used in many different senses, but largely in contradistinction to Roman Catholicism and Eastern Orthodoxy. The chief precepts are in acceptance of the bible as the only source of infallible revealed truth, the universal priesthood of all believers, and that Christians are justified, in the "eyes of God," by belief alone, rather than on the basis of good works or in dispensation by the Church. Emphasis on the preaching of ministers, with essential neglect of liturgy, is also characteristic of Protestant sects. Extreme personal morality was also earlier stressed by such sects as the Puritans. The Evangelical churches in Germany and Scandinavia are now largely those of Lutheran origin, while the Reformed Churches are those of Calvin and Zwingli. Protestantism was adopted primarily by peoples of Northwestern Europe, with the major exceptions of Southern Germans, the Irish, French and Belgians, who remained Catholic. Protestant minorities reside in France, Bohemia, Hungary and Poland.

Sects have continued to develop via the Protestant doctrine of individual conscience and interpretation of scriptures. Doctrinal disputes within sects have involved such issues as grace, predestination and the sacraments. Several Protestant movements have also claimed new revelations, e.g., the Agapemone (a now extinct sect founded in 1850), in which a mid-nineteenth century Englishman named Henry Prince claimed that the Holy Ghost resided in his body; the Mormons, and the Church of new Jerusalem also claim revelation. Other bizarre Protestant sects also hold unusual claims (cf., Christian Science, which repudiates, as an article of faith, medical treatment.)

Protestant Ecumenicity has also developed in recent years, in some cases in alliance with Orthodoxy. The alliances have been federated on local, national and international levels, (cf., the National Council of Churches of Christ in the United States of America, and the World Council of Churches).

Emphases of Protestant Churches have continued to change, perhaps due to dynamic forces of individualism operating generally within a modern free society. During the so-called period of "romanticism" in America, religious "feeling" was played up (cf., Schleiermacher). The "fatherhood" of God and the "brotherhood" of man have assumed major importance; philosophical systems, such as Existentialism, Logical Positivism and Operationism have also influenced theological thinking.

Protestantism in the United States may be broadly grouped into Fundamentalism, Neo-Orthodoxy, and Liberalism. Fundamentalism derived from the earlier surge of revivals in the 18th and 19th centuries, emphasizing literal bible interpretation, and advocating extreme moralistic codes. This movement includes contemporaries, such as Billy Graham (who also, incidentally, has adopted modern methods of big-business showmanship). The Neo-Orthodoxy movement is evidenced in varieties of contemporary evangelical churches which emphasize revelations. (cf., Barth and Niebuhr). Liberalism derives from the social gospel and modern humanistic movements, giving freer play to abstract symbolic interpretations of the bible, and emphasizing church responsibility. Liberalism cuts across many of the sects, with some clergy speaking out, even in a radical fashion (cf., Pike). Basic liberals, per se, however, are small in number and include largely the Unitarian-Universalist sect.

Each modern Protestant sect may contain elements of any or all of these aforementioned emphases. A Lutheran interpretation, for example, may be typical of the modern Protestant context. Dr. M. Marty, of the University of Chicago Divinity School, describes Lutheran youth as increasingly indifferent to the doctrine. The sixteenth century Lutheran, contrasts Dr. Marty, was much more concerned with his ultimate destiny, since he more frequently witnessed death. Today it is seen that Lutheran self-examination is necessary to restate the doctrine, for meanings have changed from Paul's and Luther's times. It must be understood, maintains Marty, that God takes the initiative in man's salvation. All Lutherans agree on the scriptures being the norm and authority of teaching; the "Word", or Christ, is revealed to us through these. Growing Lutheran unity, he avows, is evidenced in the fact that there were 60 Lutheran groups in the U.S. at the turn of the century, and now only three. Marty considers the typical Lutheran as a white middle-class suburbanite or small towner who was formerly a farmer or laborer. Politically he is Republican. He, is fiercely patriotic and religious, educating his children accordingly. The Lutheran church service appears to Dr. Marty to be similar to Episcopalian. Music is employed extensively, as in the Bach chorales. Sermons are based on biblical text, seldom oriented to social or political issues. Communion is now being observed more frequently, together with kneeling and chanting. Confession is public and spoken in groups. Baptism and the Last Supper are the only sacraments. The Lutheran minister is trained in Latin, Greek, Hebrew and German, to make first-hand interpretation of the bible. Luther's original catechism is the basis for education of Lutheran children; this is based on the Ten Commandments, the Creed, the seven parts of the Lord's Prayer, Baptism, the Lord's Supper, and some versions of confession. Lutherans, contends Marty, are not ascetic. They have no monasteries nor rules of diet, nor do they measure faith in terms of piety. They believe that one can be a good man without being Lutheran, or even having a belief in God. The question of how grace is mediated to man remains an unresolved conflict between Lutherans and Roman Catholics. Only the Bible is the norm for every Lutheran as it is for most Protestants.

The generic Protestant is an individualist who is many-faceted. Sects and points of view have continued to develop. For a brief description of a number of contemporary sects, refer to Appendix B.

As we have seen, the Christian world is yet divided three ways. Most heavily and severely bound in dogma are Roman Catholics. Orthodoxy and Protestantism also call for unity of Christian thought; but even as politico-religious blocs operate, there perhaps can be no real agreement. The avenues of difference cannot be joined, while yet that bigotry and dogma issuing from ancient paganism still prevails. Yet, the individualism that Protestantism originally nurtured may continue to penetrate the borders of dogma, and perhaps to light up new eras of inquiry and skepticism. From enlightened Protestantism may still spring the hope for new insight, to release those intellectual shackles that yet hold us firm, and constantly to revivify the enthusiasm for intensive self examination, to commission the critic who alone can bring new light to old problems, and without whom life becomes but an unyielding rigid structure, that is at once totalitarian Communism, brutal Fascism, authoritarian Catholicism, and unethical Capitalism.

Suggested Further Readings

1. Angus, S. *The Mystery Religions and Christianity,* 1925
2. Augustine *The Confessions* (Translated by F. J. Sheed), 1942
3. Baynes, N. *Byzantium: Introduction to East Roman Civilization,* 1948
4. Brezzi, P. *The Papacy: Its Origin and Historical Evolution,* (English Translation), 1958
5. Brodrich, J. *Progress of the Jesuits,* 1947
6. Brown, R. *The Spirit of Protestantism,* 1961
7. Bryce, J. *The Holy Roman Empire,* 1950
8. Budge, W. *Osiris,* 1961
9. Carpenter, E. *Pagan and Christian Creeds,* 1921
10. Cicognani, T. *Sanctity in America,* 1939
11. Cornell, G. (Associated Press) "Catholicism Taking Another Look at Luther" Oct. 22, 1964
12. Coulton, G. *Inquisition and Liberty,* 1938
13. Crosse, G. *A Short History of the English Church,* 1947
14. Daniel-Rops, H. *The Twentieth Century Encyclopedia of Catholicism,* 1963
15. Dudden, F. *Gregory the Great,* 1905
16. Ellis, J. (Ed.) *Documents of American Catholic History,* 1956
17. French, R. *The Eastern Orthodox Church,* 1951
18. Hertling, L. *A History of the Catholic Church,* 1956
19. Hitti, P. *The Arabs: A Short History,* 1956
20. Howlett, D. "Faith and History" in *Atlantic Monthly,* April, 1956

21. Howorth, H. *Saint Augustine of Canterbury,* 1913
22. Hughes, P. *A Popular History of the Catholic Church,* 1949
23. Janelle, P. *The Catholic Reformation,* 1940
24. Kerr, W. *A Handbook on the Papacy*
25. Knox, R. *The Belief of Catholics,* 1927
26. Krogman, W. *Ancient Sun Kingdoms of the Americas,* 1963
27. Larson, M. *The Religion of the Occident,* 1961
28. Lucas, H. *The Renaissance and the Reformation,* 1960
29. Maynard, T. *The Catholic Church and the American Ideal,* 1953
30. Marty, M. "Lutherans - Largest Protestant Group Re-examines Doctrines" Lecture on "Your Neighbor's Faith" Series. Buffalo Evening News, Buffalo, New York, 1963
31. Mendenhall, T. et. al., *Problems in Western Civilization,* 1956
32. McKinnon J. *Calvin and the Reformation,* 1936
33. McSorley, J. *Outline History of the Church by Centuries,* 1943
34. Miller, G. (Associated Press) "Stronger Role for Laity is Sought" October 8, 1964
35. Murphy, F. (ed.) *A Monument to Saint Jerome,* 1952
36. Neville, R. *The World of the Vatican,* 1962
37. Pallas, J. "Hellenic Church is Explained: Old Roots and a Proud History" Lecture on "Your Neighbor's Faith" series. Buffalo Evening News, Buffalo, New York. 1963
38. Putz, L. (Ed.) *The Catholic Church,* U.S.A., 1956
39. Robinson, C. *Selections from the Greek and Roman Historians*
40. Rose, H. *Ancient Roman Religion* 1949
41. Rosten. L. *Religions in America* 1963
42. Rupp, E. *Luther's Progress to the Diet of Worms,* 1951
43. Setton. K. *A History of the Crusades,* 1955
44. Shirer, W. *The Rise and Fall of the Third Reich,* 1960
45. Smith, H. *Henry VIII and the Reformation,* 1948
46. Smith, P. *Erasmus: A Study of His Life, Ideals and Place in History,* 1963
47. Stokes, A., and Pfeffer. L. *Church and State in the United States,* 1964

48. Thurston, H., and Attwater, D. (ed.) Butler's *Lives of the Saints,* 1956
49. Turberville, A. *Mediaeval Heresy and the Inquisition,* 1920
50. Verhoeven, F. *Islam,* 1962
51. Ward, J. *Anglicanism in History and Today,* 1961
52. Whale, J. *The Protestant Tradition,* 1955
53. Wedgwood, C. *The Thirty Year War,* 1939
54. Wedgwood, C. *The King's War 1641 - 47,* 1958
55. Welch, C. *Protestant Christianity,* 1954

APPENDIX A

TYPICAL CHURCH DOCUMENTS ON THE CREED

A sampling of church documents is presented that the reader might appreciate something of the mood and thinking of early Christian proponents. Question has frequently been raised as to the authenticity of such documents, in charging that they were tampered with in the original language, or in the translations, by zealous Christian redactors. However, the sampled correspondence makes sense in light of theological systems extant today. We might assume reasonable fidelity, save for possible political redactions introduced to reinforce the later power structure of the church.

Ignatius, (Bishop of Antioch) Epistle to the Smyrnaeans: (circa 75 A.D.)

"Avoid divisions as the beginning of evils. All of you follow the bishop, as Jesus Christ followed the Father and follow presbytery as the Apostles: and respect the deacons as the commandment of God. Let us not perform anything pertaining to the church without the bishop. Let that be considered a valid Eucharist over which the bishop presides, or one to whom he commits it. Wherever the bishop appears, there let the people be, just as, wheresoever Christ Jesus is, there is the Catholic Church. It is not permitted either to baptize or hold a love-feast apart from the bishop. But whatever he may approve, that is well-pleasing to God, that everything which you do may be sound and valid."

Clement's Epistle to the Corinthians (circa 175 A.D.)

" . . . the Apostles . . . went forth with confidence in the word of God and with full assurance of the Holy Spirit, preaching the gospel that the Kingdom of God was about to come. And so, as they preached in the country and in the towns, they appointed their first-fruits to be bishops and deacons of them that should believe for the scriptures say, 'I will set up their bishops in righteousness, and their deacons in faith' . . .

. . . our Apostles knew also, through our Lord Jesus Christ, that there would be strife over the dignity of the bishop's of-

fice. For this reason, therefore, having received complete foreknowledge, they appointed the aforesaid, and after a time made provisions that on their death other approved men should succeed to their ministry . . . "
Tertullianus (a Montanist, circa 200 A.D.)

"if Jesus Christ sent out the Apostles to preach no others are to be accepted as preachers but those whom Christ appointed, since 'no other knoweth the Father save the Son and he to whom the Son hath revealed him.' . . . all doctrine which accords with those apostolic churches, the sources and originals of the Faith, must be reckoned as the truth, since it preserves without doubt what the churches received from the Apostles, the Apostles from Christ, and Christ from God . . . We are in communion with the apostolic churches; there is no difference of doctrine. This is the testimony of truth . . . "
Athanasius, Patriarch of Alexandria, whose creed was adopted by the church (circa 350 A.D.)
On Atonement:

" . . . God's goodness could not acquiesce in the ruin of his handiwork

. . . But though this is unavoidable, there is on the other side the honor of God's character, so that God may appear consistent in his decree about the death . . . What then ought God to do about this matter? Demand repentance . . . ? But this would not safeguard the honor of God's character, for he would remain inconsistent if death did not hold sway over men . . . What else was needed to restore man from corruption . . . but the word of God, who in the beginning made everything from nothing?

For it was his task to restore the corruptible to uncorruption, and to maintain the honor of the Father before all. For being the Word of the Father and above all, it followed that he alone was also able to re-create everything and to be ambassador for all men with the Father.

. . . And thus, taking a body like ours, because all men were liable to the corruption of death, he surrendered it to death instead of all, and offered to the Father . . . that by all dying in him the law touching the corruption of mankind might be abolished (inasmuch as its power was fulfilled in the Lord's body), and no longer has capacity against men who are like him, and that he might turn back to incorruption men who had reverted to corruption and quicken them from death by the appropriation of his body and by the grade of his resurrection . . .

. . . The Word takes on a body capable of death, in order that, by partaking in the Word that is above all, it might be worthy to die instead of all, and might remain incorruptible through the indwelling Word, and that for the future corruption should cease from all by the grace of his resurrection . . . Hence he did away with death for all who are like him by the offering of a substitute. For it was reasonable that the Word, who is above all, in offering his own temple and bodily instrument as a substitute-life for all, fulfilled the liability in his death, and thus the incorruptible Son of God, being associated with all mankind by likeness to them, naturally clothed all with incorruption in the promise concerning the resurrection . . . "

Salvation:

" . . . wishing to help men, he naturally dwells with men as man, taking to himself a body like other men. And from things of sense, that is by the works of his body . . . so that they who were unwilling to know him from his universal providence and guidance may through the works of his body recognize the Word of God in the body and through him come to the knowledge of the Father . . .

"For this reason was he born, appeared as man, and died and rose again . . . that whithersoever men have been lured away, he may recall them from thence, and reveal to them his own true Father; as he himself says, 'I came to seek and to save that which was lost."

Creed dated 359, after Acacius, Bishop of Caesarea

" . . . We believe in one God, the only and the true God, the Father all-sovereign, creator and artificer of all things;

"And in one only-begotten Son of God, who, before all ages, and before all beginning and before conceivable time and before all comprehensible being, was begotten impassibly from God; and through him the ages were set in order and all things came into being; begotten as only-begotten, only from the only Father, God from God, like to the Father that begat him, according to the Scriptures. No one knows his begetting save the Father that begat him. We know that he, the only-begotten Son of God, at the Father's bidding came from the heavens for the putting away of sin, was born of the Virgin Mary, went about with the disciples, fulfilled all his stewardship according to the Father's will, and was crucified, died, and descended to the lower regions, and set in order all things there, and the gate keepers of Hades were frightened when they saw him, and he rose from the dead the third day and had converse with the disciples, and fulfilled all his stewardship; and when thirty days were accomplished he ascended into the heavens, and sits at the right hand of the Father, and is to become at the last day in his Father's glory, giving to each according to his works . . .

. . . But the term essence has been taken up by the Fathers rather unwisely, and gives offense because it is not understood by the people. It is also not contained in the Scriptures. For these reasons we have decided to do away with it, and that no use at all shall be made of it for the future in connection with God, because the divine Scriptures nowhere use it of the Father and the Son. But we say that the Son is like the Father in all things, as the Holy Scriptures say and teach . . . "

Jerome's Epistle to Pope Damascus (circa 376 A.D.)
(Jerome is noted for his Vulgate, Catholic version of the bible, published by Erasmus in 1516 A.D.)

Essence:

" . . . Since the East, rent asunder by feuds of long standing, is tearing to shreds the seamless robe of the Lord . . . I think it is my duty to consult the chair of Peter . . .

. . . I am terrified by your eminence, yet your benevolence attracts me. From the priest I claim the preservation of the victim, for the shepherd the due protection of the sheep. Away with all trace of pride; let Roman majesty withdraw. It is to the successor of the fisherman that I address myself, as the disciple of the cross.

As I follow no leader save Christ, so I communicate with none save your Beatitude, that is, with the chair of Peter. For this, I know, is the Rock on which the Church is built. This is Noah's ark, and he who is not found in it shall perish when the flood overwhelms all . . . "

Augustine, a Bishop of Hippo at the turn of the fourth century, wrote much that spirited the policy and doctrine of the modern Catholic Church:

Grace:

" . . . the human will is so divinely aided towards the doing of righteousness that, besides being created with the free choice of his will, and besides the teaching which instructs him how he ought to live, he receives also the Holy Spirit . . . a man's free choice avails only to lead him to sin, if the way of truth be hidden from him. And when it is plain to him what he should do and to what he should aspire, even then, unless he feel delight and love therein, he does not perform his duty, nor undertake it, nor attain to the good life. But to the end that we may feel this affection 'the love of God is shed abroad in our hearts' not through the free choice which springs from ourselves, but through the Holy Spirit which has been given us . . . the wills of men are prevented by the grace of God, and . . . it is God who makes them to will the good which they refused; for it is God whom we ask to, and we know that it is meet and right to give thanks to him for so doing . . .

. . . Assistance was bestowed on the weakness of man's will, that it might be unalterably and irresisibly influenced by divine grace; and that, weak as it was, it might still not fail nor be overcome by any adversity. So it came about that man's will, when weak and powerless, and as yet in a lowly state of good still persevered, by God's strength in that good; while the will of the first man, though strong and healthy, possessed of the power of free choice, and in a state of greater good, did not persevere in that good; and the reason was that though God's assistance was not lacking, it was the assistance without which it could not persevere even if it so willed, and not assistance of that kind by which God vouchsafed to do what he willed; but for them that were weak he reserved his own gift whereby they should most irresistibly will what is good, and most irresistibly refuse to forsake it . . . God is unable to sin; he who partakes of God has received from him the inability to sin . . . "

A Dominican friar of the 13th century, Thomas of Aquino, formulated under the influence of Aristotlian philosophy his *Summa Theologica.* This was later set up by Leo XIII as the classical exposition of Catholic doctrine.

Belief:

" . . . understanding involves assent . . . but it does not involve reasoning . . . as a result of the application of axioms to conclusions assent is given to conclusions by resolving them into axioms, and at that point the movement of reason is stayed and brought to rest . . . in belief, assent and reasoning are on, as it were, equal terms. For here assent, as has been said, is not caused by reasoning but by the will. But since the understanding is not in this way brought to its one proper termination, viz., to the vision of the intelligible object, hence it is that its motion is not brought to rest but is still employed in reasoning and inquiry on the objects of faith, however firmly it assents to them . . . and hence the understanding of the believer is said to be taken captive because it is determined by external considerations, but by its own proper processes. Hence, too, it comes that in a believer motions may surge up contrary to that which he most firmly holds, a thing which does not happen in a man who understands, or in one who knows . . . "

God Incarnate:

" . . . the nature of God is the essence of goodness . . . and hence whatever pertains to the principles of good befits God. It pertains to the principle of the good that it should communicate itself to others . . . Hence it pertains to the principle of the highest good that it should communicate itself to creation in the highest way; and the communication reaches its highest when 'he so joins created nature to himself that one person comes into being from three constitutes, the Word, the Spirit, and the flesh.' Hence it is manifest that it was fitting that God should be made flesh . . .

. . . for the restoration of human nature which had fallen through sin, nothing might seem to be required but that man should make satisfaction for his sin. But man, as it seems, could have made satisfaction for sin, for God ought not to require from man more than he is able to give; and since he is more prone to pity than to punish, as he reckons the act of sin punishable, so he ought to reckon the contrary act as meritorious. Therefore it was not necessary . . .

. . . it is of especial importance for man's salvation that he should reverence God . . . But men reverence God the more from the very fact that they consider him as raised up above all things and removed from the senses of men . . . it might seem not to be profitable for man's salvation that God should become like us by assumption of flesh.

But on the other hand, that through which the human race is liberated from perdition is needful for man's salvation. But the mystery of the divine incarnation is of this sort, according to that saying, God so loved the world that he gave his only-begotten Son; that everyone who believes on him should not perish but have eternal life. Therefore it was necessary . . .

. . . In order that man should walk towards faith with more assurance, truth itself, the Son of God, taking manhood on himself, founded and established the faith . . . God did not diminish his majesty by assuming flesh, consequently the ground of reverence towards him is not diminished; for reverence is increased by the increase of the knowledge of God. And because he wishes to come near to us through the assumption of flesh, he has drawn us the more to the knowledge of himself . . . "

Christ and Salvation:

" . . . grace was given to Christ not only as to an individual but insomuch as he is the head of the Church, that is, in order that it might from him rebound to the members; therefore the works of Christ have the same effect with respect both to himself and to his members, as have the works of another man. Now it is clear that any man established in grace, who suffers for righteousness sake, merits salvation for himself by that very suffering . . . Hence Christ through his passion merited salvation not only for himself but for all his members.

. . . a thing is properly called a sacrifice when it is done to pay the homage properly due to God, to propitiate him. Hence . . . a true sacrifice is every work which is performed in order that we may inhere in God in holy fellowship, a work, that is, directed to that end of good in which we can attain true blessedness. Now Christ, . . . offered himself for us in his passion; and it was this voluntary undergoing to the passion which, above all, rendered it acceptable to God. Hence it is manifest that the passion of Christ was a true sacrifice . . .

. . . man was bound, through sin, in two respects; first, in servitude to sin . . . The devil, by inducing man to sin, had overcome him and therefore man was assigned to the devil as a slave. Secondly, in respect to the incurring of a penalty . . . according to the justice of God.

. . . Therefore, since the passion of Christ was sufficient and superabundant for the sin of human race and the penalty incurred, his passion was a kind of ransom, by which we were freed from both these obligations . . . "

On the Sacrament of Bread and Wine:

" . . . all conversion which takes place according to the laws of nature is formal . . . But God . . . can produce not only a formal conversion, that is, the supersession of one form by another in the same subject, but the conversion of the whole being, that is, the conversion of the whole substance of A into the whole substance of B. And this is done in this sacrament by the power of God, for the whole substance of bread is converted into the whole substance of Christ's body . . . Hence this conversion is properly called transubstantiation . . . it is apparent to sense that after consecration all the accidents of bread and wine remain. And this indeed happens without reason, by divine providence. First because it is not customary but abhorrent for men to eat man's flesh and to drink man's blood. Therefore Christ's flesh and blood are set before us to be taken under the appearances of these things which are of frequent use, namely bread and wine. Secondly lest this sacrament should be mocked by the infidels, if we ate our Lord under his proper appearance. Thirdly, in order that, while we take the Lord's body and blood invisibly, this fact may avail towards the merit of faith . . . "

Pope Pius' Iteration of Infallibility - 19th century (The Vatican Council of 1870 decreed this. Pius was also noted for his Bull Ineffabilis Deus and decree on the Immaculate Conception).

" . . . adhering faithfully to the tradition received from the beginning of the Christian faith tradition, the glory of our Divine Savior, the exaltation of the Catholic religion, and the safety of the Christian peoples, teach and define as a dogma divinely revealed; That the Roman Pontiff, when he speaks ex cathedra, though the divine assistance promised him in blessed Peter, is endowed with that infallibility with which the divine Redeemer has willed that held by his Church—in defining doctrine concerning faith and morals—should be equipped: And therefore, that such definitions of the Roman Pontiff of themselves—and not by virtue of the consent of the Church—are irreformable. If anyone shall presume to contradict this our definition, let him be anathema."

APPENDIX B

PROTESTANT SECTS AND ORGANIZATIONS

Protestantism is unique among the other Christian bodies, in that scores of individual groups operate, each perhaps not tightly bound nor always a closed system, but presenting varied doctrine and emphases. The Eastern Orthodox and Roman Catholics, by contrast, are largely universal in precepts. Some minor variations are found, as in the discipline of the Uniates, or in the Syrian rites, or the rebellious National Polish Catholics in America; but by and large all are consistent in dogma.

Protestant sects number over 200; most are of European origin with such exceptions as Eddy's Christian Science, Miller's Jehovah's Witnesses, Smith's Mormonism, and the various Hillbilly groups, all of American origin.

The reason for sects are many, due perhaps to politico-religious demagoguery of the founders (cf., evangelistic revivalists, Billy Sunday, Father Divine, etc.), or perhaps interpersonal conflicts and resentments, or even legitimate and reasonable premises. The very act of communicating the religion may also be frequently responsible.

Nuances of word meanings, for example, colloquialisms, idioms, folksy phrasings, and the very context of utterances, change appreciably within the same tongue even during the brief span of a decade. Witness words like "mom", once an affectionate reference to the maternal aspect of the family, that, since Wiley, has come more to mean a sinister, insidious self-centered person; or "daddy", once, too, only an intimate, affectionate, respectful reference to the paternal aspect, becoming a flippant allusion to any older person.

In formal and historical writing, the "zeitgeist", or the contemporary mood of speech and word meanings, may be frequently overlooked; from tongue to tongue, these changing and differing significances among words are necessarily obscured in theological formulations. Jesus of Nazareth spoke of blessings and man's redemption. His tongue was Aramaic. The gospels were written in Greek nearly a century later. The Greek was translated into Latin for the Romans. Subsequent versions of Luther's German, Wyclif's English, or Waldo's French introduced unique language idioms and meanings. Theological insistence upon accuracy can thus only be arbitrary. In such whimsy as this, and passionate partisanship in the emotionally-conditioned dogma, sects were born. Following are briefly described samples of such extant sects:

AMERICAN BAPTIST ASSOCIATION - made up of "Landmark", "United", and "Missionary" Baptist sects. The forerunners, the "Anabaptists", were so called because of insisting upon rebaptizing those who came to join their ranks from Catholicism. Many Baptists claim their origins came not from reformers, but from dissenters who never did accept the system of Catholicism; e.g., Donatists, Novationists, Paulicians, Albigenses, and Waldenses.

AMERICAN EPISCOPAL - founded in America by such men as William White in the 18th Century for autonomy of the American Episcopal Church in separating from the English Church. Consecration by the Archbishop of Canterbury was denied after the American Revolution, so the Scottish Episcopal Church gave sanction. Evangelicalistic aspect stresses the Bible first, the Church second. Sect is predominately located east in New York, Pennsylvania, and Virginia.

AMERICAN LUTHERAN - merged synods of Buffalo, New York, Iowa, and Ohio in the mid-twentieth century; composed of Prussian and German Lutherans. The Iowa Synod was originally organized in the mid-19th century of German origin; the Buffalo Synod was developed about the same period by Prussian immigrants.

ANABAPTISTS - among the earliest of cleavages within Protestantism, and the least tolerated by all the sects. They suffered at the hands of both the Reformation groups and of the Roman Church. The founder, Zwingli, differed with Luther on such theological points as infant baptism. From 1517 to 1530, a period when both Luther and Zwingli won large numbers of converts, Anabaptists were persecuted by soldiers of the Roman Church; some 2000 were also executed by members of the reform groups. The reformers' methods of execution were those of the Inquisition, the same force, cruelty and inhumanity. The number of

Anabaptists grew, however, and the movement spread throughout Switzerland, Germany, Austria, and Holland. The Anabaptists later developed into several separate sects, such as Baptists and Congregationalists.

AUGUSTANA LUTHERAN CHURCH - American Sect founded by Swedish Lutherans predominately settled in Illinois and Wisconsin; it was named by Eric Norelius. Membership is made up largely of English, German, Swedish, and Norwegian Lutherans.

ASSEMBLIES OF GOD - organized early in the 20th Century in Hot Springs in the pentecostal motif. Baptism in the Holy Ghost, speaking in tongues as the spirit gives utterances, and the imminence of resurrection are the essential beliefs. The group originated in revival movements and now has a half million members spread throughout the South and Midwestern United States. Theological basis for the church is "Baptism in the Holy Ghost", accompanied by speaking in tongues as the "Spirit gives utterance." Organized early in this century, it grew out of intense revivalism in the preaching of the "Second Coming."

BAPTIST - No single origin is ascribed. Many claim John Smyth first organized it in Holland; Smyth believed that baptismal rites belong to believers rather than infants. Another stream is traced back to John Spilsburg, a former Congregationalist. Calvinistic Baptists believed in predestination and practiced immersion. In present day America, an American Baptist Convention grew out of the Northern Baptist Convention. The Southern Baptist Convention came from the original General Missionary Convention. The latter have remained relatively aloof from inter-denominational tendencies. There are notably some seven million negroes in this group.

Origin of the Baptist sect is thus somewhat obscured, though it is likely theologically rooted in the Anabaptists, which also claim the contemporary Menonites. Some facets of the sect may have originated in the early English Separatists as well as the John Smyth creed that baptism is no blind infant ritual, but for believers only.

On the American continent, Roger Williams is often credited with establishing the first Baptist Church in Providence, Rhode

Island, after having been driven from the Massachussets Bay Colony in the 17th Century for his radical views. Others credit John Clarke for an earlier Newport, Rhode Island Church. The first Baptist Association met in Philadelphia, in a Calvinistic tone.

The General Missionary Convention for American Baptists first met in 1814. In 1824 the General Tract Society and Publication Societies were formed, and the American Baptist Home Mission Society in 1832. In 1905 the Baptist World Alliance was formed, and in 1907, the Northern Baptist Convention (American Baptist Convention) became a limited corporation.

In 1845 the Southern Baptist Convention separated from the General Mission Convention; and since, the southern religious attitudes have become traditionally strict in their solitary adherence to the Baptist Creed with emphasis on revivalism.

Baptist schools include the following:

Brown University in Rhode Island, after the benefactor, Nicholas Brown, a Baptist inspired institution, dedicated to liberalism and religious freedom.

Colby University in Maine founded in 1813.

Baylor University in Texas, instituted in 1845 at the Texas Baptist State Convention.

Denision University in Ohio founded in 1831 by the Ohio Baptist Education Society.

Vassar College, established in 1861 as a woman's college in New York, founded by Baptists but non-sectarian.

Chicago University, a university for general education under Baptist supervision, with non-sectarian requirements, founded in 1857.

BAPTIST GENERAL CONFERENCE OF AMERICA - organization founded in the Mid-19th Century by Swedish Missionary Gust of Palmquist, for American Swedish Baptists.

CHRISTIAN REFORM - American Sect formed by Dutch immigrants to the United States, seceding from the State Church of the Netherlands early in the 18th Century, and settling largely in Western Michigan. Organization is similar to that of the Presbyterian Church, with ministers, elders and deacons; each congregation is largely autonomous.

CONGREGATIONALISM - original Puritans, the Separatists or Pilgrims, who formed under such leaders as Robert Browne in the 16th Century. Variety of creeds developed, based on simple friendship rather than organization; competed with Presbyterians, but later joined them against the Quakers. Congregationalism was dominant among Puritans who immigrated to Massachussetts, and throughout the New England Colonies. Calvinism was the predominant theology; autonomy marked the movement, with ministers subject to local regulation. Many ministers supported institutions of higher learning. Later, Congregational Churches in New England, New York and New Jersey, were united into a Federation of Churches for the movement west.

Congregationalism originated in England. Each congregation set its own creed. Growth was checked in England due to persecution. Due to the tyranny of the later beheaded Charles I, and his supporter, the Archbishop Laud, Congregational and Presbyterian Puritans migrated to New England early in the 17th Century. Congregationalism became the dominant way in the New World and remained so in the New England States up until the 19th Century when it joined with New Jersey Presbyterians for church expansion westward. Calvinism was the dominant theology, spiced with liberalism.

The original Mayflower Group had earlier migrated to Holland, but found life there strange and foreign. However, rather than return to their own England where they had not been tolerated, they sought to settle in the New World. The London Virginia Company agreed to support their New World journey and the crown agreed to their colonization; thus, they returned to England and set sail in the Fall of 1620.

Their organization was civil in the Plymouth Colony rather than religious. At first the Puritans sought converts among the Indians, as exemplified by John Eliot who preached among them, and translated the Bible into their language.

In 1636, Puritans of the Massachusetts Bay Colony founded Harvard for ministerial training. Congregational and Presbyterian Puritans, steeped in Calvinism and predestination doctrine, also founded such schools as Yale (after Elihu Yale), Oberlin College in Ohio and Mount Holyoke College in Massachussetts.

As the schools developed as institutions of higher learning, several became extremely dangerous to the dogma. At Harvard, Jonathan Mayhew (18th Century) opposed the Trinitarian Doctrine, for example, and Calvinistic Congregationalists forthwith withdrew support.

Horace Bushnell helped dethrone the Calvinism in the 19th Century that had been dominant in the New England Congregationalist Churches. He held that it was normal religious growth, rather than marked conversion experience, that mattered. This view was antedated by such 17th Century German mystics as Jacob Bohme and Johann Arndt, who held that inspiration of the Bible is little different from that of any good person. This also became the forerunner of Quakerism and such philosophical systems as those of Hegel and Schopenhauer.

Several Congregationalists were also active in early social reform. Henry Ward Beecher, early 19th Century Congregational minister, suffered much abuse for his unpopular anti-slavery stand. Congregationalist John Fee founded Berea College, the first interracial school in the country.

CHRISTIAN REFORMED CHURCH - originated in the Netherlands where a group of congregations seceded from the State Church during the mid-19th Century in reaction to ecclesiastical reorganization and doctrinal latitudinarianism. Emigrating to the United States of America, they immediately organized into the Reformed Church in America, and thence denouncing doctrinal laxity and reformed practices. They are largely found in Western Michigan and New Jersey. Calvin College is located in Grand Rapids, Michigan.

CHURCH OF CHRIST - diverged from the Disciples of Christ around 1840. Founders objected to the use of musical instruments in the church and the increasing power of titles and pastors. The church is self-governing. Highly evangelistic, the New Testament is considered true and completely adequate revelation. It is one of the largest Christian bodies in the western and southern parts of the United States, first officially listed in the United States Census of 1906.

THE CHRISTIAN PAGAN

CHURCH OF CHRIST SCIENTISTS - (Christian Scientists) founded by Mary Baker Eddy early in the 19th century, with claims of inspiration in biblical metaphysics by personal physical healing through the mind. Eddy published: "Science and Health with Key to the Scriptures," and formed a group to practice primitive Christianity in Massachusetts. An actively proselytizing sect, membership has spread throughout the world.

CHURCH OF GOD IN NORTH AMERICA - founded by John Winebrenner of Harrisburg, Pennsylvania in 1828, in revivals from Armenian and Baptist doctrines. Characterized chiefly by immersion and foot bathing at the Last Supper rites. Originally spread to Maryland from Pennsylvania; now found elsewhere.

CHURCH OF CHRIST OF LATTER DAY SAINTS (Mormons) - American sect founded by the prophet Joseph Smith who claimed revelation in a holy vision to form an organized church. Church is highly organized with a presidency, apostles, patriarch and priesthood. Belief is in the traditional trinity, atonement, prophecy and healing. Polygamous practices were prohibited by the United States Government in 1890. Theirs is a history of persecution in America (Missouri and Illinois). They themselves were later implicated in the massacre of Missourians going west. Major settlement is in Salt Lake City, Utah where they settled under the leadership of Brigham Young; also located in Illinois, Pennsylvania, Missouri, and Arizona.

They moved on the basis of revelation, first to Kirkland, Ohio, thence to Independence, Missouri to convert the American Indians. Driven from Missouri by the militia, the Mormons themselves mobilized, but, in battle, Smith and others were captured and ordered to be executed; but the captors failed to carry out the orders. The Mormons then migrated to Illinois, where Smith suffered martyrdom. Brigham Young assumed leadership after Smith's death. Young had a vision of a nation in the far west and the group migrated in search of such an image. It was so that they settled near the Great Salt Lake in Utah.

Later, in retribution, they attacked Missourians and others migrating west when camping near their Salt Lake Community. All were massacred when the Mormons joined Indians in the slaughter, save a few children.

The Mormons believed in polygamy as a reward for the extra devout. Having an abundance of progeny was next to godliness, in providing bodies for the myriad angels awaiting incarnation. President Buchanan in 1857 dispatched an army to Utah for statehood. The Mormons resisted with pillages on the troops, but finally surrendered the territorial seal to receive a new governor. The polygamous practice was also outlawed.

CHURCH OF LUTHERAN BRETHREN - organized at the turn of the 19th Century from the free church movement in Norway, holding that Church people should be separated from the rest of the world. Very active in missionary work.

CHURCH OF THE BRETHREN - originated in Schwarzenau, Germany in the 18th Century, and in Holland under such leaders as Alexander Mach. Later settled in Pennsylvania in the United States. Practices were those of primitive Christianity. They are marked by non-conformity in garb, bearing witness to worldly indulgences. Popularly called "Dunkards", "Tunkers", or "Dumplers" in Pennsylvania.

CHURCH OF THE NAZARENE - Methodist background, organized early in the 20th Century in Texas. Theological stress is on holiness or sanctification, baptism with the Holy Spirit, and pentacostal (i.e., as in the descent of Christ upon the apostles) power of Christian experience. Almost 4,500 churches are centered throughout the Midwest, Texas, Massachusetts, Missouri, Kansas, and California.

COVENANTER CHURCH - reformed Presbyterian, organized by ministers of the Reformed church late in 18th Century from the Presbytery of Scotland and Ireland. It is small in number; they acknowledge the Westminister confession of faith and the Catechisms. The church has been active in civil affairs, education, and anti-slavery. Their belief is fundamentally in the lordship of Jesus Christ. As a nation, the sovereignty of Christ is not subscribed to by the American Constitution. These, as dissenters, seek a constitutional amendment to this end.

DISCIPLES OF CHRIST - founded by the Irish Alexander and Thomas Campbell in the 18th Century as dissenters from established Presbyterianism. In the United States they are largely located in the midwest. Belief is in the rejection of creeds, with emphasis on the New Testament, and the divine sonship of Jesus. Baptism is practiced.

In America, the sect was earlier associated with the Baptists in belief and practice. They felt there should be unity, and that differences were merely in human opinions. Walter Scott formulated the "five finger" exercise to conversion, in "faith", "repentance", "baptism", "remission of sins", and "gift of the holy spirit." His work as an evangelist on the Ohio frontier did much to establish the sect.

ECUMENICAL MOVEMENT - World Council of Protestant Churches formed in 1948 in Amsterdam, Holland, to discuss issues of church unity and common bounds of Christian Faith. Movement is composed of some 165 Protestant, Anglican, and Orthodox Church bodies from more than 50 countries.

The council proposed to study and discuss issues involving church unity, to bear witness together to their common allegiance to Jesus Christ. The council's presidential body is made up of five ministers from all parts of Europe and America.

EVANGELICAL AND REFORMED CHURCH - made up from a merger early in the 20th Century of the old German Reform Church, with the Evangelical Synod (originally the Evangelical Union Church of Prussia). Membership is located primarily in the Mississippi Valley, Pennsylvania, and Missouri.

EVANGELICAL CHURCH - founded by Jacob Albright in the 18th Century among German Americans in Pennsylvania. Recently merged with the United Brethren in Christ.

EVANGELICAL COVENANT CHURCH OF AMERICA - organized late in the 19th Century by Swedish Lutheran laymen. The Church is non-creedal, but subscribes to the primacy of Bible teachings, viz., that "He will be born again into a new hope." Primarily located in Midwestern United States, Minnesota, Illinois, Iowa, Nebraska, and Kansas.

EVANGELICAL LUTHERAN JOINT SYNOD OF WISCONSIN - organized in Wisconsin in the Mid 19th Century. John Muehlhaeuser took issue with the Missouri Church doctrine, with groups of his followers organizing in Minnesota, Michigan, and Wisconsin. Belief is in the inspiration of the scriptures and inerrant word of God.

PROTESTANT ORGANIZATIONS

FINNISH EVANGELICAL LUTHERAN - made up of immigrants from Northern Norway in the mid 19th century, largely settled in Minnesota, Iowa, Northern Michigan, and including the mid-western Scandinavian groups.

FREE METHODIST - originated in Pekin, New York, in the mid 19th century by a group of ministers attempting to restore principles of Methodism based on Wesleyan doctrine, Christian perfection, simplicity and piety of life, and a freedom of spirit in worship. This was, also, incidentally, the first church with free seats, where those before were bought or rented. Headquarters are in Indiana.

HILLBILLY CHRISTIANS - Broad designation for such groups as the "Shakers", so-called in derision, alluding to the tremble in religious esctasy characteristic of their practices. This particular group is called the United Society of Believers organized from the original Quakers. Hand motions and spiritualistic communications with the deceased are practiced. Many southern religionists are described as reverent and uninhibited. Hellfire and damnation sermons are common practice, including baptism and anointing of feet; high-pitched religious singing and frenzy, including faith-inspired poison snake handling.

The Shakers date back to mid-18th century England; in America, settling in New York, New England, Kentucky, and Ohio. Chief practices are wordless songs, marching, hand motions, and spiritual communication.

Southern religious character is extremely fundamental. Sermons are of condemnation and admonition about the damnation of souls. Men and women sit apart. Practices are again fundamental in the washing of each others feet, hysterical "rebirth," a kind of momentary "possession by the spirit."

Hardshell Baptists pray and sing as though possessed, in all day communion, in a simple and familiar faith demonstration. In the Church of God at Chattanooga, Tennessee, the handling of poison snakes is practiced, fondling and draping them about their necks in a roped off area.

HUGUENOTS - a French Protestant sect of the 16th and 17th Centuries, Calvinistic in origin. The Massacre of St. Bartholomew, under Catherine de Medici, is infamous, in which thou-

*s*ands of Huguenots were killed in treachery, having entered the city of Paris ostensibly in peace; they were sought out and murdered during a full week of persecution. The sect had attracted nobility with political motives, and in vying for political control, entered into deadly conflict.

In the early 16th century, Protestantism was making headway in France. Luther's influence had spread, and other Germans, Swiss and English reformers were being heard. The Hugeunot Church became established as an early French Protestant Sect that had attracted nobility with political ambitions. This Protestant group became identified as politically ambitious, and a threat to the monarchy. A plot was uncovered to seize the king, and several thousands of Huguenots were picked up and executed. There continued for nearly half a century religious wars, massacres, and retaliations.

Under the rule of Catherine de Medici, a treacherous conspiracy took place (a further blight on Christian history). Religious freedom was pretended. The king's sister, a Catholic, was to be married to a Huguenot army officer. Thousands of Huguenots were invited to attend the wedding feast. On August 24, 1572, the eve of the Feast of St. Bartholomew, the visiting Huguenots and families were mercilessly killed. Some 30,000 were massacred in a full week of treachery.

Toleration was slow to come. In France, King Francis II condemned Protestantism. Even suspects were arrested. Hundreds of executions took place. The king was said to have relished the fanfare of a public burning of heretics. A brief respite came in the Edict of Nantes in 1598 under King Henry IV when some religious freedom was allowed. Then after Henry died, the religious wars broke out again and the Edict was revoked. Huguenots were driven into exile by the thousands. It was not until late in the 18th Century when religious freedom was won for Protestants in France.

INDEPENDENT FUNDAMENTAL CHURCHES - organized in the second quarter of the 20th Century by a Moody Bible School graduate, W. McCarrell. The Church stands for "Christian Fundamentals", denouncing worldly methods of finance and reform. Soul-winning work, revivals, and Bible studies are the major activities of the participants.

PROTESTANT ORGANIZATIONS

The Churches of America were organized in 1930 in Illinois, with Chicago as headquarters. The organization was made up of independent churches, as that of the Reverend W. McCarrell's Independent Bible Institute (a former Congregational minister). His church stood apart from worldly methods of finance, for separation from the world. The Cicero, Illinois Church has a "fishermans club" of layworkers who call upon individuals to see the light. Their activities include traveling, preaching in gospel tents, organizing Bible schools, and sending out foreign missionaries.

INTERNATIONAL CHURCH OF THE FOURSQUARE GOSPEL - founded by Aimee Semple McPherson in the first quarter of the 20th Century, pentecostal in character. McPherson was a missionary in China, and evangelistic in temperament. The foursquares is a Biblical term, meaning the gospel facing East, North, South, and West. There are four symbols; the cross is the symbol of salvation through the blood of Christ; the cup, a symbol of divine healing; the dove and the torch of the Holy Spirit. Angelus Temple in Los Angeles was one of the original church structures, a fabulous one-and-one half million dollar building. Among McPherson's compositions are hymns such as "Why Are They Whipping My Jesus?"

JEHOVAH'S WITNESSES - founded by Charles Taze Russell late in the 19th Century in Allegheny, Pennsylvania. Theology stresses the "Second Coming". The sect publishes the famous "Watchtower", and "Awake" magazines having world-wide circulation. The faith has become one of an "assembly of nations".

In 1813 a self-educated seaman named William Miller decided from his Bible reading that the world was to end in 1844. The Millerites, followers of Miller, awaited the year with eager anticipation, disturbing others as well with their admonitions. The Millerite movement disbanded after 1844; however new harbingers appeared as they probed scripture passages for the accurate date. Charles Taze Russell searched scripture to confirm the date selected by a Second Adventists group and annunciated their error. The real date was 1914, he proclaimed, and immediately won a multiple of followers. World War I had thus been designated as the beginning of world conflagration leading toward world's end.

The sect is a rapidly growing one, now highly evangelistic, each member serving as a door-to-door disciple, and promising the "glory of God's Kingdom" to each. World wide, they have been extensively persecuted in the United States. Some 15,000 were mercilessly tortured in Nazi Germany.

Jehovah is said to reside in the constellation Plaiades. Satan, as a fallen angel, is considered to be the hidden ruler of every government based on force. They oppose Roman Catholicism, Orthodoxy, Judaism, Protestantism, symbols, evolution, entertainment of the Trinitarian doctrine, and nationalism. They now look to the "Bomb" for the conflagration, but promise joy and plenty to all believers in their doctrine.

LAMBETH CONFERENCE (1884 and 1920) — Council of the Church of England meeting for unity:

". . . We, Archbishops, Bishops Metropolitan and other Bishops of the Holy Catholic Church in full communion with the Church of England, in Conference assembled, realizing the responsibility which rests upon us at this time, and sensible of the sympathy and prayers of many, both within and without our own communion, make this appeal to all Christian people.

. . . The causes of division lie deep in the past, and are by no means simple or wholly blameworthy. Yet, none can doubt that the self-will, ambition, lack of charity among Christians have been principal factors in the mingled process, and that these, together with blindness to the sin of disunion, are still mainly responsible for the breaches of Christendom. We acknowledge this condition of broken fellowship to be contrary to God's will, and we desire frankly to confess our share in the guilt of this crippling the Body of Christ and hindering the activity of His Spirit . . .

. . . The time has come, we believe for all the separated groups of Christians to agree in forgetting the things that are behind and reaching out towards the goal of a reunited Catholic church. The removal of the barriers that have arisen between them will only be brought about by a new comradeship of those whose faces are definitely set this way . . .

. . . The vision that arises before us, is that of a Church genuinely Catholic, loyal to all truth, and gathering into its fellowship all who profess and call themselves Christians within whose visible unity all the treasures of faith and order . . . shall be possessed in common and made serviceable to the whole Body of Christ . . .

. . . We do not ask that any one Communion should consent to be absorbed in another. We do ask that all should unite in a new and great endeavor to recover and to manifest to the world the unity of the Body of Christ for which He prayed . . ."

LUTHERAN FREE CHURCH - organized late in the 19th Century by such men as George Sverdrup in Minnesota, coming from Norwegian Lutheranism. The church has no constitution, but is organized on the creed that theirs is the right faith in the Kingdom of God on Earth. Located chiefly in the North-Central States on the Northwestern Coast of the United States, and in Western Canada.

MENNONITES - originating in claims of martyrdom, in the 16th century, in Switzerland; originally Anabaptists. Swiss founder, Conrad Gregel, was influenced by Zwingli, but broke with him because of too-slow progress. The name comes from Menno Simmons, a Dutch Roman Catholic Priest, and the group stood for separation of Church and State, and opposition to militarism. In the United States, they are located chiefly in Pennsylvania east of the Mississippi, and in Canada in the Province of Ontario.

METHODISM - founded by John Wesley in the 18th Century at Oxford, England. Originally called the "Holy Club" and "Bible Moths". The word "Methodism" means exact method, according to Wesley, as laid down in the Holy Scriptures. To Wesley, Morovians seemed too aloof; his own Anglicanism seemed too cold and formal. He preached throughout England for changed lives, and regeneration. The group was originally stigmatized as fanatical. The evangelist George Whitehouse, preacher par excellence, held forth among heathens and criminals. Early American Methodist groups were already established throughout Eastern Pennsylvania, in New York, and Maryland in the 18th Century, when an evangelist, Francis Asbury, came to America as Wesley's missionary. Methodist schools are many, including Dickenson College, Ohio Weslyan, and Wilberforce University. The famous Chautauqua Institute in western New York, was founded by Methodists, now an interdenominational summer resort and cultural center. Methodist are the largest single protestant population in the United States.

MISSOURI SYNOD LUTHERAN CHURCH - founded midway in the 19th Century and located largely in Michigan, Missouri, and Ohio. Pioneer leaders in the St. Loius Churches included such men as C. Waether. Divers groups of immigrant Lutherans vowed to remain united in the doctrine that the Pope of Rome fulfills the anti-Christ prophecy. Church ministry is considered to be of divine ordinance, with powers of the word of God bestowed upon them in accordance with scriptures. Educational institutions and parochial schools are the most extensive in American Protestantism.

This Lutheran sect numbers over two million members in the United States, formed from the congregations of Missouri, Michigan and Ohio. Creed is conventional as described in the Lutheran Book of Concord dating back to 1586, and affirming the doctrine that the anti-Christ is fulfilled in the Pope of Rome and his dominion, and in abrogation of the Sabbath and holy days. They hold that the Holy Scriptures are complete in truth, and final, and the hour of judgment is near.

MORAVIAN - originated in an area of Czechoslovakia by the followers of John Hus in the 15th Century. Hus took issue with Roman Catholic practices, in the repudiation of war, political power, human laws, and of the papacy. In America, the sect is predominantly located in Bethlehem, Pennsylvania, and Winston-Salem, North Carolina.

NATIONAL ASSOCIATION OF FREE WILL BAPTISTS - originally founded in both England and the United States in New England, Delaware, and the Carolinas. Doctrine is in "free will", to distinguish it from the "fatalistic" predestination of Calvinism, holding that the human will is free to yield or resist truth and the Spirit. Each church is the voice of authority; immersion is practiced, together with the Lord's Supper and the washing of saints' feet.

PENTECOSTAL HOLINESS CHURCH - organized early in the 20th Century, merged in North Carolina with the Fire Baptist Church. Stated belief is in entire sanctification, instantaneous definite second work of grace, the Pentecostal Baptism of the Holy Ghost, and fire appropriated by faith on the part of the fully cleansed believer, giving evidence by his speaking with another tongue. Belief is also in divine healing, and the imminent second coming. Membership is located primarily in the Southern and Western United States.

PROTESTANT ORGANIZATIONS

PRESBYTERIANISM - stemming from the reformation movement in England and Scotland, and associated earlier with Calvin. Word is from "presbuteros", meaning "elders", which govern the church in a "session". Developed in Scotland under John Knox. Theology is traditionally conservative. Early churches in the United States (17th Century) were formed in Maryland, New Jersey, and Pennsylvania. There are more than 40 Presbyterian colleges in the United States, including Princeton.

QUAKERS - arose in 17th Century England; the Quakers had neither clergy nor churches. Theirs was an "inward light". Sacred places became wherever they met and gathered, in the homes of friends, or in yards and grounds; they were first called the "Society of Friends". The word "Quaker" was applied facetiously by a judge; George Fox, a founder of the society, stood before the magistrate, and when questioned on his belief, he told the judge that he should respect and even tremble at the word of the Lord. Thus came the word "Quaker". Quakers were persecuted in England, and many migrated to the New World; they received no better treatment there. Quaker William Penn began a Quaker colony in what has now become Pennsylvania and New Jersey. Quakers have influenced other groups, and have since modified many of their own beliefs.

The Quakers espoused a variety of mysticism, an "inner light". Beginning in the 17th Century, such men as George Fox decreed the hypocrisy and artificiality in the churches of the day. It is essentially a primitive Christianity with no creed, holding that the scriptures only are inspirational; God is the soul of every man, and simplicity is the good life committed to "Truth". Under William Penn's organization, their numbers expanded in the United States. William Penn, born in London in 1644, was liberal in his outlook. He argued with Angelican Church principles, entering a Huguenot college in France and specializing in Church History. For his radical views, he suffered ostracism, imprisonment, and the terror of the Tower of London.

Penn later converted to Quakerism, "the inner light", writing many books. Wealthy by heritage, he was given a land grant in America and was named by the King as Governor of the Province of Pennsylvania. He envisioned a colony where religious freedom and equality might prevail, and formed his colony with the guarantee of religious freedom and review of grievances.

Contemporary Quaker groups include:

1) Hicksites, after Elias Hicks, formulated in the original tradition, holding a general conference or fellowship of six yearly meetings.
2) Wilburites, after John Wilbur, also traditional and conservative.
3) Orthodox, having yearly meetings in Philadelphia
4) Independents

Quakers are predominantly located in the eastern United States. The Orthodox Group in Philadelphia founded Haverford College in 1833, and a later midwestern group founded Earlham College in Richmond, Indiana.

REFORMED PRESBYTERIAN - also called the "Covenanter Church", numbering approximately 5,000. Originally formed by Scotch and Irish ministers in reformed Presbytery. Their beliefs, though a small sect, are important as an example of the influence a creed might have on the indivdual; for they believe in the Lordship of Jesus Christ, and his directives in the individual's life, the Church and the Nation. The group has pressed for United States constitutional changes to recognize the sovereignty of Christ.

REVIVALISTS - interdenominationalists, such as D. Moody and other non-ministerial individuals, who preached throughout the United States and England in the mid-nineteen hundreds. Institutions, such as the Moody Bible Institute and Missionary Training, have become widely influential in religious affairs. Others notable were: Billy Sunday, a gymnastic revivalist, and former professional baseball player; Gypsy Smith, a contemporary of Moody, and self-educated evangelistic Englishman who was non-orthodox - "I learned by living . . . the world needs only love and hope." Gypsy is credited with obtaining more converts and to have reached more than any other in his time; Billy Graham, a modern evangelist crusading in massive auditoriums, and via radio and television throughout the world.

SALVATION ARMY - founded by William Booth in the mid-nineteenth century. It was organized as " . . . an army fighting for peace and love . . . " eventually spreading throughout the world. Booth was a Methodist minister in England. He intended no separate organization, but, rather, to minister to those refused membership in the established churches. Semi-military lines were set up in England in 1865, and in the U. S. in 1880, portraying "Christianity in action."

Beliefs are conventional in the Biblical doctrine of the Trinity, Atonement, Repentance in faith, eternal happiness of the righteous, and endless punishment of the wicked.

Activities include the "Golden Agers Club," "Missing Friends Bureau," Booth Memorial Homes and Hospitals, Emergency Disaster Service, and Service to the Armed Forces. The preaching is always fundamental in righteousness and salvation through the Lord Jesus Christ.

SEVENTH DAY ADVENTISTS - founded in America by the Reverend William Miller, a Baptist minister, in the mid-nineteenth century. The "Second Coming," an ancient Christian hope, was given renewed emphasis early in the 19th century in America. Miller espoused the prophecy that the "coming" would occur about 1843. Subsequently, the movement grew into a distinct sect, with headquarters in Battle Creek, Michigan. Small in number, they are zealously missionary in practice. Co-operation in patriotic matters is confirmed. (cf., Jehovah's Witnesses.)

UNITARIAN - principles disavow the Trinity of God, affirming Jesus and the Holy Spirit as less than co-equals with God. Formally organized in the 18th century in England, theirs was a radical departure from the Trinitarianism of the official Protestant Church creed. Early creedal differences occurred when the King's Episcopal Church was organized in revising the liturgy, and discarding the Nicene Creed. Michael Servetus, confronting Calvin in the 16th century, was burned alive for stating what he considered to be errors in the Trinitarian Doctrine. Boston became the site of the first Unitarian Church in America, formed from a non-creedal church in the Pilgrims' colony at Plymouth early in the 19th century. William Channing voiced the more modern Unitarian position by stating that authority of an ultimate nature should not be the word of the past revealed in scriptures, but of experience and reason — essentially a doctrinal denial of the authority of the Bible.

UNITARIAN-UNIVERSALIST CHURCH - sects merged in the 1950s. Both are traceable to the 3rd century Paul of Samosata, and the 4th century Arians. These heresies early questioned the Trinitarian doctrine, holding that Jesus and the Holy Spirit were less than co-equal with the God of Unity. The Socinians of Unitarian Creed were formed in Poland, named after Faustus Socinus. There they were banned, as well as in England in the 16th and 17th centuries for the Unitarian heresy. Michael Servetus was later executed for the same heresy after publishing his *Errors of the Trinity.*

Late in the 18th century, the King's Chapel Liturgy was revised in Boston omitting the Athanasian and Nicene Creeds and Trinitarian passages. William Channing, in 1819, delivered a sermon in a Baltimore Unitarian Church as the voice of liberalism in the Church. He held that truth was not the voice of the past revealed in scriptures, but of experience and reason. Ralph Waldo Emmerson, two decades later, in an address at the Harvard Divinity School, re-iterated the view as a theological position. The Bible no longer stood for them as the ultimate authority.

Headquarters of the American Unitarian Association was organized in 1825. At the turn of the century, congresses of the religious liberals were held in London, Amsterdam, and Geneva. Today many Protestant ministers are cognizant and sympathetic toward the Unitarian view, though Trinitarianism is the official Christian view.

Universalism stems from the teachings of Clement and Origen in the 2nd and 3rd centuries in Alexandria. The doctrine is " . . . universal salvation under the God of Love and Justice . . . " American Universalism harks back to James Relly in the 18th century; Relly was the author of a treatise on Union and anti-Calvinism. His influence subsequently brought John Murray to America, who, seeking freedom from persecution, preached that Christ's Atonement was not limited to the elect. Universalists important to the American movement were Dr. Benjamin Rush, a signer of the Declaration of Independence and the first to organize a non-sectarian Sunday School, i.e., the first day Sunday School Society in America; Hosea Ballon, in the early 19th century, wrote his famous *Treatise on Atonement* (a Unitarian view), Clara Barton, founder of the American Red Cross, is also noted as an early Universalist.

UNITED BRETHREN IN CHRIST - founded by Phillip Otterbein, a German missionary, in the 18th century. Headquarters of the Church are in Dayton, Ohio. Creed is that of the Dutchman James Arminius (16th century) who opposed strict Calvinism. Theology is similar to that of British Wesleyanism and American Methodism.

UNITED LUTHERAN CHURCH OF AMERICA - direct successor and heir to major Lutheran bodies, including the General Synod of the Evangelical Lutheran Church in the U.S.A., the General Council of the Evangelical Lutheran Church in North America, and the United Synod of the Evangelical Lutheran Church in the South. Over 2½ million are encompassed in this body.

Lutherans first arrived on the American continent in 1619. The Dutch and Swedes moved to Delaware, and the Germans along the Hudson. The Salzburgers of the Nordic Alps settled in Georgia, the Saxon immigrants in Missouri, and in the Midwest, the Scandinavians; those of the Norwegian Synod settled in Iowa, with Danes and Finns coming later.

Henry Melchior Muhlenburg arrived in America during the first half of the 18th century. His Lutheran influence was widespread in New York, New Jersey, Maryland, Virginia, the Carolinas, Georgia and Pennsylvania. He is referred to as the father of the American Lutheran Church.

Samuel Schmucker, in the early 19th century, introduced a major liberal element among American Lutherans. He had planned a union of churches, but later yielded to new conservative Lutheran immigrants. Charles Krauth notably led this conservative movement against Schmucker.

UNITED PRESBYTERIAN CHURCH OF NORTH AMERICA - originated in the Covenantors of Scotland in the mid-16th century. In attempting to force an episcopacy on the Scots, England was trounced, with the Scotch gaining economic, civil and religious freedom. Many also came from Ireland. In the mid-18th century many settled and established churches in Pennsylvania. Recently, Presbyterian Churches have begun a merger to adhere to the common faith of Westminister standards, including anti-secret societies, closed communion and psalms in worship.

In 1546 Wishart was burned to death for heresy, and John Knox was condemned to a French galley. Knox returned two years later to form a covenant loyal to the "Word of God." Late in the 16th century, under King James, greater freedom was enjoyed. Then, in 1638, the Church of England again attempted to force a rule of service on the Presbyterians, who successfully revolted. After Charles I was de-throned, and under Cromwell, Presbyterianism grew. In the years following, however, from Charles II to James II, extensive persecution gave the group its later martyrs.

U. S. Presbyterianism began with the English Puritans, and the Scotch and Irish. Early 17th century Presbyterian settlements in Maryland and New England, New Jersey and Pennsylvania flourished. Francis Makemi, who is credited with establishing American Presbyterianism, was arrested by Governor Corbury of New York for practicing the ministry without a license. His license, insisted Makemi, was good throughout the empire. Makemi won his case, as well as that for religious freedom throughout New York.

The early Presbytery agreed upon mutual aid and encouragement for existence in the wilds of America.

The history of Presbyterian education is essentially the history of Princeton College, formed by Alumni of the William Tennent Log College in Pennsylvania, a ministerial school. Residents of Princeton offered a plot of land and money to encourage settlement. It was accepted in 1753. The Princeton Theological Seminary was formed in 1812. Presbyterians have founded over 40 colleges in the U. S., including theological seminaries, the College of Wooster in Ohio, Lafayette College in Pennslyvania, Parsons College in Iowa, and Macalaster College in Minnesota.

The first bible on the continent was printed by Presbyterians from the original Greek. This resulted from a resolution by the

Continental Congress when the British blockade prevented importing bibles.

At a recent conference in Buffalo, New York, widespread Protestant merging was proposed by Presbyterian groups to other such sects as Methodists, Episcopalians, etc. Presbyterianism is a militant group, pitted against moral and social evils, and known for missionary zeal.

UNIVERSALISM - sect recently merged with Unitarianism. Stems historically from second and third century Alexandria, standing for salvation under a God of Love and Peace. James Relly is credited with modern Universalism stemming from the 18th century. His thesis held that salvation is not limited to the elect. Among famous Universalists were Clara Barton and Benjamin Rush.

The creed is akin to that of Unitarianism in the ideal that reason and experience are ultimate; Universalists, however, abide by the trinitarian form. Merged sects number approximately one half million in America.

VOLUNTEERS OF AMERICA - originated in America late in the 19th century by Mr. and Mrs. B. Booth; coming out of the Salvation Army, they objected to London rule. The society is presently active in maternity and aged homes, Summer camps, and prison reform.

"Y.M.C.A." - no specific nor diverse religious creed is involved. Intention was to recruit those early in the period of the industrial revolution who had become indifferent to religious and Christian ways. The basic philosophy is in bridging differences between all races and creeds.

The Y.M.C.A. was founded in London in 1844 by dry-goods clerks, George Williams and Edward Beaumont, as a layman movement in the revolution of industry to encourage young men who had no religion. The sect is evangelical, ecumenical and puritanical. It grew in America to include educational functions, with physical facilities. Membership numbers two to three million, including many Roman Catholics despite Vatican warning.

"Y.W.C.A." - formed in England during the mid-nineteenth century, of Protestant origin. It was presumably founded to meet the needs of young women working in shops and factories, solicitous of their religious welfare. Practically, it was organized to house nurses returning from the Crimean War. Mrs. Marshall Roberts set it up in America as the "Ladies' Christian Association" in 1858.

The interests are varied, including activities to encompass family interests, interracial relations, training in practical arts and skills, etc.

Forerunners of the Y.W.C.A. included the Emma-Roberts Prayer Union for Spiritual Welfare, and Mrs. Kinnaird's General Female Training Institute, established in England in 1855. Mrs. Boyd later set up a branch of the English version of the Y.W.C.A. in Boston.

ZIONITES - Christian Catholic Church. founded in Chicago in 1896 by John Alexander Dowie. The center is in Zion, Illinois. Industries are operated on a co-op basis, as well as religious and educational activities.

GLOSSARY

Abihisasta: a Brahmanist who must suffer long penance as a social outcast.

Absolution: Roman Catholic sacrament granting a communicant remission of sins, through penance, etc.

Absolutism: advocacy of a rule by unrestrained standards or principles standing alone without a modified substantive, with no restriction, exception or qualification.

Act of Supremacy: enacted in 1534 A.D. by English King Henry VIII, usurping papal authority in England.

Agnostic: position that nothing is known nor can be known about the existence of God, or about things outside of human experience.

Agnus Dei: medallions bearing the image of the lamb as a symbol of Christ, believed by Roman Catholics to protect the wearer from malign influences. Widely worn during the period of the "Black Death."

All-Saints Day: Nov. 1st, Roman Catholic holy day of obligation. Commemorates all lesser saints, as well as holy men and martyrs.

Americanism: a growing trend in religious liberty among American Roman Catholics, headed by Cardinal Gibbons of Baltimore. Condemned as heresy by Pope Leo XIII in 1899. Thenceforth administrative authority was bound more firmly to Rome.

Anti-clericalism: a term applied during the 19th and 20th centuries to a political movement in Europe and hostile to the Roman Catholic Church. Occurs as a reaction to militant clericalism, cf., that in France, England, Italy, Russia, Mexico. ". . . twenty four hours of disorder (in Spain) could mean the assassination of every bishop, priest and nun that could be found . . ." Cardinal Spellman.

Aphrodite: daughter of Zeus, Greek goddess and lover of Adonis, and who spent six months alternately with him among the dead. Her worship was often marked by sexual excesses. Her counterpart in the East was Cybele, Ishtar and Astarte.

Apocalypse: a depiction of eschatological conditions of a Zoroastrian type, transformed in Hebrew scriptures.

Apocalyptical Revelation: a method evident in biblical writings of ascribing authorship to a traditional figure who lived during an earlier period. Writing was thus attributable to fulfilled prophecy.

Apocrypha: hidden or supressed scriptures. Early-century Christian forgeries coming after the canonical New Testament. Fourteen books included in the Roman Catholic bible, but not accepted as genuine by Jews and Protestants. Writings or statements of doubtful origin or authority, hence, false, counterfeit or sham.

Apollonarianism: a fourth-century heresy holding Jesus to be simply a divine personage without a dual nature.

Apostolic Delegate: representative from the Vatican to Washington, D.C.

Aramaic: Arabic and Amharic. Language of Jesus.

Arameans: Semitic group in the biblical Aran in the middle of the Euphrates Valley and neighboring territories.

Archeology: science of excavating and interpreting ancient cultural ruins.

Ascension Day: May 27th, or forty days after the resurrection. Roman Catholic holy day.

Ash Wednesday: opens penitential Lenten season — forty days not counting Sundays preceding Easter. Observed by Roman Catholics and several Protestant denominations. Catholic ceremonies include marking forehead with ashes from palms burned after Palm Sunday from previous year.

Babel: Babylonian city where Noah's descendants attempted to build a tower that would reach to heaven. For this their words were made incomprehensible. (cf., fables about the origin of languages.)

Baptism: (Gr: dipping) practice of purification by water (cf., ancient Hindu practice). Ceremony invoking the grace of God to regenerate the soul, free it from sin, and make it a part of the Church.

Battle of the Scrolls: controversy between theologians and historians concerning the Dead-Sea Scrolls found in recent decades.

Bhikkhus: Buddhist monks, precursor to the Christian.

Bishop John Chrysostom of Constantinople: early Church father famous for establishing the date of Christmas. In the fourth century he decreed: ". . . on this day (the 25th of December) the birthday of Christ was lately fixed at Rome in order that

GLOSSARY

while the heathen were busy with their profane ceremonies, the Christians might perform their sacred rites undisturbed . . ."

Black friday: festival day of the mystery cult of Cybele. Day of blood, when Cybele's lover, Tammuz, died. After 3 days he was resurrected. (cf., Attis festival day and the Christian Easter.)

Brotherhood Week: sponsored by National Conference of Christians and Jews for furthering mutual understanding among races and creeds.

Canon: religious scriptures.

Catholic Charms: objects and practices believed to protect the individual from all forces under the control of evil spirits, e.g., earthquakes, cyclones, floods, droughts, famines, fires, shipwrecks, drownings, etc.

Catholic Public Schools: U.S. public schools, operated by public funds in Kentucky, Ohio, New Mexico, Missouri, etc., and staffed by Roman Catholic nuns.

Chiliasm: belief that Christ and his saints will reign on earth for a thousand years after the Parousia, i.e., He will establish His earthly kingdom.

Christmas: Dec. 25th, most important and widely celebrated event in Christian year marking the birth of Jesus, and based on ancient pagan festivals and celebrations.

Clericalism: pursuit of power (political) by an ecclesiastical hierarchy through secular channels for social control, e.g., ". . . the Roman Catholic Church, convinced through its divine prerogatives of being the only true Church, must demand the right of freedom for herself alone, because such right can only be possessed by truth, never error . . ." Civilta Cattolica, 1948.

Concordat: agreement between the Roman Catholic Church and a nation or state, usually calling for mutual support.

Confirmation: sacrament to formalize the individual's Christian faith; consisting of laying on of hands and anointing with chrism (oil and balm).

Confession: Roman Catholic practice in which, by private pronouncement of sin, the clergy are believed to have the power of forgiveness.

Consubstantiation: belief that Christ's body and blood are combined in the eucharist.

[333]

Creation: Hebrew and Babylonian epics. The Babylonian god, Ea, established his dwelling place first over the ocean and made land, as did the Hebrew god.

Crucifixion: rites practiced largely in Sicily in the deposition of Christ from the cross, in conduct of the passion drama, in its sorrow and grief.

Curia Romania: papal administrative body, made up of cardinals in residence at Rome, having power to judge, to command and legislate.

Cybele: mother of the gods; nature goddess from Asia to Rome, guardian of cities and nations; prototype of the Virgin Mary.

Day of Atontment (Yom Kippur): most solemn of Jewish holy days, devoted to prayer, fasting and repentance.

Dead-Sea Scrolls: documents of leather, linen, and copper, containing transcripts and copies of Old Testament books; belonging to the Qumran community about the Dead sea, and part of the Essenic sect dating at about the turn of the Christian era.

Deluge: overwhelming biblical flood, destroying every living thing. Found among Hebrew writing (Gen. 6-8), but of earlier Sumarian origin.

Docetism: doctrine that Christ was never born or resurrected, but simply a power or spirit which the deity sent to the world to perform a specific task, thence returning to the supreme lord of spirits. (This is in the tradition of Greek Gnosticism.) He was thus hostile to the Hebrew God, Yahweh.

Dominicans: Roman Catholic order founded in 1216 as the Order of the Preachers, attempting conversion of the Albigenses. Acquinas became a Dominican. The order was principally in charge of the Inquisition. Especially attached to ritual of the rosary. Their habit is white.

Dualism: Zoroastrian belief that the universe is antithethical — evil versus good, matter versus spirit, darkness versus light, cold versus warmth, and the God of Light versus the power of darkness.

Ea: major god in ancient Babylon.

Easter: traditional holy Christian day marking the resurrection of Jesus. Occurs on the first Sunday after the first full moon after March 21st. Derived from "Eastra" a Latin form of "Astarte," and celebrated between December 25th and the Spring Equinox. This period was earlier the mystical forty day search for the Egyptian

GLOSSARY

god Osiris by his wife, Isis; later becoming the Season of Lent terminating with Easter. (cf., also the Attis-Cybele cult)

Eastern Orthodox Christmas: January 7th, date observed by followers of the Julian Calendar.

Eastern Orthodox Easter: Eastern Church commemoration of the resurrection of Jesus.

Eastern Orthodox Holy Friday: Eastern Church celebration of Good Friday, or the last day of Jesus' life.

Eastern Orthodox Holy Thursday: Eastern Church celebration of the Last Supper and the Sacrament of Holy Communion.

Eastern Orthodox Lent: Eastern Church period of commemoration of Jesus' forty days in the wilderness.

Eastern Orthodox New Year's Day: first day of the new year marked by the older Julian calendar.

Eastern Orthodox Palm Sunday: first day of Eastern Church's holy week.

Eastern Orthodox Feast of the Epiphany: Eastern Church celebration based on Julian Calendar.

Eighth   Day of Tabernacles: climax of Jewish holy season.

Eleusinian Mystery: originated as part of an early agrarian festival; fasting, ritualistic purification in the sea were practiced. Annual cycle of seasons, birth and death, and immortality were symbolized.

Epiphanes: meaning "the appearance of God."

Epiphany: January 6th, originally celebrated as Jesus' birthday.

Eschatology: final things, the afterlife, the last judgement, hell, heaven, purgatory, etc.

Essenic Sect: one of three religio-political sects extant at the time of Jesus (cf., Pharisaic and Sadducean). Ideology and theology of this sect were most closely allied with that of the Gospel Jesus.

Eunuch: castrated priests in the rites of Attis in early Rome.

Excommunication: official act of punishment, excluding one from social intercourse and economic activity.

Exorcism: ritual driving out evil spirits. In Roman Catholicism, method of driving out the devil is regulated by Canon Law.

Fast of Ab (Tishah B'Ab): Jewish day of mourning in memory of destruction of the Temple in Jerusalem.

Feast of the Assumption: Roman Catholic and Eastern Orthodox holy day commemorating the Virgin Mary; celebrates her departure from earth and her assumption into heaven.

Feast of the Epiphany: observed twelve days after Christmas, in commemoration of the baptism of Jesus, the visit of the three wisemen to Jerusalem, and the miracle of Cana.

Feast of the Immaculate Conception: Roman Catholic holy day, celebrating the Virgin Mary's freedom from sin at the moment of her conception.

Feast of Weeks (Shabuot): marks giving of the Law (Torah) on Mount Sinai. (Also called Pentecost as the fiftieth day after the Passover).

First Amendment to the U. S. Constitution: ". . . Congress shall make no law respecting an establishment of religion, or prohibiting the free exercise thereof; or abridging the freedom of speech, or of the press; or of the right of the people to peaceably assemble, and to petition the government for a redress of their grievances . . ."

First Sunday in Advent: begins season when Christians prepare for the anniversary of Jesus' birth on Christmas.

First Two Days of Passover (Pesach): Eight-day celebration marking deliverance of Jews from slavery in Egypt. "Seder" services in Jewish homes on the eve and first night of Passover, recount the story of Exodus.

Flagellants: groups punishing themselves by whipping. Includes such devotees as Dominicans, Jesuits, and the Augustinian order. Saints such as St. Antony and St. Vincent Ferrer, also practiced. Practice was extensive during the Middle Ages.

Good Friday: commemorates last day of Jesus' life. Three hours of crucifixion from noon to 3 p.m. are observed with special services of silence and devotion.

Hababli: also known as Hillel the Babylonian and Hazaken the Elder (ca. 60 B.C. to 10 A.D.) Great doctor of Jewish law, who came to Palestine at the age of 40 when he was chosen president of the Sanhedrin.

Hades: ruler of the underworld over the dead; the underworld was separated from the world of the living by the rivers Styx, Lethe, Acheron, etc.

GLOSSARY

Halloween (See also All-Saints Day): feast of Roman Catholics and Anglican Churches glorifying all God's Saints. The Roman Catholic Church has an octave and vigil of fasting and abstinance as a principal feast. The seventh-century Pantheon at Rome was dedicated to Our Lady and all martyrs. The vigil (Halloween) is celebrated on October 31st as an old Celtic custom in celebration of the beginning of Winter. In Britain, fire building and fortune telling continue as the custom. In America, masquerading is popular, with tales told of witches and ghosts. All-Souls day, following on November 2nd, is a time when Roman Catholics pray for the faithfully departed suffering in purgatory. This latter tradition originated around the 11th century. This is also traceable to the Abbot of Cluny who began a still-practiced Roman Catholic custom of leaving lights on in the cemetary.

Hunakkah (Feast of Lights): Nov. 30, Jewish holy day beginning an eight day festival, and marking first recorded battle for religious liberty, and rededicated Temple worship by the Maccabees. In Jewish homes, candles are lit for eight nights.

Herod Archelaus: son of Herod the Great; succeeded his father in the year one A.D., and maintained his position against an insurrection raised by the Pharisees. When his heirship was disputed by his brother, Antipas, Archelaus went to Rome where his authority was confirmed by Augustus, who made Archelaus the Ethnarch of Judea, Samaria, and Idumaea. Brothers Antipas and Philip were made Tetrarchs over the other half of Herod's dominions. After a nine year reign, Archelaus was deposed by Augustus for tyranny and banished to Vienne in Gaul where he died.

Heirarchy: authoritative officialdom of the Church, holding delegated power over worship and administration of the sacraments and over all its members.

Holy Grail: medieval legend, variously written to be a chalice, a cup or dish. Christians claimed it to be a chalice of the Last Supper, that could provide food and healing. Largely involved in Arthurian legend in England.

Holy See: throne of the Church, located in Vatican City adjacent to Rome, Italy.

Holy Thursday: marks last supper and holy communion.

Holy Water: belief among Roman Catholics that water blessed by a priest can be used to give help, drive away diseases, and put demons to flight. ". . . the Church beseeches the Almighty to endow Holy Water with virtue that it may protect those who use it against attacks of the devil . . ." Legislation on the

Sacraments in the New Code of Canon Law. The practice originated together with the use of incense, around the 9th century, derived from earlier pagan custom.

Ignostic: position that the word "God" has no meaning and therefore cannot be considered in belief or disbelief.

Ikhnaton: meaning "profitable to Aton." Egyptian King who assumed this name in espousing an early monotheism — the religion of Aton, circa 1400 B. C.

Immortality: condition of deathlessness ascribed to each individual soul. Found in several religions, but is a cardinal tenet of Christianity and Islam.

Imprimatur: license to print or publish where censorship of the press is practiced.

Index: list of publications in Roman Catholicism forbidden to be read (Index librorum prohibitorum), exercised by the Holy See on anything challenging the faith.

Innocent III: pope (1198-1216) first claiming to be Vicar of Christ.

Inquisition: medieval ecclesiastical tribunal for the preservation of the faith, instituted in 1227 A.D., under Gregory IX. Later a similar purge was undertaken in Spain, though not officially authorized by Rome. Remnants lasted until 1787, dissipating with Protestant toleration.

Israel: name given Jacob after he had wrestled with the angel (Gen. 32:28). Also compare the Crete belief in Gilgamesh.

James the Just: early Jerusalem Church leader, whom Protestants claim to have been Jesus' brother, and who was heir apparent to the Christian Church.

Jerome: most learned and eloquent of Latin fathers at the turn of the 5th century, A. D. Completed his commentary, polemic and ascetic, on the scriptures, and the Vulgate, a revision of former versions of the Bible. This was later edited by Erasmus in 1516 A.D., to become the standard for the Roman Catholic Church in 1592 under Pope Clement. (Later Latin revisions were introduced under Pius X at the turn of the 20th century.)

Jewish New Year: (Rosh Hasanah) marks the beginning of Jewish year. (The Christian 20th century is carried into the year 5700). Ten Days of Penitence is observed, closing with the Day of Atonement.

GLOSSARY

Jupiter: the Roman counterpart of Zeus, king of the gods — sky god, god of rain, thunder, lightening, hospitality, truth and justice.

Law of Contact: primitive magical practice holding that whatever is done to an object will affect the person that the object was next to. Analysis is from a false premise in natural law.

Law of Similarity: primitive rite based on the assumption that by building an image or likeness of an object or individual, any effect can be produced. The logic is without analysis and is implicit.

Legion of Decency: Roman Catholic group censoring, condoning or condemning movies, books, etc. Accused by non-Catholics of being most critical of anything putting the Church in a bad light.

Legates: Roman Catholic cardinals representing the pope at all nationally important functions.

Lent: Christian fast period in Roman, Orthodox and Angelican Churches for 40 days between Ash Wednesday and Easter. Originally a fast of 40 hours, until the time of Gregory the Great when it was made a fast of 36 days. Some time later, Ash Wednesday and the remainder of the week were added. According to the St. Joseph's Daily Missal, Ash Wednesday marks the beginning of the Season of Lent which is in preparation for Easter. It was so arranged that 40 days would precede the feast as a reminder of Jesus' fast in the desert. Penitents earlier did penance in sack cloth and ashes in the old law. Now the priest merely blesses the ashes with prayers, sprinkles the communicant with holy water, incenses him, and with his thumb, presses ashes onto his forehead exclaiming, "Remember, man, you are dust and to dust you shall return." According to Mark, after the baptism of Jesus, He went into the wilderness, and was tempted by Satan for 40 days. Lent is based upon a synthesis of such religious traditions as the great temptations of Zoroaster and Gautama. In the Apocalypse of Abraham, the prophet was similarly tempted by Azazel.

Mars: Roman God of war.

Mass: the eucharistic ritual of the Roman Catholic Church, based on the doctrine of Transubstantiation. High mass includes priests, deacon, choir, and incense. Low mass is without the latter.

Mazdeism: the prehistoric religion from which Zoroastrianism evolved.

Medicine Man: a sorcerer supposed to possess mysterious healing powers, e.g., Siberian Shaman, African witch doctor, etc. Also includes tribal priests with supernatural powers. They are presumed to use supernatural healing agencies.

Mental Reservation: Catholic law permitting Catholics to lie, if by doing so they can further Catholicism. Such is not sinful.

Metaphysical Dualism: Zoroastrian belief, influencing that of Christianity, that matter and flesh are derived from Ahriman (the Devil), and that spirit and soul are derived from the Supreme God.

Mithraism: sun religion in Rome and elsewhere bearing many similarities to Christianity, e.g., baptism and the sacred banquet. Mithraism declined per se late in the 3rd century A.D.

Monita Secreta Societatis Jesu: secret instructions of the Society of Jesus (Jesuits). Rules and regulations, and guiding principles of the Jesuit Order for promoting dogma and dealing with lay Catholics.

Monophysitism: fifth century heresy regarding Christ as human.

Mysteries: ancient cults with a ritualistic soteriology.

Mummification: belief in an afterlife, with the body being preserved so that the soul might return to it.

Nazareth: a city in Galilee, from which Jesus came. Many scholars, since no records of such a city are extant, variously interpret such references to bear significance to the root word, meaning "offshoot" of David; hence, a Messianic sect heralding the coming of another divine leader as was the son of Jessie, David. Thus, this might have been one of the Essene communities which entertained such a belief.

Neptune: Roman God of the sea.

New Year's Day: Protestant, Roman Catholic and Orthodox holy day marking the Feast of the Circumcision. Also known as Octave Day of Christmas.

Nicholas III: pope from 1277 to 1280, first to assume role as the Vicar of Christ.

Nuncios: fully accredited ambassadors or ministers of the Vatican State to foreign lands. First rank over all other delegates is expected.

Omens: signs or augery believed to overshadow the future. Roman religion required trained priests to interpret the meaning of signs.

Omophagia: ritualistic eating of raw flesh as a eucharist.

Original Sin: belief that the fall of Adam (refer to Genesis) made him irrevocably corrupt, transmitting his degeneracy to all mankind.

GLOSSARY

Palm Sunday: Sunday before Easter, sixth and last week in Lent; from the biblical strewing of palms before Jesus. Opens holy week lasting to Easter. Special significance for Christians as the last week of Jesus' life.

Papacy: seat of Roman Catholic Church power residing in the office of the pope (see also Holy See). The papacy faltered or came near collapse in three periods: (1) the early vying for control with the Church of Constantinople, (2) the "Babylonian captivity" in Avignon, France, and (3) the Napoleonic seizure. In the first case, the struggle for power was almost lost to Constantinople but for extenuating political circumstances in Rome. In the second case, Pope Clement V, in 1309, deserted Rome for Avignon and the domination of France. All were subordinated to French kings until the year 1378 — Catherine of Siena and Bridget of Sweden persuaded Gregory XI to move the office back to Rome where rival popes vied for power until the Council of Constance. In the last case, Pope Pius VII claimed high rights for the papacy in the face of Napoleonic political seizures. Napoleon ordered the pope to be imprisoned. Then, early in the nineteenth century, the papacy seemed to be doomed, until Napoleon fell. Since then it has climbed steadily in power.

Paleography: science concerned with the dating of ancient manuscripts.

Parousia: a second appearance of the sacrificial savior god-man, when he will establish the saintly kingdom, bringing eschatological conditions. Hence the second coming of Christ.

Passion: ritualistic death of the soter, making possible redemption.

Parochial Education: a vast system of education within (particularly) the Roman Catholic Church, which refuses the state permission to educate children of Catholic parents without special permission of its bishops. Such schools serve as educational arms of the Church, operated by its various orders.

Patriarchs: biblical founders of the tribes and autocrats including Abraham, Isaac, Jacob and his twelve sons.

Pelagianism: fifth-century heresy, rejecting "original sin" paedobaptism and reprobation.

Penance: Roman Catholic sacrament absolving penitent of sin by his confessor priest. Priest must inflict punishment for guilt (usually prayers). Practice is taken from Hellenic text (John 20. 19-23).

THE CHRISTIAN PAGAN

Pentacost: commemorates descent of the holy spirit upon the Apostles fifty days after the resurrection and first Christian baptism. Originally a Jewish celebration of the closing of the grain season and the beginning of the Passover. Christians adopted the celebration, instituting the belief that fifty days after the Passover, the Holy Ghost descended upon the disciples. It is now the seventh Sunday after Easter (cf., the British Whitsunday).

Phallic Religions: cults involving, in some form, worship of the male genital organ. The tree and the serpent in the religion of Tammuz, the Tree of Knowledge in the Genesis story of Creation, the Maypole, the rod of Aaron, the cross of Osiris and of the Aztecs are such symbols. Followers of the ancient phallic religions worshiped with licentious rites.

Pope: Roman Catholic pontiff possessing absolute infallible authority over spiritual and moral matters.

Pope Gregory the Great: early pope (540-604 A.D.) to whom the Church is indebted for complete organization of public ritual and systematization of sacred chants.

Population Explosion: mushrooming growth of population through acceleration of birth rate and deceleration of death rate. Roman Catholic growth is attributed to such accelerated population expansion through birth-control policies, e.g., in the U. S., Roman Catholics are expected to be in the majority by the turn of the century.

Primitive Christianity: practices as in the early Christian Church, such as communal living, yielding up wealth, etc.

Pseudepigraphy: apocalyptic writings attributed to a writer who had already died prior to the period of writing, e.g., the Book of Daniel.

Purgatory: Roman Catholic theological state after death where souls destined for heaven are purified of taint. Those dying who are still unpunished for minor sins, martyrs excluded, must be cleansed. Those in purgatory are still members of the church, and may be helped, as in life, by prayers (cf., the Requiem Mass). Hell is permanent, while purgatory is temporary.

Purification Rituals: removal through ritual of what the religion deems to be unclean, e.g., Candlemas commemorating the purification of Mary after the birth of Jesus (Luke 2:22).

Purim (Feast of Esther): Jewish day of merrymaking (March 18) marking defeat of Persian tyrant, Haman, who sought to secure

GLOSSARY

his power by making scapegoats of the Jews. Book of Esther is read in synagogue; gifts are exchanged and presents distributed to the poor.

Quebec: French Canadian city, reported as favored for a future site of the Holy See.

Qumran Sect: Community about the Dead Sea at the time of Christ practicing a variety of Judaism in the Essenic format. Dead-Sea scrolls were found in the area.

Race Relations Sunday: Feb. 14th, sponsored by National Council of Churches to emphasize brotherhood ideal in race relations.

Reformation Day: Oct. 31st, observed in many Protestant Churches to mark the beginning of Protestant Reformation in 1517.

Rejoicing of the Law (Simhat Torah): Jewish holy day when reading of the Law (Torah) is concluded and begun anew in the synagogues. The day is celebrated with festivity and the spirit of reverence.

Roman Calendar: old calendar when the year ended in February.

Rosary: Roman Catholic prayer with beads used as counters (cf., Moslem and Buddhistic practices). Communicants meditate on the lives of Jesus and Mary. Popularity is ascribed to its simplicity and stereotypy: one dwells on an episode, recites the Lord's Prayer, "Hail Mary" ten times, and Gloria Patri once.

Sacraments: sacred sign in Roman Catholic belief that it was instituted by Jesus. Includes: Eucharist, Baptism, Confirmation, Penance, Extreme Unction, Matrimony and Order. All but Baptism and Penance can be bestowed only on those in a "State of Grace."

Sacrifice: ancient religious practice of killing or eating a divine animal or god-man. Modern Christian Mass is symbolic of such earlier practices.

Saturn: Roman god of sowing and husbandry.

Saturnalia: festival of Saturn. Likely celebrated in December even before Caesar's calendar reforms. Called the "Carnival." Likely originally a paying of homage prior to the sowing season, i.e., by cramming his belly, by swilling and guzzling before sowing, the husbandman believed that he imparted vigor to the seed.

Scapular: piece of cloth of a prescribed shape worn by Roman Catholics in the belief that it will protect them from malign influences.

Science: according to Frazer, a solution of the mysteries of the universe rejecting religious theories of nature as inadequate, but frequently postulating an inflexible regularity in natural events; the order is derived from patient and exact observations.

Seasons: great changes that annually occur across the surface of the earth. Primitive man attempted to hasten or retard the changes through magical rites. Food and reproduction are generally found to have been basic concerns in attempting to regulate the seasons.

Semite: Caucasian racial types, now Jews and Arabs, but formerly Babylonians, Assyrians, Aramaeans, and Phoenicians.

Semitic: Mediteranean cultures of the Middle East with inflectional languages; records are extant of great antiquity, including Phoenician and Hebrew.

Septuagint: early Greek translation of Old-Testament scriptures.

Shrove Tuesday: last day of merrymaking before Ash Wednesday and Lenten Season, usually observed by Roman Catholics.

Sin: lesser ancient Babylonian god.

Sinai Covenant: tradition that God appeared to Moses giving him the Decalogue or Ten Commandments, and other detailed legislation; these documents are now indicated to have been written at least four centuries later than the exodus to Sinai, circa 1300 B.C.

Soshans (Saoshyant): a divinely generated personage to appear 3,000 years after Zoroaster, and who would establish the universal kingdom of righteousness; this was the prototype of the Son of Man in the Book of Daniel.

Soter: incarnate god-man who has died in atoning for sinful humanity. In mass, the body and blood must be consumed by communicants to become divine and immortal in absorbing the essence of the god.

Soul: vital elements of the body, thought to live within it. For several religions concerned with animism and spiritism the soul is all important, e.g., as in Christianity.

St. Anthony: saint credited with power for finding lost things.

St. Blase: saint credited with special powers for curing throats.

St. George: saint usually pictured in the act of piercing a dragon in saving a king's daughter. The dragon's breath, according to legend, caused pestilence whenever it approached a town. George advised the townspeople to be baptized to be saved from the pestilence; finally he slayed the dragon.

St. Jude: patron saint of the sick. Where Roman Catholicism is prevalent, classified ads are frequently found in local papers: "Thanks to St. Jude for favors granted."

St. Patrick's Day: Mar. 17th, when traditional festivities honor the patron saint of Ireland.

Sumer: southern part of ancient Mesopotamia; in 3,000 B.C., a flourishing urban culture existed.

Sumerians: ancient Aryans about the Iranian-Euphrates region, preceding the Semitic-Babylonian Empire.

Syllabus of Pius IX: eighty-five propositions issued in 1864, holding the Roman Catholic religion to be supreme over the state and individual.

Synoptics: the New Testament gospels of Mathew, Mark and Luke, which carry essential similarities and consistencies.

Synthesis: a harmonious unity developed from combining different religious elements to form a new religion.

Tabernacles (Sukkoth): Sept. 21, harvest festival of thanksgiving, taking its name from booths or tabernacles, in which Jews lived following their traditional deliverance from Egypt.

Taboos: prohibition of an act under pain of punishment by supernatural powers.

Thanksgiving day: fourth Thursday in November. Tradition marks Pilgrims' celebration thanking God for their survival in the New World.

Taurobolium: baptismal bath in the blood of a bull. Practiced as symbolism in such religions as Osiris, Dionysus, or Attis.

Theotokos: Roman Catholic doctrine, originating in the fourth century, declaring Mary as the Mother of God.

Tide Superstitions: sea-shore peoples' belief in things associated with the ceaseless ebb and flow of the tide, e.g., that no creature can die except at ebb tide.

Torah: the five books of Moses.

Transubstantiation: elements symbolizing the body and blood of the god-man are believed to become literally transformed into his essence before the eyes of the celebrants.

Treasury of Merit: Roman Catholic practice of charging relatives of the deceased in order to get the latter out of, or, to reduce the torments of, purgatory.

Twelfth Night: popular celebration of twelve days from Christmas to Epiphany; likely relics of the ancient intercalary days which were inserted into the calendar at midwinter to equalize the short lunar year with the solar year.

Unitarianism: Christian form denying the Trinity, believing that God exists only in one person. Arianism and Monarchian heresy were early forms. Servetus (1553) was first of the Reformation Unitarians in Geneva and Socinus in Poland. In America, reason and conscience were taken to be the only guides to religious truths (cf., Emerson, Parker, and Channing). Non creedal. Merged with Universalists in 1961.

Vatican City: temporal state ruled by the pope, constituting the claim of the Roman Catholic Church for temporal and political power.

Venus: Roman version of the Greek Aphrodite, originally goddess of gardens, wife of Mars.

Virgin Mary: virgin mother of Jesus whom Christians call "Our Lady;" Protestants frequently criticize the Cult of Mary in the Roman Catholic Church.

Yahweh: name of Jewish creator-god; earlier written "YHWH." Later became Jehovah.

Zeus: king of the gods in ancient Greece.

INDEX

INDEX

INDEX

Pope, 206, 222, 230, 250f, 253, 280, 283, 285f, 307
Pope Gregory, 204, 206, 243
Pope Gregory VII, 288
Pope Gregory VIII, 270
Pope Gregory IX, 263
Pope Innocent III, 262, 270
Pope Julius II, 247
Pope Leo, 243
Pope Leo III, 267
Pope Leo X, 247
Pope Leo XIII, 289, 304
Pope Paul III, 274
Pope Pius V, 256
Pope Pius IX, 289, 307
Pope Urban II, 269, 288
Prayer, 286, 287
Presbyterianism, 258, 311, 312, 323
Priest (s) (hood), 95, 253
Printing, 248, 255
Protestant (ism), 227, 290-95, 308-30
   origin of word, 292
Ptolemy, 36
Puritans, 257, 258f, 291, 312f
Pythagorian Heresy, 234
Pythagorian Synthesis, 147, 172
Pythagorus, 134

Q

Quakers, 312, 313, 323
Qumran (See Khirbet Qumran)

R

Rabbis, 65
Reformation, 231, 239, 246, 255, 263
Reformed Presbyterian Church, 324
Reinhart, 252
Religion, 14
Renaissance, 212, 246, 249
Resurrection, 13, 129, 141, 148, 150, 185, 197f, 203, 204, 301
Revivalists, 324
Roman Catholicism, 47, 285-90
   Conflict, 227
   Education, 277
   Tenets, 222, 277f
Rom (e) (ans), 37, 61, 117, 155, 174, 192, 197, 199, 206, 207, 209-223
Romulus, 209
Russian Orthodox, 284f

S

Sacraments, 101, 261
Sacrifice, 16, 64, 90, 114, 306
Sadducees, 37, 58, 120, 123, 197

Salvation, 147, 261, 301, 305
Salvation Army, 324
Saturn (alia), 159, 162f, 172, 179
Saul (See also Paul of Tarsus), 29, 181, 187
Sayings of Jesus, 51
Secular (ized), 15, 38, 269
Separation Fear, 17
Separatists, 257, 310
Septuagint, 49
Sermon of the Mount, 55, 78
Seventh-Day Adventists, 325
Sicarii, 38, 61
Simons, Menno, 264
Sin, Original, 305
Skepticism, 295
Soter (iology), 39, 161, 171, 185, 186, 205, 302, 304
Soul, 147, 152
St. Anthony, 242
Stephen, 181, 187, 197
St. Jerome, 242
St. Martin, 242
Sumer, 23
Sweden, 251
Synod of Whitby, 290
Synoptics, 49, 50

T

Taurobulian, 163
Teacher of Righteousness, 58f, 88, 94
Temple, 76, 77, 92f, 119, 122, 198, 238
Tertullian, 205, 234, 235
Tezcatlipoca, 165f
Thanksgiving, 15
Theodosius, 217, 220, 223
Thinking, 44
Thirty-Year War, 271-74
Thomas Aquinas, 205, 304
Titus, 25, 39
Toleration Act, 259
Tower of London, 254
Treaty of Westphalia, 273
Trinitarianism, 50, 313, 314

U

Unitarian (ism), 325
Unitarian-Universalist Church, 294, 326
United Brethren in Christ, 327
United Lutheran Church of America, 327
United Presbyterian Church of North America, 327
Universalism, 329